UNDERSTANDING THE PARABLES OF *Jesus Christ*

UNDERSTANDING THE PARABLES OF *Jesus Christ*

JAY A. PARRY • DONALD W. PARRY

SALT LAKE CITY, UTAH

Other Books in This Series

Understanding Isaiah

Understanding the Book of Revelation

Understanding the Signs of the Times

Understanding Death and the Resurrection

Visit us at DeseretBook.com

Library of Congress Cataloging-in-Publication Data

Parry, Jay A.
Understanding the parables of Jesus Christ / Jay A. Parry and Donald W. Parry.
p. cm.
Includes bibliographical references.
ISBN-10: 1-59038-626-4 (hardbound : alk. paper)
ISBN-13: 978-1-59038-626-2 (hardbound : alk. paper)
1. Jesus Christ—Parables. 2. Parables. 3. Church of Jesus Christ of Latter-day Saints—Doctrines. 4. Mormon Church—Doctrines. I. Parry, Donald W. II. Title.
BT375.3.P37 2006
226.8'06—dc22 2006021889

Printed in the United States of America
R. R. Donnelley and Sons, Crawfordsville, IN

10 9 8 7 6 5 4 3

Contents

Acknowledgments

We offer our heartfelt thanks to all those who helped to bring this book to fruition. We are grateful to Carli Anderson for conducting research into the parables of the New Testament and Thomas K. Sowards for comparing Greek source material of the parables with the King James translation and the Joseph Smith Translation. We also express gratitude for the wonderful people at Deseret Book: Cory Maxwell, who offered continuing encouragement and support; Richard Peterson, whose thoughtful editing was most welcome; Shauna Gibby, who gave the book its professional design; Laurie Cook, who contributed her professional skills as a typesetter; and Lisa Mangum, who helped to shepherd the book through much of the publishing process.

Introduction

"There is nothing in all literature equal to the parables of Christ."[1] This statement by Elder Howard W. Hunter demonstrates the significant place that Jesus' parables have in our scriptural writings. Jesus' parables are significant because they address both the unbelieving and the faithful at the same time; the unbelieving receive one message and the faithful another, but both benefit. His parables are universal in their application—they reach across time, borders, and boundaries so that people of all eras, regardless of their geographical locale, profit from their teachings. His parables are simple and profound at the same time. "They are so simple a child can understand, yet profound enough for the sage and philosopher."[2] And his parables contain moral and spiritual teachings that benefit all of God's children, regardless of religious affiliation. One need not be a Christian to appreciate the value of Jesus Christ's parables; people of all faiths may benefit from them.

Characteristics of Christ's Parables

Each of Christ's parables has most, if not all, of the following characteristics:

1. They are based on commonplace events. Jesus' parables feature images from everyday life, from nature, and from typical situations that could be found in the first century A.D. environment of Palestine. For example, when Jesus uttered the parables, he referred to a number of occupational groups, such as builders, shepherds, farmers, fishermen, and laborers in a vineyard. He drew upon such commonplace but significant events as marriage, feasting, planting, and harvest. He spoke of an assortment of plants and animals, including wheat, tares, mustard seed, fig tree, sheep, and goats. His teachings recalled such common things as a coin, a pearl, a hidden treasure, clothing, food, and wine, a Samaritan and a Pharisee, virgins, a widow, a king's son, and a wayward son.

In presenting the parables, Jesus drew upon life's experiences. As Elder Hugh B. Brown explained, Jesus' "parables were not woven from fancy. They were word pictures of what he had observed as he lived among the people. He had seen the sower at work in the field, the shepherd with his sheep, the repentant son returning to his father, the barren fig tree; he knew the publican and the Pharisee and had attended wedding feasts where foolish virgins had no oil in their lamps. He taught from the richness of his own life."[3]

2. They are very short stories. In terms of length, Christ's parables are quite succinct. For instance, the well-known parable of the prodigal son (Luke 15:11–32) contains only about five hundred words, and the parable of the ten virgins (Matthew 25:1–13) has just over two hundred words. A number of parables contain fewer than one hundred words. The parable of the pearl of great price (Matthew 13:45–46) has less than three dozen words, and the parable of the mustard seed (Luke 13:18–19) has approximately fifty-four words. His parables are so compact that they contain no unnecessary words or redundant phraseology. Every word provides meaning to the parable; no words are wasted.

All human characters portrayed in the parables are important to the story; none are superfluous. For example, the parable of the ten virgins features a number of themes that are vital to the story: the kingdom of heaven, virgins, the number *ten,* lamps and oil, the bridegroom, and marriage. Nonessential elements, such as the virgins' names, their parents, hometowns, ages, ethnic backgrounds, political viewpoints, occupational interests, and social standings are not part of the story.

3. As short narratives, they are designed to hold one's attention. Parables, similar to any good narratives, have the ability to draw readers (or hearers) into the story, thus engaging their attention. They provide readers with pictures or images of day-to-day existence so that they can then relate to a true-to-life situation. For example, when we read the parable of the prodigal son, many of us relate or feel akin to one or more of the characters. Our own life may be like that of the prodigal, or the forgiving father, or the elder son.

4. They have a point of comparison. "The word *parable* is Greek in origin, and means a setting side by side, a comparison."[4] This principle of comparison is a major feature of Christ's parables. In each parable a person or thing represents a moral principle or a spiritual truth. The parables of the hidden treasure (Matthew 13:44), the pearl of great price (Matthew 13:45–46), and the gospel net (Matthew 13:47–53), for example, feature earthly things—a treasure, a pearl, and a fishing net. Each of these three ordinary items is compared to the kingdom of heaven. The meaning of each of these will be addressed in the pages that follow.

Not only do the people or things in the parables represent moral principles or spiritual truths, but the parables' characters are often comparable to us, the readers of the parables. For example, when we read the parable of the lost sheep, we may feel that we are connected to the attitudes and approaches of the shepherd—or of the sheep. Or we may feel linked to the characters in other parables when we, like them, have used leaven in cooking, labored for a employer, planted seeds in a garden, experienced wealth or poverty, lost a valuable coin, attended an important wedding, or feasted at a wedding meal.

5. They feature symbolic elements. Jesus' parables feature a variety of events (such as harvest, feasts, marriage), things (leaven, tares, treasure, pearl, fishing net, wheat, mustard seed, fig tree, pounds), people and their status or occupations (fishermen, servants, masters, friends, widow, farmers, virgins, shepherds, builders, tax collectors), and animals (sheep, goats, fatted calves). All these may serve as symbols of eternal truths. In the parable of the Pharisee and the publican, for example, the Pharisee symbolizes all who are proud. In the parable of the pearl of great price, the pearl represents the gospel and its inestimable value. In the parable of the ten virgins, the virgins signify Church members. And in the parable of the prodigal son, that son symbolizes each of us when we stray from God's righteous paths.

6. They are often associated with Old Testament images. Many of the themes, characters, or images in the parables have connections to the Old Testament. For example, the parable of the lost sheep (Matthew 18:11–14) recalls numerous Old Testament passages about shepherds, sheep, and related pastoral themes. One well-known psalm opens with "the Lord is my shepherd. . . . He maketh me to lie down in green pastures: he leadeth me beside the still waters" (Psalm 23:1–2). The parable of the great supper (Luke 14:16–24) has thematic links to feasts and festivals that belonged to the ancient Israelites, their calendar, religious system, and temple practices. These festivals include Passover (Exodus 12:3–20), Pentecost (Exodus 23:14–17; Numbers 28:26), the feast of tabernacles (Numbers 29:12–38), and Purim (Esther 9). The greater our understanding of the parables' connections to the Old Testament, the more we appreciate the parables and their meaning.

7. They teach gospel principles. Parables are designed to teach us various gospel principles or to reinforce our understanding of gospel truths that we have already been taught. Elder Howard W. Hunter explained, "Each of the parables spoken by the Savior seems to teach a principle or give an admonition regarding the attributes necessary to qualify for exaltation. Some of these are faith, repentance, baptism, development of talents, forgiveness, perseverance in doing good, being a profitable steward, charity, mercy, and obedience. These parables were usually given by him to add to the knowledge of persons already spiritually enlightened, particularly the disciples, although they were sometimes directed to other persons and audiences."[5]

8. Their teachings conform to established truths. The doctrines and teachings of the parables are in harmony with those of Jesus and his apostles and to the teachings of all the scriptures. Any interpretation of the parables that contradicts the doctrines of the gospel is inappropriate and lacks a foundation.

9. The parables appeal to people from all ages of the world. People of every generation are able to appreciate parables and find personal application in them. From Jesus' contemporaries who actually heard Jesus utter the parables to twenty-first century Christians who read the parables, all may apply the parables' teachings and principles to themselves. In this sense, the parables are timeless in their value and relevance. As President Rudger Clawson taught, parables "seem almost to cover our human experience."[6]

10. They do not have geographical boundaries. Most of the subjects of the parables—a coin, shepherd, pearl, farmer, wheat, fisherman, sheep, a wayward child, leaven, and so forth—are so commonplace that peoples of various geographical locales may appreciate and understand them. Most nations and peoples know of sheep and shepherds, farmers, and coins. In this sense, parables have a universal appeal.

11. They contain multiple levels of meaning. One reader finds basic understanding in the parables and another locates deeper meanings. One message is readily found on the surface, while additional truth can be found by those who dig deeper. In a way, parables are coded messages that reveal their meaning to the righteous who study those messages. The keys to the cipher are righteous living and the assistance of the Spirit.

12. They are intentionally open ended. Jesus purposely left details out of each narrative, which details were not necessary for his audience. In the parable of the prodigal son, for example, we do not hear the older brother's reaction to the father's plea that he join the family and friends in the feast. Does the older brother follow his father's footsteps and offer up forgiveness, joining the festivities with joy because his brother has returned—or does he pout, or does he become a prodigal himself? Likewise, in the parable of the hidden treasure, we do not know the relative value of the treasure, its specific contents, whether it was sold and, if so, to whom and for how much. These elements were purposely omitted from the parable because they are extraneous. In fact, the inclusion of any of these elements might actually detract from the parable's essential meaning.

Why Did Jesus Christ Teach in Parables?

One reason that Jesus Christ taught in parables was to conceal the truth from those who were spiritually unprepared. According to the LDS Bible Dictionary, parables "veil the meaning. The parable conveys to the hearer religious truth exactly in proportion to his faith and intelligence; to the dull and uninspired it is a mere story, 'seeing they see not,' while to the instructed and spiritual it reveals the mysteries or secrets of the kingdom of heaven. Thus it is that the parable exhibits the condition of all true knowledge. Only he who seeks finds."[7]

Jesus himself gave the above reason for using parables. After he spoke the parable of the sower, "the disciples came, and said unto him, Why speakest thou unto them in parables? He answered and said unto them, Because it is given unto you to know the mysteries of the kingdom of heaven, but to them it is not given. For whosoever hath, to him shall be given, and he shall have more abundance: but whosoever hath not, from him shall be taken away even that he hath. Therefore speak I to them in parables: because they seeing see not; and hearing they hear not, neither do they understand" (Matthew 13:10–13). We note that Jesus' disciples asked him, "Why speakest thou unto *them* in parables?" not "Why speakest thou unto *us* in parables?"

On another occasion Matthew recorded that Jesus said to unbelievers, "Unto you that believe not, I speak in parables; that your unrighteousness may be rewarded unto you" (JST, Matthew 21:34).

Jesus spoke parables to veil the mysteries from the wicked. Those who do not understand the parables are those who fail to use their spiritual eyes to see and understand and their spiritual ears to hear and comprehend the spiritual message of the parables. As noted, "They seeing see not; and hearing they hear not, neither do they understand."

After saying these words to his inquiring disciples, Jesus cited a passage from Isaiah: "By hearing ye shall hear, and shall not understand; and seeing ye shall see, and shall not perceive: For this people's heart is waxed gross, and their ears are dull of hearing, and their eyes they have closed; lest at any time they should see with their eyes, and hear with their ears, and should understand with their heart, and should be converted, and I should heal them" (Matthew 13:14–15; see Isaiah 6:9–10). The reason why Jesus' unbelieving contemporaries would not understand his parables was that "this people's heart is waxed gross," another way of saying they were nothing less than wicked.

Latter-day prophets and apostles provide additional witnesses as to why Jesus taught in parables. Joseph Smith taught: "The very reason why the multitude, or the world, as they were designated by the Savior, did not receive an explanation upon His parables, was because of unbelief. To you, He says (speaking to His disciples), it is given to know the mysteries of the Kingdom of God. And why? Because of the faith and confidence they had in Him."[8]

One reason that Jesus veiled his message may have been to temporarily protect himself and his newly established kingdom. In many of the parables he refers explicitly to the "kingdom of heaven" (Matthew 13:3–23; 13:24–30; 22:1–14; 25:1–13; 25:14–30) or the "kingdom of God" (Mark 4:26–29; Luke 21:29–33), but he consistently veils the doctrine that he himself is the King of that kingdom. If Jesus had made explicit statements regarding his kingship during his mortal ministry, it is likely that the civil and religious leaders of his day would have brought him to trial (possibly for treason or sedition) much earlier than they actually did, bringing an end to his ministry before its completion. Ultimately, "one of the reasons they crucified Jesus," writes one biblical commentary, "was because of His challenging parables and the claims of his Kingdom."[9]

Another reason that Jesus veiled his message was to show mercy to the unbelievers. According to Elder James E. Talmage: "There is plainly shown an element of mercy in the parabolic mode of instruction adopted by our Lord under the conditions prevailing at the time. Had He always taught in explicit declaration, such as required no interpretation, many among His hearers would have come under condemnation, inasmuch as they were too weak in faith and unprepared in heart to break the bonds of traditionalism and the prejudice engendered by sin, so as to accept and obey the saving word. Their inability to comprehend the requirements of the gospel would in righteous measure give Mercy some claim upon them, while had they rejected the truth with full understanding, stern Justice would surely demand their condemnation."[10]

Just as parables conceal truth from the spiritually unprepared, parables also disclose truth to those who are spiritually able to receive it. Jesus' words regarding the wicked whose "heart is waxed gross" do not apply to his disciples, whom he calls blessed. "But blessed are your eyes, for they see: and your ears, for they hear" (Matthew 13:16). "Parables reveal truths to those whose hearts are open and receptive. . . . Parables are majestic teaching devices, and they do reveal truth, and they do add light and understanding to those who already have the gift of understanding, as well as to those who are sincerely seeking truth."[11]

As Mark recorded in his gospel, "And with many such parables spake he the word unto them, as they were able to hear it. But without a parable spake he not unto them: and when they were alone, *he expounded all things* to his disciples" (Mark 4:33–34; emphasis added).

How Many New Testament Parables Are There?[12]

Parables formed a significant part of Jesus' teaching ministry during his mortal life. He uttered them in a range of settings—from a boat anchored near the shore, in a private residence, in the home of a chief Pharisee, while journeying to Jerusalem, in the temple, and while sitting on the Mount of Olives. He spoke them to a variety of audiences—to his disciples, to Jewish rulers, to multitudes, to a Pharisee named Simon, and to Jerusalem in general. According to one source, parables "make up approximately 35 percent of [Jesus'] recorded sayings,"[13] referring to those uttered in mortality. During one part of Jesus' mortal ministry, Mark observed that "without a parable spake he not unto them" (Mark 4:34).[14] Matthew also wrote, "All these things spake Jesus unto the multitude in parables; and without a parable spake he not unto them: that it might be fulfilled which was spoken by the prophet, saying, I will open my mouth in parables; I will utter things which have been kept secret from the foundation of the world" (Matthew 13:34–35).

Scholars do not always agree on what constitutes a parable or even exactly how many have been preserved in the New Testament.[15] Some are generous in their approach when they count a metaphor, proverb, simile, saying, or allegory as having a parabolic form. For example, biblical scholar David Wenham treats John 10:1–18 ("I am the good shepherd") and John 15:1–8 ("I am the vine, ye are the branches") as parables, when most consider these passages to be allegories.[16] Wenham also treats the metaphors of Matthew 5:13–16 ("Ye are the salt of the earth"; "Ye are the light of the world") as having parabolic forms.[17] Richard Lloyd Anderson wrote, "What illustrations really qualify as parables? 'Light of the world,' 'salt of the earth,' 'candle' (the Greek word for lamp), 'under a bushel'? Although these are often classified as parables, they are really only simple comparisons, for the parable involves an entire story that moves to a dramatic close."[18]

To complicate the question of what constitutes a parable, a few scholars also cite the parables recorded in the apocryphal Gospel of Thomas when they compare and contrast these of the synoptic gospels, Matthew, Mark, and Luke. For instance, the Gospel of Thomas's version of the parables of the foolish rich man, the wicked husbandmen, the pearl of great price, and the sower are similar to those belonging to the New Testament, but there are also notable differences. And further, this gospel includes the parable of a woman with a jar, which is not located in the synoptic accounts. How should students of Jesus' parables deal with Thomas's gospel and its parables? In this book we have followed the path of most scholars who have elected to deal only with those of the canonized Gospels.

In this book, we feature thirty parables. The combined lists of parables of Elders McConkie and Talmage, along with those in the LDS Bible Dictionary,[19] have influenced our decision of what constitutes a parable. The thirty parables are listed, together with scripture references, in Table 1.

Jesus did not provide titles or names for the parables; such identifiers are recent characterizations. Most of the names are more or less standard in the English-speaking Christian community, across religious affiliations and creeds. "The good Samaritan," for example, is a well-known name of the parable found in Luke 10:25–37; "the prodigal son" is a standard designation for the parable recorded in Luke 15:11–32, although the word *prodigal* is not commonly used in everyday speech; and "the ten virgins" is a universally understood designation of the parable set forth in Matthew 25:1–13. In this book, we have adopted standard names for the parables (see table).

We have attempted to arrange the parables in chronological order, using the LDS Bible Dictionary's "Harmony of the Gospels" as a guide (see BD, 684–96).

TABLE 1

NAME OF THE PARABLE	REFERENCE
The Sower and the Soils	Matthew 13:3–9, 18–23; Mark 4:3–9, 13–20; Luke 8:5–8, 11–15
The Seed Growing by Itself	Mark 4:26–29
The Wheat and the Tares	Matthew 13:24–30, 36–43
The Mustard Seed	Matthew 13:31–32; Mark 4:30–32; Luke 13:18–19
The Leaven	Matthew 13:33; Luke 13:20–21
The Hidden Treasure	Matthew 13:44
The Pearl of Great Price	Matthew 13:45–46
The Gospel Net	Matthew 13:47–50
The Lost Sheep	Matthew 18:11–14; Luke 15:3–7
The Lost Coin	Luke 15:8–10
The Prodigal Son	Luke 15:11–32
The Unmerciful Servant	Matthew 18:23–35
The Good Samaritan	Luke 10:30–37
The Friend at Midnight	Luke 11:5–8
The Foolish Rich Man	Luke 12:16–21
The Barren Fig Tree	Luke 13:6–9
The Great Supper	Luke 14:16–24
The Unrighteous Steward	Luke 16:1–8
Lazarus and the Rich Man	Luke 16:19–31
The Unprofitable Servant	Luke 17:7–10
The Importunate Widow and Unjust Judge	Luke 18:1–5
The Pharisee and the Publican	Luke 18:9–14
The Laborers in the Vineyard	Matthew 20:1–16
The Pounds	Luke 19:12–27
The Two Sons	Matthew 21:28–32
The Wicked Husbandmen	Matthew 21:33–41; Mark 12:1–9; Luke 20:9–16
The Royal Marriage Feast	Matthew 22:1–14

The Fig Tree	Matthew 24:32–34; Mark 13:28–29; Luke 21:29–31
The Ten Virgins	Matthew 25:1–13
The Talents	Matthew 25:14–30

Personal Application of Parables

Parables are for people of all ages of the world. All of us, regardless of the era in which we live or our geographical boundaries, can apply to our own lives the principles and spiritual truths of the parables. Elder Dallin H. Oaks set forth the following insightful principle: "A scripture is not limited to what it meant when it was written. . . . [It] may also lead to current revelation on whatever else the Lord wishes to communicate to the reader at that time. We do not overstate the point when we say that the scriptures can be a Urim and Thummim to assist each of us to receive personal revelation."[20]

Robert L. Millet added, 'While it is always wise to seek to understand exactly what a speaker had in mind (in this case, Jesus' intended interpretation of a parable), it is also the case that each of us brings our own background, strength, and need to the reading of a parable. In that sense, a parable can have many applications. Thus one person could read a particular parable and come away feeling peace and gratitude, while another might read the same parable and feel smitten in his or her conscience and eager to become more sensitive and caring.[21]

It is not enough for Christ's disciples to gain knowledge of gospel doctrines or to have a great understanding of God's truths. As followers of Jesus Christ, each of us must apply that knowledge to our own life until our behavior becomes aligned with God's divine purposes. When we apply gospel knowledge, we invite the Spirit to become part of our lives. After learning of God's word, we apply that truth to our lives by exchanging bad habits for productive actions, evil thoughts for proper and uplifting thoughts, the tendencies of the natural person for those of a spiritual being. That effort is enhanced as we dedicate ourselves to God, as we more fully become his sons and daughters, and as we partake of the power of his atonement.

The discussion of each parable in this book includes a section labeled Personal Application, in which we provide ideas of how each of us may apply that particular parable to our own lives. As you liken the parable's story and principles to yourself, the Spirit may help you see other ways you can apply to your life the truth the Savior has given us. In the end, biblical commentators can reveal only limited levels of meaning to the reader. It is the individual's responsibility to more fully grasp the parable's meaning and to apply it. As in all gospel study, understanding the parables and their application depends on our level of personal spiritual preparedness.

How Does One Interpret or Understand Parables?

The following keys assist us in understanding or interpreting the parables:

1. We must live the life of a disciple of Jesus Christ so that we can be enlightened by the Holy Spirit. The Holy Ghost is a revealer of truths and the power by which we can more fully understand the scriptures.

2. We must look at the parable's greater context or the circumstances that brought forth the parable. Joseph Smith explained, "I have a key by which I understand the scriptures. I enquire, what was the question which drew out the answer, or caused Jesus to utter the parable? . . . To ascertain its meaning, we must dig up the root and ascertain what it was that drew the saying out of Jesus."[22] Knowing the parable's setting contributes to our understanding of the parable.

3. In some cases, the scriptures themselves provide an interpretation of a parable. Occasionally, Jesus interpreted a parable after presenting it (for example, see Matthew 13:18–23), or he interpreted the parable after his disciples asked about the parable's meaning (see Matthew 15:15). The Doctrine and Covenants also provides interpretation of some parables. For example, Doctrine and Covenants 35:15–16 speaks regarding the parable of fig tree; Doctrine and Covenants 86:1–7 casts light on the parable of the wheat and tares; and Doctrine and Covenants 101:43–62 has some parallels with parable of the wicked husbandman.

4. Joseph Smith (see *Teachings,* 63–64, 94–102, 276–77) and other

latter-day authorities have provided commentary and insights into the meaning of some of the parables. A number of these authorities are cited throughout the book.

5. A great number of the parables pertain to the kingdom of God. (Some commentators have claimed that all of the parables, to a greater or lesser extent, touch upon God's kingdom.[23]) Such parables define the kingdom of God. They prepare us to enter the kingdom by teaching us about faith, love, service, obedience, priesthood authority, moral agency, and many other principles. They instruct us regarding the Lord's earthly and heavenly kingdoms and explain his life, ministry, atoning sacrifice, death, and resurrection. They teach us that Christ's kingdom is governed by love rather than by power and force, remind us to focus on spiritual riches rather than earthly wealth, and charge us to care for the fatherless and widows rather than ignore the poor and needy.

6. Avoid overinterpreting the parable. Richard Anderson provided this key: "Avoid the temptation to make every small detail of a parable have significance. Try to understand the main comparisons Jesus intended without bending his story to illogical lengths. It is a safe rule to err on the side of simplicity in interpreting parables."[24]

Robert J. Matthew provided this additional insight: "The message of a parable may be compared to a flash of light, like a beacon on a hill. Some parables are more literal than others, but all of them may be pressed beyond the limits of the original intent of the author. It is unnecessary to strain or to stretch the interpretation of an item in a parable to get more out of it than was originally intended. Interpreters sometimes engage in pulverizing a passage until it has but faint resemblance to its original form. There is little to be gained through defining and refining a parable until it is reduced to dust and powder—a process that is exhausting to the reader as well as to the text. Proper interpretation will draw out the intended meaning without belaboring a passage as if squeezing the last bit from a tube of toothpaste."[25]

7. *Lege, lege, lege, labore, ora, et relege*. This motto from the alchemists of the Middle Ages means "read, read, read, work (or experiment), pray, and reread."[26] This motto clearly applies to our study of the parables. We cannot grasp the full meaning of the parables through a simple reading; rather we must diligently study them, pray

about their meaning, and apply the principles they teach in our own lives.

As we prayerfully apply these keys to our study, the deeper meaning of the parables will be unfolded unto us—and we will grow in wonderful ways in our understanding of our God and his glorious purposes.

CHAPTER 1

THE SOWER AND THE SOILS

Matthew 13:3–9, 19–23

And he spake many things unto them in parables, saying, Behold, a sower went forth to sow;

And when he sowed, some seeds fell by the way side, and the fowls came and devoured them up:

Some fell upon stony places, where they had not much earth: and forthwith they sprung up, because they had no deepness of earth:

And when the sun was up, they were scorched; and because they had no root, they withered away.

And some fell among thorns; and the thorns sprung up, and choked them:

But other fell into good ground, and brought forth fruit, some an hundredfold, some sixtyfold, some thirtyfold.

Who hath ears to hear, let him hear. . . .

Hear ye therefore the parable of the sower.

When any one heareth the word of the kingdom, and understandeth it not, then cometh the wicked one, and catcheth away that which was sown in his heart. This is he which received seed by the way side.

But he that received the seed into stony places, the same is he that heareth the word, and anon with joy receiveth it;

Yet hath he not root in himself, but dureth for a while: for when tribulation or persecution ariseth because of the word, by and by he is offended.

He also that received seed among the thorns is he that heareth the word; and the care of this world, and the deceitfulness of riches, choke the word, and he becometh unfruitful.

But he that received seed into the good ground is he that heareth the word, and understandeth it; which also beareth fruit, and bringeth forth, some an hundredfold, some sixty, some thirty.[1]

This parable is typically called "the sower and the seeds," but it could more accurately be called the parable of the soils. In the story there is only one sower and one kind of seed. But there are many soils on which the seeds fall.

The image of a man sowing would have been very familiar to those who heard this parable. In fact, there may have been a farmer within eyesight doing that very thing. Those walking through the countryside of Palestine would have commonly seen fields of growing grain—and they would have been familiar with rocky places and patches of ground choked with weeds and thorns, where seeds would struggle to grow.

Sowing in Palestine was typically done in the fall, often in October, which may have been when this parable was uttered. The farmer would carry his seeds in a bag and would scatter them by hand, flinging them in every direction. Because of this method of sowing, the seed would fall on all kinds of ground: on the edges of the field as well as on the hard-packed trails that crisscrossed it; on a thin layer of soil overlaying rocky surfaces; among the thorns that were so prevalent in Palestine; and on the desirable good ground.

All of this, of course, was used as a metaphor for life, as was the case with all parables. The seed was the word of God, sent forth by Christ and carried by his servants, while the soils represented the different states of the hearts of men.

It is a common usage in the scriptures to compare the word of God to a seed planted within us. Paul wrote to the Colossians, "Ye heard before in the word of the truth of the gospel; which is come unto you, as it is in all the world; and bringeth forth fruit, as it doth also in you, since the day ye heard of it" (Colossians 1:5–6). In his epistle, James wrote, "Humbly accept the word planted in you, which can save you" (NIV, James 1:21). And Peter said that the righteous have been "born again, not of corruptible seed, but of incorruptible, by the word of God, which liveth and abideth forever" (1 Peter 1:23).

This comparison of God's word to a seed goes back to Isaiah: "For as the rain cometh down, and the snow from heaven, and returneth not thither, but watereth the earth, and maketh it bring forth and bud, that it may give seed to the sower, and bread to the eater: so shall my word be that goeth forth out of my mouth: it shall not return unto me void, but it shall accomplish that which I please, and it shall prosper in the thing whereto I sent it" (Isaiah 55:10–11).

This is one of the few parables that Jesus explicitly interpreted. Mark records, "And when he was alone, they that were about him with the twelve asked of him the parable. And he said unto them, Unto you it is given to know the mystery of the kingdom of God: but unto them that are without, all these things are done in parables. . . . And he said unto them, Know ye not this parable? And how then will ye know all parables?" (Mark 4:10–11, 13). Jesus then gave them the interpretation they had requested.

Commentary

> ***Matthew 13:3*** *And he spake many things unto them in parables, saying, Behold, a sower went forth to sow;*

Farm houses were unknown in Palestine in the time of Jesus. Instead, farmers (who constituted much of the rural population) lived together in towns, and then "went forth" to tend to their farms.

The act of sowing, as is made clear in subsequent verses, symbolizes the act of preaching the word and testifying of the truthfulness of the gospel.

> ***Matthew 13:4, 19*** *And when he sowed, some seeds fell by the way side, and the fowls came and devoured them up. . . . When any one heareth the word of the kingdom, and understandeth it*

not, then cometh the wicked one, and catcheth away that which was sown in his heart. This is he which received seed by the way side.

The wayside would have brought to mind the roads or paths that led around and through the farmer's fields, which were not accommodating to the seeds that were sown. When seeds fell on such hard and unprepared ground, they would have been unable to take root at all. Instead, the birds would cluster around and eat them all.

So it is with those whose hearts are hardened by sin or rebellion or the false traditions of their fathers. When people surrender themselves to enslaving addictions, when they hearken to the whisperings of the evil one, when they love darkness more than light, they allow "the wicked one" to catch "away that which was sown" in their hearts. Landing on such inhospitable ground, the precious gospel seed can take no root and is instead devoured by the fowls, or the devil and his helpers.

Joseph Smith said regarding the seeds that fell by the wayside, "Men who have no principle of righteousness in themselves, and whose hearts are full of iniquity, and have no desire for the principles of truth, do not understand the word of truth when they hear it. The devil taketh away the word of truth out of their hearts, because there is no desire for righteousness in them."[2]

Matthew 13:5–6, 20–21 *Some fell upon stony places, where they had not much earth: and forthwith they sprung up, because they had no deepness of earth: And when the sun was up, they were scorched; and because they had no root, they withered away. . . . But he that received the seed into stony places, the same is he that heareth the word, and anon with joy receiveth it; Yet hath he not root in himself, but dureth for a while: for when tribulation or persecution ariseth because of the word, by and by he is offended.*

When a seed falls upon ground that has only a thin layer of soil, it cannot properly get root. In time, when the sweltering sun beats down, the seed will be scorched and die.

Likewise, when converts receive testimonies on a superficial level but do not give their whole hearts to Christ, when they come to a shallow understanding of the truths of the gospel, they will be only lukewarm in their commitment. In time those with such hearts will be offended and fall away.

Trials can also be a great cause of people falling away from the truth they once so joyfully embraced. Paul spoke of how people have widely differing responses to the word of the gospel: "To the one we are the savour of death unto death; and to the other the savour of life unto life" (2 Corinthians 2:16). So likewise do some have diametrically differing responses to trials.

In this parable, the scorching of the sun is a symbol for tribulation. Because the seed has no root system, it has no way to sustain itself through the inevitable times of difficulty.

It is notable that the Lord said this person has "not root *in himself*." Such a person does not have the internal strength to resist the trials and afflictions of life—which strength comes through making God and his word essential elements in life. Those who have no such root are "offended" when "tribulation or persecution" arise.

Luke added the truth that those who receive the seed in stony places are the people who "for a while believe, and in time of temptation fall away" (Luke 8:13).

The sun is a blessing to those who are well rooted—trials can strengthen us and help us to become all that the Lord desires of us. But that same sun, symbolizing trials, can cause those who are not deeply rooted to fall away. The different responses to the same trials often depend on our relationship to God and his word.

> ***Matthew 13:7, 22*** *And some fell among thorns; and the thorns sprung up, and choked them. . . . He also that received seed among the thorns is he that heareth the word; and the care of this world, and the deceitfulness of riches, choke the word, and he becometh unfruitful.*

Thorns are common in Palestine, being found on thistles, brambles, and certain other bushes. In this parable, the thorns were not evident when the sowing was done. The thorns "sprung up" after the seeds were sown.

The soil in which the thorns grow must be good soil or the thorns would likely not be so abundant. But the seed is forced to compete with the thorns for nourishment—and the seed of gospel truth loses the competition, for the thorns "choke the word."

"So it is of the saints who think more of the honors of men, the educational standards of the world, political preferment, or money and property, than they do of the gospel. They know the Lord's work has been established on earth, but they let the cares of the world choke the word."[3]

In addition to the cares of this world and the selfish pursuit of riches, Luke adds the "pleasures of this life" as being among the things that choke the seeds. As a result, they "bring no fruit to perfection" (Luke 8:14).

> ***Matthew 13:8, 23*** *But other fell into good ground, and brought forth fruit, some an hundredfold, some sixtyfold, some thirtyfold. . . . But he that received seed into the good ground is he that heareth the word, and understandeth it; which also beareth fruit, and bringeth forth, some an hundredfold, some sixty, some thirty.*

The only seeds that ultimately bore fruit were those that fell on good ground. All others ceased growing before they could reach sufficient maturity. But even good ground is not all the same. Some good ground bore three times as much fruit as other such ground.

A key to the difference in the amount of fruit that is produced may be found in a metaphor Jesus used late in his life. Regarding plants and their fruits, Jesus said, "Abide in me, and I in you. As the branch cannot bear fruit of itself, except it abide in the vine; no more can ye, except ye abide in me. I am the vine, ye are the branches: He that abideth in me, and I in him, the same bringeth forth much fruit: for without me ye can do nothing. . . . If ye abide in me, and my words abide in you, ye shall ask what ye will, and it shall be done unto you. Herein is my Father glorified, that ye bear much fruit; so shall ye be my disciples" (John 15:4–5, 7–8).

Those who more fully abide in Christ, and allow Christ to abide in them, are those who "bear much fruit."

It is remarkable that in this parable the sower (Christ and his followers) scatter so many good seeds that never take root and bear fruit. But so it is in reality: missionaries will sow many seeds of testimony, service, and example as they serve the Lord. Most of those seeds will fall on unresponsive or unproductive soil. Nevertheless, the seeds that fall on good soil will bear such a rich harvest that the labor is worth all the sacrifice and effort expended.

To have your seeds multiply thirtyfold would have been considered a very good crop in the ancient world. But in this parable, some of the seeds bore even more fruit, as much as one hundredfold. The Lord would have us bear abundantly, as Paul said: "Be ye stedfast, unmoveable, always abounding in the work of the Lord" (1 Corinthians 15:58).

***Matthew 13:9, 18** Who hath ears to hear, let him hear. . . . Hear ye therefore the parable of the sower.*

Jesus frequently used this expression. In other words, he was saying, There is a meaning here that is important to seek out and to understand. Don't hear this only as a simple story from the life of a farmer but understand that it has an application to each person listening, one worth comprehending.

Personal Application

This parable describes four kinds of soils, each one representing the different states of the hearts of those who hear the word of God.

First is the "wayside heart," which is too hard to receive the word. How are hearts so hardened? They may be fettered by false religious or philosophical traditions. Or they may be bound by sin. Because of their hardened state, people with such hearts will reject the word outright. They won't give place at all to the gift of truth the sower brings them. Instead, they cast off that truth, leaving it for the birds, or Satan and his followers, to quickly take it away.

Those with this heart hear the word, but they give it no heed.

Second is the "thin-soil heart," which receives the word joyfully, but only briefly. The word enters into this heart but does not take root. Even though there is a thin covering of soil on the ground, beneath that soil is rock.

People with this heart hear the word and heed it—but only for a short season because they are not firmly rooted in the truth.

Third is the "thorn-infested heart," which doesn't allow room for the word. Before the seed has much chance to grow, the thorns quickly spring up and choke the tender plant.

People with this heart hear and heed, but their reaction to external influences soon causes them to turn away.

Fourth is the "good-soil heart," which is the open and prepared heart. It receives the word and provides for its nourishment and allows it to grow and bear good fruit.

Those with this heart hear the word, heed it, and endure to the end, bearing the fruit of righteousness.

One of the primary differences between the different kinds of soils (hearts) is their preparation. The soils that rejected the word were intrinsically no different from the good soil, except that the good soil had been prepared. It had been plowed, unlike the hard soil on the wayside. It had had the rocks removed, including those hiding under the surface. It had many of the thorns pulled out of it. That doesn't mean that our lives will be free of trials and tribulations. But when we bind ourselves to God, receiving his word with joy and commitment, we will have the strength and ability to retain his word in our hearts.

We prepare our hearts to receive God's word by having a desire, by being humble and open, by trusting in God and clinging to his gospel even when things are difficult, by refusing to be turned or distracted by the cares of the world or "the deceitfulness of riches."

President James E. Faust lamented the fact that, despite much success in preaching the gospel around the world, "at the same time, the ground seems to be hardening, and many are less receptive to things of the Spirit." But we don't have to simply give in to the forces that fight against God and his plan. "For the seeds of faith to sprout in our lives, we must avoid Satan's grasp," President Faust said. "We also need to prepare our own seedbed of faith. To do this we need to plow the soil through daily humble prayer, asking for strength and forgiveness. We need to harrow the soil by overcoming our feelings of pride. We need to prepare the seedbed by keeping the commandments to the best of our ability. We need to be honest with the Lord in the payment of our tithing and our other offerings. We need to be worthy and able to call forth the great powers of the priesthood to bless ourselves, our families, and others for whom we have responsibility. There is no better place for the spiritual seeds of our faith to be nurtured than within the hallowed sanctuaries of our temples and in our homes."[4]

Once we have received the seed in our hearts, we must thoughtfully care for it. Alma taught us how this is done. He said, "We will compare the word unto a seed. Now, if ye give place, that a seed may be planted in your heart, behold, if it be a true seed, or a good seed, if ye do not cast it out by your unbelief, that ye will resist the Spirit of the Lord, behold, it will begin to swell within your breasts." Through that process, Alma said, we would come to know that the seed was good, "or that the word is good." We would note that it enlarged the soul, enlightened the understanding, and tasted delicious (Alma 32:28).

But that would be only the beginning of the process. We must recognize the light of truth in the word. We must "nourish it with great care, that it may get root, that it may grow up, and bring forth fruit." If we instead "neglect the tree, and take no thought for its nourishment, behold it will not get any root; and when the heat of the sun cometh and scorcheth it, because it hath no root it withers away, and ye pluck it up and cast it out (Alma 32:37–38)."

If we cast the seed away at that point, that would not mean that the seed was not good; it would simply show that "your ground is barren." But if we do "nourish the tree as it beginneth to grow, by [our] faith with great diligence, and with patience, looking forward to the fruit thereof, it shall take root; and behold, it shall be a tree springing up unto everlasting life (Alma 32:41)."

When we finally partake of that fruit, we will discover that it is "most precious" and "sweet above all that is sweet, . . . and pure above all that is pure." Then, Alma says, "Ye shall feast upon this fruit even until ye are filled, that ye hunger not, neither shall ye thirst" (Alma 32:42).

Nephi taught that we enter into the kingdom "by the word of Christ with unshaken faith in him." Then, having entered in, we must "press forward, feasting upon the word of Christ, and endure to the end" (2 Nephi 31:19–20).

CHAPTER 2

The Seed Growing by Itself

Mark 4:26–29

And he said, So is the kingdom of God, as if a man should cast seed into the ground;

And should sleep, and rise night and day, and the seed should spring and grow up, he knoweth not how.

For the earth bringeth forth fruit of herself; first the blade, then the ear, after that the full corn in the ear.

But when the fruit is brought forth, immediately he putteth in the sickle, because the harvest is come.

Mark alone records this parable, which Jesus pronounced to the twelve apostles after the departure of a "great multitude" (Mark 4:1). Inasmuch as the apostles were given sacred knowledge beyond that provided to the masses, Jesus said to them: "Unto you it is given to know the mystery of the kingdom of God: but unto them that are without, all these things are done in parables" (Mark 4:11); also, "If any man have ears to hear, let him hear. And he said unto them, Take heed what ye hear: with what measure ye mete, it shall be measured to you: and unto you that hear shall more be given. For he that hath, to him shall be given: and he that hath not, from him shall be taken even that which he hath" (Mark 4:23–25). In other words, the apostless were expected to more fully receive into their hearts the truths Jesus taught and to apply them in their lives.

After saying these words, Jesus gave the parable of the seed growing by itself. This parable is but one passage where God uses seeds or agriculture to reveal truths to his people. For example, Isaiah recorded the parable of the farmer (Isaiah 28:23–29), Jacob quoted Zenos' allegory of the olive tree (Jacob 5), and Alma likened God's word to a seed that eventually became a tree (Alma 32). During his mortal ministry, Jesus presented several other parables that pertained to the topic of farming: the parable of the sower and the soils (Matthew 13:3–9, 18–23; Mark 4:3–8, 13–20; Luke 8:5–8, 11–15), the parable of the wheat and the tares (Matthew 13:24–30, 36–43), the parable of the mustard seed (Matthew 13:31–32; Mark 4:30–32; Luke 13:18–19), and the parable of the laborers in the vineyard (Matthew 20:1–16). In many such scriptural passages, God plays a central role—as Planter, Farmer, Vinedresser, Vineyard Owner, Harvester, and so forth. For example, in Isaiah's parable of the farmer, the Lord scatters his people as if they were seeds, and at the appropriate time "the Lord will gather and thresh his people [now ready to be harvested] in order to bring an increase to himself."[1]

Commentary

> ***Mark 4:26*** *And he said, So is the kingdom of God, as if a man should cast seed into the ground;*

The kingdom of God, or the Church of Jesus Christ, is likened to a seed that a farmer scatters upon the ground. As noted, farming was a common occupational endeavor in ancient Palestine, and these scenes represented familiar images to Jesus' hearers.

In this parable it is a farmer who casts the seed. The farmer represents any of the Lord's authorized ministers—apostles, full-time missionaries, Church members—who spread the gospel throughout the earth. The seed planter also refers to the mortal Jesus Christ, who was the ultimate sower. However, we cannot say of the Lord that "he knoweth not how" the seed springs up and grows, even though the parable applies that truth to his servants. According to the parable of the wheat and the tares, "He that soweth the good seed is the Son of man" (Matthew 13:37), or Jesus Christ (see also Isaiah 60:21; Jeremiah 12:2).

The seeds are symbolic of people. Again, the parable of the wheat and the tares details that the "good seed are the children of the kingdom" and the "tares are the children of the wicked one" (Matthew 13:38). Other scriptural passages also support the concept that seeds symbolize people when they refer to "the seed of the righteous" (Proverbs 11:21), "a seed of evildoers" (Isaiah 1:4), "the seed of men" (Daniel 2:43), and "the holy seed" (Isaiah 6:13). Also, those who receive and magnify their priesthood responsibilities become "the seed of Abraham" (D&C 84:34). When we are born again, we become "not of corruptible seed, but of incorruptible, by the word of God, which liveth and abideth for ever" (1 Peter 1:23; see 1 John 3:9). The lineage of Jesus, too, was compared to a seed, when Paul wrote that Jesus "was made of the seed of David according to the flesh" (Romans 1:3).

> ***Mark 4:27–28*** *And should sleep, and rise night and day, and the seed should spring and grow up, he knoweth not how. For the earth bringeth forth fruit of herself; first the blade, then the ear, after that the full corn in the ear.*

After the farmer scatters the seed upon the soil, the seed germinates and grows to become seedlings and then mature plants. Eventually the seeds produce grains or fruits or vegetables that are worthy of harvest. Meanwhile, as the seed is growing in the soil, time passes, represented in the parable by the farmer sleeping every night and rising every day. The minerals in the soil, the moisture from the earth and from sky above, and the sun shining on the soil all serve to cause the seeds to grow and to produce the crops. Jesus emphasizes the marvel that is associated with the growing crops when he says that the farmer "knoweth not how" the seed grows and springs forth into a full grown plant.

Jesus also points out that it is the earth "herself" that brings forth the fruit. It is not because of the farmer's power to produce fruit—it is a miracle. The farmer's sole action was to cast the seed upon the ground. This same miracle applies to the Church's growth, which continues day and night, miraculously, in a manner that is beyond human comprehension. The parable shows, then, the partnership that exists between God and men. Men cast the seed in the beginning of the planting season, and then they harvest the crops with the use of the sickle.

God's role is to cause the seeds to spring up and mature while the men sleep and in a manner that they do not understand. Even as the seed "should spring and grow up" without the farmer knowing how, so the Church grows miraculously without people fully comprehending how.

This parable has two primary applications.

1. The parable compares the steady growth of a seed to the spiritual growth of God's kingdom. Like the seed, the kingdom has small beginnings, but it continues to grow in a process that is gradual and constant until it reaches spiritual fruition and is ready for the harvest. Over the years this seed produces more seeds, and they multiply and grow so that eventually there is a large crop. The same is true of the kingdom of God, which began with a single individual and continues to grow into a great host of people. Daniel's vision of "the stone which is cut out of the mountain without hands" is a similar illustration of the small beginnings of God's kingdom that grows "until it has filled the whole earth" (D&C 65:2; see Daniel 2:34–45).

2. The seed of this parable may also be likened to the total and complete conversion of a disciple of Jesus Christ. The seed of faith is first planted in the disciple's heart and then God cares for that seed and provides nourishment. In time that person, like the seed, spiritually matures and produces fruit, or good works. As Paul explained, "I have planted, Apollos watered; but God gave the increase" (1 Corinthians 3:6).

A comparable passage to this interpretation of the seed growing by itself is found in Alma 32, where God's word is compared to a seed that is planted in one's heart. The seed grows until it becomes a tree of life and eventually produces the most precious, sweet, white, and pure fruit that one can feast upon (see especially Alma 32:28–29, 41–42).

> ***Mark 4:29*** *But when the fruit is brought forth, immediately he putteth in the sickle, because the harvest is come.*

Jesus' parable concludes with the crop's growth to maturity and the use of a sickle to accomplish the harvest. A sickle is a tool with a wooden handle and a curved blade used to cut tall grass and fully grown grain. Mention of the sickle reveals that the seed cast to the earth is a grain seed. Sickles are used to harvest grains, not dates, olives, figs, grapes or other crops common to Palestine. The harvest is a symbol of missionary work in the New Testament (see Mark 4:29; Luke 10:2; John 4:35) and the Book of Mormon (Alma 17:13; 26:7), where God himself serves as "the Lord of the harvest" (Alma 26:7). The Doctrine and Covenants also has many passages regarding the harvest. A familiar theme pertains to the crops' maturity, set forth as the familiar expression, "The field is white already to harvest" (D&C 4:4; 6:3; 33:3, 7).

One passage connects the work of the harvest with the salvation of the harvester: "For behold the field is white already to harvest; and lo, he that thrusteth in his sickle with his might, the same layeth up in store that he perisheth not, but bringeth salvation to his soul" (D&C 4:4; see also 6:3). Several passages link the harvest with the last days. For example, Doctrine and Covenants 33:3 states, "For behold, the field is white already to harvest; and it is the eleventh hour, and the last time that I shall call laborers into my vineyard" (see D&C 6:3; 33:7; 101:64). The favorite tool of the harvest is the sickle: "Whoso desireth to reap, let him thrust in his sickle with his might" (D&C 6:3); and, "Thrust in your sickles, and reap with all your might, mind, and strength" (D&C 33:7).

The harvest theme is also connected with God's judgments upon the wicked at the second coming of Christ. The Lord's earthly ministers conduct the early work of the harvest, sowing seeds and harvesting the wheat with their sickles; in the end of days, at the time of the judgment, angels serve as God's reapers when they take their sickles and conduct the final harvest of the wicked. According to the parable of the wheat and tares, "The reapers are the angels. . . . The Son of man shall send forth his angels, and they shall gather out of his kingdom all things that offend, and them which do iniquity" (Matthew 13:39, 41; see also Joel 3:13; Revelation 14:14–16; D&C 45:2; 56:16). A revelation to Joseph Smith speaks of the harvest and the eventual burning of the tares: "Therefore, let the wheat and the tares grow together until the harvest is fully ripe; then ye shall first gather out the wheat from among the tares, and after the gathering of the wheat, behold and lo, the tares are bound in bundles, and the field remaineth to be burned" (D&C 86:7).

Personal Application

The parable of the seed growing by itself demonstrates that both God and mortals have a role in the growth of his kingdom. A mortal casts the seed into the ground; God, working with the creative forces that he instilled in the natural world, causes the seed to spring up and grow and to eventually bring forth fruit. Missionary work, too, is a work that embraces the work of mortals who join with God's powerful forces. We as mortals often plant gospel seeds in the hearts of our children, our neighbors, or even strangers; and God works with those people, perhaps for years or decades, until many become his faithful sons and daughters. "Seeds sown in the soil of the earth and seeds sown in the souls of men, both spring forth by a power greater than that of the sower."[2]

In a talk titled "Planting Gospel Seeds of Spirituality," Elder David B. Haight told of a woman who spent much of her life planting gospel seeds. Her plantings were cared for and increased by God's eternal power, though the mortals "knoweth not how," until many souls had received the blessings of the gospel. Elder Haight related: "Some years ago such a precious seed was planted in fertile soil in Germany."

Robert Frederick Lippolt and his family lived in a small city in central Germany. Robert, a house painter, provided a modest living for his family. "One Sunday, while on her way to the Protestant church, Robert's wife was approached by Mormon missionaries, who invited her to attend sacrament meeting. She attended and was impressed."

She eventually was baptized and became a faithful member of the Church. Their daughters also were touched by the Spirit and were baptized. But Robert resisted the message, even becoming antagonistic toward the Church.

Anxious to get away from the Mormons in Germany, Robert moved his family to Mexico, and then to Brazil. Everywhere she went, Robert's wife spread the good news of the gospel. And people listened.

"Bitterness filled Robert. He hated the Mormons. He prevented his children from going to public school, for fear they would learn to read and would thus be further indoctrinated with Mormon literature.

"Finally, in desperation, he took his family away from civilization to the interior of Brazil. They settled in the remote, peaceful valley of Ipomeia, in the state of Santa Catarina."

In that new location, Sister Lippolt asked that an official representative of the Church visit her area. A mission president came and realized the missionaries could enjoy "much success . . . among the German-speaking people of Brazil. From the tiny seeds sown by missionaries in Germany and carried across the Atlantic, the First Presidency established a mission in Brazil in February 1935. The work now flourishes. Hundreds, then thousands heard the good news. Now [1973] there are four missions in Brazil and four stakes of Zion."

And the husband? "Even Robert Frederick, the once bitter husband and father, was eventually touched by the seed of truth, for at the age of 83 he was carried in his wooden rocking chair to the nearby River Rio de Peixe and baptized a member of The Church of Jesus Christ of Latter-day Saints."

Elder Haight concluded: "Mothers and fathers need to plant the seeds of the gospel firmly in the hearts of their children, to create in them a desire to serve and also to know how to serve—seeds of hard work, seeds of courtesy, seeds of thrift.

"Then, deep in their hearts, your sons and daughters need to have planted the more valuable seeds of spirituality—the seeds of cleanliness, the seeds of love, the seeds of virtue, the seeds of courage."[3]

CHAPTER 3

The Wheat and the Tares

Matthew 13:24–30, 36–43

Another parable put he forth unto them, saying, The kingdom of heaven is likened unto a man which sowed good seed in his field:

But while men slept, his enemy came and sowed tares among the wheat, and went his way.

But when the blade was sprung up, and brought forth fruit, then appeared the tares also.

So the servants of the householder came and said unto him, Sir, didst not thou sow good seed in thy field? from whence then hath it tares?

He said unto them, An enemy hath done this. The servants said unto him, Wilt thou then that we go and gather them up?

But he said, Nay; lest while ye gather up the tares, ye root up also the wheat with them.

Let both grow together until the harvest: and in the time of harvest I will say to the reapers, Gather ye together first the tares, and bind them in bundles to burn them: but gather the wheat into my barn. . . .

Then Jesus sent the multitude away, and went into the house: and his disciples came unto him, saying, Declare unto us the parable of the tares of the field.

He answered and said unto them, He that soweth the good seed is the Son of man;

The field is the world; the good seed are the children of the kingdom; but the tares are the children of the wicked one;

The enemy that sowed them is the devil; the harvest is the end of the world; and the reapers are the angels.

As therefore the tares are gathered and burned in the fire; so shall it be in the end of this world.

The Son of man shall send forth his angels, and they shall gather out of his kingdom all things that offend, and them which do iniquity;

And shall cast them into a furnace of fire: there shall be wailing and gnashing of teeth.

Then shall the righteous shine forth as the sun in the kingdom of their Father. Who hath ears to hear, let him hear.

This parable starts off simply enough: A man went out to sow seeds in his field. He made sure they were good seeds; weed seeds were removed before the sowing took place. But then something sinister happened: an enemy came into his field at night and sowed weed seeds among the wheat seeds.

Because the enemy acted under cover of darkness, apparently the man and his servants were unaware of his wicked act. But when the plants began to grow, the weeds became apparent.

The servants were ready to immediately go into the field to try to pull out the tares. But because the plants were growing so closely together, and because the wheat plants and the tares were so similar in appearance, the owner of the field instructed his servants to wait. The wheat and the tares would be separated at the time of harvest. At that time the wheat would be stored in the barn and the tares would be burned.

After Jesus concluded the parable, his disciples waited until they could be alone with him, then asked for an interpretation. Jesus' interpretation was plain and to the point: the sower was Christ himself; the field represented the world; the good and bad seed represented the good and bad people of the world; the enemy represented Satan; the reapers at harvest time are the angels of God; and the harvest is symbolic of the end of the world.

"We learn by this parable," Joseph Smith wrote, "not only the setting up of the Kingdom in the days of the Savior which is represented by the good seed, which produced fruit, but also the corruptions of the Church, which are represented by the tares which were sown by the enemy, which His disciples would fain have plucked up, or cleansed the Church of, if their views had been favored by the Savior. But He, knowing all things, says, Not so. As much as to say, your views are not correct, the Church is in its infancy, and if you take this rash step, you will destroy the wheat, or the Church, with the tares; therefore it is better to let them grow together until the harvest, or the end of the world, which means the destruction of the wicked, which is not yet fulfilled. . . .

"The harvest and the end of the world have an allusion directly to the human family in the last days. . . . As, therefore, the tares are gathered and burned in the fire, so shall it be in the end of the world; that is, as the servants of God go forth warning the nations, both priests and people, and as they harden their hearts and reject the light of truth, these first being delivered over to the buffetings of Satan, and the law and the testimony being closed up, as it was in the case of the Jews, they are left in darkness, and delivered over unto the day of burning; thus being bound up by their creeds, and their bands being made strong by their priests, [they] are prepared for the fulfilment of the saying of the Savior—'The Son of Man shall send forth His angels, and gather out of His Kingdom all things that offend, and them which do iniquity, and shall cast them into a furnace of fire, there shall be wailing and gnashing of teeth.' We understand that the work of gathering together of the wheat into barns, or garners, is to take place while the tares are being bound over, and [incident to] preparing for the day of burning; [and] that after the day of burnings, the righteous shall shine forth like the sun, in the Kingdom of their Father."[1]

Elder Bruce R. McConkie saw this parable as a great overview of God's work from the time of Christ to the time of the exaltation of the righteous Saints: "In giving the parable of the wheat and the tares, Jesus was actually summarizing the doctrines of the apostasy, the restoration of the gospel in the latter-days, the growth and development of the latter-day kingdom, the millennial cleansing of the earth, the glorious advent of the Son of Man, and the ultimate celestial exaltation of the faithful."[2]

Commentary

***Matthew 13:24** Another parable put he forth unto them, saying, The kingdom of heaven*

The kingdom of heaven is the kingdom of God on the earth, or the Church of Jesus Christ. Through this parable Jesus is teaching an important truth about his kingdom.

***Matthew 13:24, 37** is likened unto a man which sowed good seed. . . . He answered and said unto them, He that soweth the good seed is the Son of man;*

In the parable of the sower and the soils, the seeds represent the word of God, but here the good seed symbolizes those people who receive the word in their hearts, or those who have come unto Christ and his kingdom.

Jesus Christ is the father of our salvation. He is the chosen administrator of the Father's plan, the source of the power, through the Atonement, that enables us to return to the Father's presence. He brings good things into the world. When we yield our hearts unto him, his power can help us to grow up in righteousness, help us come to repentance and a change of heart, help us to be good. Through Christ, we can be sown as good seed in the world.

Latter-day revelation sheds further light on this parable. As the Lord said to Joseph Smith, "Verily, thus saith the Lord unto you my servants, concerning the parable of the wheat and of the tares: Behold, verily I say, the field was the world, and the apostles were the sowers of the seed" (D&C 86:1–2). As we learn here, the sower is not only Christ, but also his apostles—and by extension, all those who go forth preaching the word and bringing souls unto Christ.

Matthew 13:24, 38 *in his field: . . . The field is the world;*

The world, this earth on which we dwell, has been provided to give us all we need to rise to the spiritual stature our Heavenly Father intends for us. It is capable of growing good seed; with the help of the sower, we can become godly. Or, if we choose, we can grow as tares.

The world is the setting in which the Lord's missionary force works. We are to cover the entire earth with the message of Christ and the restoration of his gospel. As we sow good seeds (as in this parable), we are not planting truth in the field; we are planting righteous souls in all parts of the earth.

Matthew 13:25, 38–39 *But while men slept, his enemy came and sowed tares among the wheat, and went his way. . . . [T]he good seed are the children of the kingdom; but the tares are the children of the wicked one; The enemy that sowed them is the devil;*

The tares here mentioned are typically viewed as the darnel weed, which is a species of bearded rye grass. When the two species of plants are young, they look very much like wheat. And as the darnel weed grows, its roots typically intertwine with the roots of the wheat. Thus, it is difficult to separate the two while they are growing without damaging the wheat. If darnel is harvested with the wheat and mixed into bread, it will bring a bitter taste; it causes dizziness and can act as a violent emetic. The darnel must therefore be separated from the wheat at harvest time.

Satan has taken upon himself a destructive mission in this world. It is his plan and desire to hurt us, to distract and disturb us, to seek to weaken us. In some cases he will seduce good seed into changing into bad. Other good seed he will weaken or harm by taking some of their nourishment. He often does this through his servants (the bad seed), who seek to turn us from our spiritual obligations and opportunities—receiving God's word in our lives, communing with God in prayer, and serving God and man in a spirit of love.

The adversary has sought from the beginning to sow these tares among the wheat. No sooner had Adam taught the gospel among his posterity than "Satan came among them, saying: I am also a son of God; and he [Satan] commanded them [Adam's posterity], saying: Believe it not; and they believed it not, and they loved Satan more than God. And men began from that time forth to be carnal, sensual, and devilish" (Moses 5:13).

Truly the devil is our enemy.

But the Lord does not leave his children defenseless; he sends his Spirit to help them understand the truth: "And the Lord God called upon men by the Holy Ghost everywhere and commanded them that they should repent" (Moses 5:14).

When Jesus walked in mortality he warned that people can become children of Satan, rather than children of God: "Ye are of your father the devil, and the lusts of your father ye will do," he said to the wicked among the Jews. "He was a murderer from the beginning, and abode not in the truth, because there is no truth in him. When he speaketh a lie, he speaketh of his own: for he is a liar, and the father of it" (John 8:44). As is the father, so are the children. They give their lives to lust, to lies, careless of damage to those around them. In doing so, they are as weeds among the wheat, seeking to harm and hinder the growth of all that is good and of God.

What do the tares look like? Outwardly, they look just like the wheat. But inwardly they are carnal and sensual; they love falsehood (whether in religion, science, philosophy, or governmental system) more than they love truth. The tares include those who belong to spiritual Babylon, "the mother of abominations" (D&C 88:94).

Paul spoke accusingly of those who "walked according to the course of this world, according to the prince of the power of the air, the spirit that now worketh in the children of disobedience" (Ephesians 2:2). The spirit of those who follow Satan is the same spirit that leads people to choose to be sown as tares in the earth.

This parable teaches us four important truths about "the children of the kingdom":

1. They are utterly dependent on Christ. He is the sower, and they are his seed. They come into the kingdom because of him.

2. God is named as "their Father." He has prepared a place in his eternal kingdom for them.

3. They are called "righteous." They have chosen to follow the path that is good and true.

4. They not only enter the Father's kingdom, but they "shine forth as the sun" there. They are glorified and enter a kingdom of glory.

Similarly, the parable teaches us truths about "the children of the wicked one":

1. They are sown by the devil. He plays an important role in their becoming unprofitable, evil plants.

2. They "offend" the Lord and are "them which do iniquity." They choose to act contrary to the law and will of God.

3. They shall be burned at the time of the destruction of the wicked, and then they shall be cast into hell.

Obviously, the course of being "good seed," of being wheat, is the course of happiness—while the path of the wicked, the tares of the world, leads to misery and destruction.

Doctrine and Covenants 86:3 shows that this parable has application not only to the growth of the Church in the time of Christ, but also to the time of the great apostasy: "And after they [the apostles] have fallen asleep the great persecutor of the church, the apostate, the whore, even Babylon, that maketh all nations to drink of her cup, in whose hearts the enemy, even Satan, sitteth to reign—behold he soweth the tares; wherefore, the tares choke the wheat and drive the church into the wilderness."

In this interpretation, those who sow the tares are the servants of Satan, as well as Satan himself. The result is that the true believers in Jesus Christ are persecuted and driven into hiding. Thus began the great apostasy, when the tares grew freely in every habitable corner of the earth.

> ***Matthew 13:26–27*** *But when the blade was sprung up, and brought forth fruit, then appeared the tares also. So the servants of the householder came and said unto him, Sir, didst not thou sow good seed in thy field? from whence then hath it tares?*

As noted, tares are not benign weeds. They are harmful. They take of the sustenance intended for the wheat, thereby weakening the good plants.

Even though in their early stages tares are indistinguishable from wheat, in their more mature form, one can easily tell the difference, for they bear different kinds of fruit. In the Sermon on the Mount, Jesus taught his followers how to distinguish good people from bad:

"Ye shall know them by their fruits. Do men gather grapes of thorns, or figs of thistles? Even so every good tree bringeth forth good fruit; but a corrupt tree bringeth forth evil fruit. A good tree cannot bring forth evil fruit, neither can a corrupt tree bring forth good fruit. Every tree that bringeth not forth good fruit is hewn down, and cast into the fire. Wherefore by their fruits ye shall know them" (Matthew 7:16–20).

The Lord sows only good seed, as his servants noted. If there are ever tares in the world—or in the Church—they do not flow from Christ or his work, but from those who are his enemies.

> ***Matthew 13:28–29*** *He said unto them, An enemy hath done this. The servants said unto him, Wilt thou then that we go and gather them up? But he said, Nay; lest while ye gather up the tares, ye root up also the wheat with them.*

The Lord's true servants have deep concern for his kingdom. When they see things amiss, they desire to set them right.

Yet it is very difficult, if not impossible, to tell the difference between wheat and tares when the plants are young. In the same way, it is sometimes impossible to tell the true followers of Christ from hypocrites, or those who follow with their lips but not their hearts. Hence, the Lord tells his followers to wait until the fruit is manifest before the gathering of the tares takes place.

In latter-day revelation the Lord has given us this continuing interpretation of the parable:

"But behold, in the last days, even now while the Lord is beginning to bring forth the word, and the blade is springing up and is yet tender—Behold, verily I say unto you, the angels are crying unto the Lord day and night, who are ready and waiting to be sent forth to reap down the fields; But the Lord saith unto them, pluck not up the tares while the blade is yet tender (for verily your faith is weak), lest you destroy the wheat also" (D&C 86:4–6).

The world in the last days is full of sin and corruption; tares have been sown everywhere, and they commonly outnumber the wheat. During these days when the Church is being established in various parts of the world, it is often small and relatively weak. Because the righteous as a body are still young and tender (and because their faith yet needs to be strengthened), the Lord delays the harvest of the tares until the time is right.

> ***Matthew 13:30, 39–40*** *Let both grow together until the harvest: and in the time of harvest I will say to the reapers, Gather ye together first the tares, and bind them in bundles to burn them: but gather the wheat into my barn. . . . [T]he harvest is the end of the world; and the reapers are the angels. As therefore the tares are gathered and burned in the fire; so shall it be in the end of this world.*

Comparing the end of the world to a harvest is a common analogy in the scriptures (see Hosea 6:11; Revelation 14:15; D&C 45:2). It is a time of judgment (see Revelation 20:12–13). It is a time when the righteous will be rewarded and the wicked will be punished, a punishment that is often symbolized by fire and burning. The end of the world, of course, is not the end of the physical earth. It is the end of the world of wickedness. As Joseph Smith was inspired to write in his translation of the Bible, "The harvest is the end of the world, or the destruction of the wicked" (JST, Matthew 13:39).

The Lord added through Joseph Smith: "Therefore, let the wheat and the tares grow together until the harvest is fully ripe; then ye shall first gather out the wheat from among the tares, and after the gathering of the wheat, behold and lo, the tares are bound in bundles, and the field remaineth to be burned" (D&C 86:7).

In this latter-day revelation, as in the Joseph Smith Translation, the wheat is shown to be gathered first. This inspired change to the record in the New Testament reflects the reality of the latter-day work the

Lord is doing: he is first gathering the pure in heart into his kingdom; then, later, he will gather and burn the tares.

When Christ comes again, a literal fire will burn the earth and every corruptible thing on its face (see 1 Nephi 22:15–17). This fire will purify the face of the earth and prepare it to be a paradisiacal glory for those who continue to dwell here.

But even now some of the harvesting is occurring, as the wheat is being identified and gathered "into my barn." Angels restored priesthood keys to Joseph Smith, who in turn sent forth priesthood holders to reap the world. As the Lord said in Doctrine and Covenants 4:4, "Behold the field is white already to harvest; and lo, he that thrusteth in his sickle with his might, the same layeth up in store that he perisheth not, but bringeth salvation to his soul."

The reaping of the tares is yet to happen, but even now "the angels are waiting the great command to reap down the earth, to gather the tares that they may be burned" (D&C 38:12). But not only angels will participate in the reaping. The Joseph Smith Translation indicates that "the reapers are the angels, or the messengers sent of heaven." That same translation then ends the parable by saying, "For the world shall be burned with fire" (JST, Matthew 13:40, 44).

> ***Matthew 13:41–42*** *The Son of man shall send forth his angels, and they shall gather out of his kingdom all things that offend, and them which do iniquity; And shall cast them into a furnace of fire: there shall be wailing and gnashing of teeth.*

One of the great principles of the gospel is that Israel, the true children of the kingdom, will be gathered. Through that gathering they will be able to receive ordinances and covenants, participate together in the blessings of the temple, and strengthen one another in a Zion society.

But here we learn that the wicked also shall be gathered. They will be separated from the Lord's kingdom and consigned to a punishment of misery and torment (the place called hell, represented by a furnace of fire), until the day of redemption, when they will be blessed to live in a kingdom of glory, although it will be a lower kingdom than they might have received. (Some, however—the sons of perdition—will be cast forever into outer darkness.)

Again the Joseph Smith Translation makes important changes: "For in that day, before the Son of man shall come, he shall send forth his angels and messengers of heaven." And rather than making reference to the furnace of fire, that translation reads concerning those "things that offend, and them which do iniquity," that the Lord's angels " . . . shall cast them out among the wicked" (JST, Matthew 13:42–43).

> ***Matthew 13:43*** *Then shall the righteous shine forth as the sun in the kingdom of their Father. Who hath ears to hear, let him hear.*

Shining as the sun alludes to the blessings of dwelling in the Father's presence, in the celestial kingdom. As Joseph Smith learned by revelation: "These are they whose bodies are celestial, whose glory is that of the sun, even the glory of God, the highest of all, whose glory the sun of the firmament is written of as being typical" (D&C 76:70).

Malachi uses judgment language that is similar to that found in this parable: "For, behold, the day cometh, that shall burn as an oven; and all the proud, yea, and all that do wickedly, shall be stubble: and the day that cometh shall burn them up, saith the LORD of hosts. . . . But unto you that fear my name shall the Sun of righteousness arise with healing in his wings" (Malachi 4:1–2).

Personal Application

This parable has a number of immediate applications for Saints in the latter days. We have the privilege of participating both in the sowing and the harvesting. We can represent God and his angels in seeking out souls who will turn their hearts to Christ. And we can help to gather that good wheat into the kingdom.

At the same time, we need to make sure we are good seeds ourselves, that we are growing up as wheat and not as tares, that we are following Christ rather than the adversary.

We choose to be wheat by coming unto Christ with all our desire, by receiving the ordinances and covenants of the gospel, and by continuing in righteousness until the end.

We also choose to be wheat by rejecting the wiles of Satan. As noted in the parable, Satan often works in the dark. He comes at us when we are not looking, when our attention is turned elsewhere. When we are focusing on reading the scriptures more in our lives, for example, he may seek to prompt an increase in anger in our hearts. It is almost proverbial how he seems to cause problems when we're getting ready to have family home evening or go to the temple.

Satan also will attack us when we are sleeping spiritually. Prophets have repeatedly warned us against spiritual slumber. For example, Jacob pleaded, "O my brethren, hearken unto my words; arouse the faculties of your souls; shake yourselves that ye may awake from the slumber of death; and loose yourselves from the pains of hell that ye may not become angels to the devil, to be cast into that lake of fire and brimstone which is the second death" (Jacob 3:11).

Earlier, his father, Lehi, had cried out to his children in the same vein: "O that ye would awake; awake from a deep sleep, yea, even from the sleep of hell, and shake off the awful chains by which ye are bound, which are the chains which bind the children of men, that they are carried away captive down to the eternal gulf of misery and woe. Awake! and arise from the dust, and hear the words of a trembling parent" (2 Nephi 1:13–14).

After Satan does his evil work, he will typically slink away (he "went his way"). He often likes to work anonymously, without getting credit. He seeks the Father's honor, but not immediately. For now he will hide his true identity. Satan falsely declared to Moses that he was the Only Begotten (Moses 1:19). He told Korihor he was an angel of God (Alma 30:53; see 2 Corinthians 11:13–14). So will he seek to deceive us. When Satan gives us thoughts, feelings, or ideas, he will tell us that they are from God—or that they are our own. He will sow tares in our lives and then slink away and let them grow. With the Lord's help, we can develop the gift of discernment, one use of which is to help us more fully understand our own thoughts and feelings.

It is important to note that there are two sowers in this parable: Jesus (and his followers) and Satan (and those who follow him). We can choose in whose hands we will place ourselves. We can choose to be the children of the kingdom, rather than the children of darkness. When we do, we will, in the end, be blessed to "shine forth as the sun in the kingdom of [our] Father."

CHAPTER 4

THE MUSTARD SEED

Matthew 13:31–32

Another parable put he forth unto them, saying, The kingdom of heaven is like to a grain of mustard seed, which a man took, and sowed in his field:

Which indeed is the least of all seeds: but when it is grown, it is the greatest among herbs, and becometh a tree, so that the birds of the air come and lodge in the branches thereof.

Jesus presented this parable to a large group of disciples near Capernaum, a small town located on the northern shore of the Sea of Galilee. So great was the multitude that Jesus "went into a ship, and sat; and the whole multitude stood on the shore" (Matthew 13:2). The parable of the mustard seed is the third of several parables, all about seeds and planting, that Jesus delivered to this group; it follows the parables of the sower (Matthew 13:3–9, 18–23) and the wheat and tares (Matthew 13:24–30, 36–43).

Three of the Gospel writers—Matthew, Mark (4:30–32), and Luke (13:18–19)—recorded this parable. Matthew opens the parable with a simple statement, "The kingdom of heaven is like to a grain of mustard seed."

This parable forms a pair with the parable of the leaven. Both open with the same formula: "The kingdom of heaven is like . . ." (Matthew 13:31, 33); both feature a human character, one a man and the other a woman (Matthew 13:31, 33); both associate the verb *take* with the human character, "which a man took" and "which a woman took" (Matthew 13:31, 33). The central element of both parables is a small amount of substance—one compares the kingdom of heaven to a tiny seed, and the other compares a little leaven. Both things grow to great size (when compared with the beginning size)—a large tree and an expanded loaf. (For more parallels, see the discussion on the parable of the leaven on page 36.)

The parable of the mustard seed also parallels the parable of the seed growing by itself (Mark 4:26–29). Both parables compare the kingdom of God to a seed that grows into a mature plant, and both seeds eventually yield produce that is beneficial to humankind.

Commentary

> ***Matthew 13:31*** *Another parable put he forth unto them, saying, The kingdom of heaven is like to a grain of mustard seed, which a man took, and sowed in his field:*

Jesus compares a mustard seed to the kingdom of heaven, or the Lord's church. At first the comparison seems to be very unlikely because of the smallness of the mustard seed and the greatness of God's kingdom. But as we will see below, the comparison is fitting.

As Jesus compared the kingdom of God to a seed that grows into a large tree, some of his hearers may have recalled Old Testament passages wherein trees were compared to kings and kingdoms. King Nebuchadnezzar and his kingdom, for instance, were compared to a great tree, a tree that "was strong, and the height thereof reached unto heaven, and the sight thereof to the end of all the earth," and fowls lived in its branches and beasts under its shadows (Daniel 4:10–24). Similarly, speaking to Ezekiel, the Lord compared the great and mighty Assyrian nation to a tall cedar, which was taller than all other trees. Fowls also nested in this tall tree (Ezekiel 31:3–9; see also Judges 9:7–16). At the end of the world, however, none of the earthly kingdoms will continue to grow. Only God's kingdom will flourish and provide fruit for the kingdom's inhabitants.

Matthew 13:32 *Which indeed is the least of all seeds: but when it is grown, it is the greatest among herbs, and becometh a tree,*

Jesus presents a contrast by using the words *least* and *greatest.* A mustard seed was the least[1] or the smallest of all seeds used by farmers at the time of Jesus Christ, but the plant that grew from that seed would eventually become the "greatest among herbs." As a mature tree it would grow to a height of eight to ten feet. The comparison of God's kingdom to the smallest of seeds may have shocked Jesus' hearers, who were anticipating a kingdom large and powerful enough to prevail over all other kingdoms, including the Roman Empire, which dominated at the time the parable was uttered. Certainly the comparison of the kingdom to a mature cedar or a mighty oak would have been more appropriate. But the parable particularly applied to the kingdom of God that would be established in the last days and that would continue to grow through the Millennium. This kingdom is The Church of Jesus Christ. Even though the seed of that kingdom was initially planted in Jesus' day, it eventually went dormant and remained so for centuries, until it sprouted with the restoration of the gospel.

Joseph Smith taught this interpretation in an unmistakable manner when he said: "The Kingdom of Heaven is like unto a mustard seed. Behold, then is not this the Kingdom of Heaven that is raising its head in the last days in the majesty of its God, even the Church of the Latter-day Saints, like an impenetrable, immovable rock in the midst of the mighty deep."[2]

In the same sermon, the Prophet Joseph Smith taught: "Let us take the Book of Mormon, which a man took and hid in his field, securing it by his faith, to spring up in the last days, or in due time; let us behold it coming forth out of the ground, which is indeed accounted the least of all seeds, but behold it branching forth, yea, even towering, with lofty branches, and God-like majesty, until it, like the mustard seed, becomes the greatest of all herbs. And it is truth, and it has sprouted and come forth out of the earth, and righteousness begins to look down from heaven, and God is sending down His powers, gifts and angels, to lodge in the branches thereof."[3]

Again, on the same occasion, Joseph Smith explained that the parable's fulfillment would take place in the last days: "And again, another parable put [Jesus] forth unto them, having an allusion to the Kingdom that should be set up, just previous to or at the time of the harvest, which reads as follows—'The Kingdom of Heaven is like a grain of mustard seed, which a man took and sowed in his field: which indeed is the least of all seeds: but, when it is grown, it is the greatest among herbs, and becometh a tree, so that the birds of the air come and lodge in the branches thereof.' Now we can discover plainly that this figure is given to represent the Church as it shall come forth in the last days."[4]

Speaking of a tiny mustard seed is a wonderful way to describe the humble beginnings of the Church. It began with one man, Joseph Smith, who did not receive a formal education. At first the Church was utterly obscure when compared to the mighty nations and kingdoms that then existed upon the earth, with their kings and queens, presidents and prime ministers, and advanced governmental structures and judicial systems. These nations and kingdoms possessed national treasures: vast plots of land, fleets of ships, navies and armies, castles and palaces, and millions of tax-paying citizens who vowed support to their leaders.

Although the beginning of the Church was as a very small seed, through the decades it has grown to become a tree, with branches large enough to host birds. In the language of a revelation to Joseph Smith, the kingdom of God is destined to gain strength, become great, and obtain favor among the kingdoms of the world. Further, the kingdom will have its own armies, called "the army of Israel" and "the armies of Israel," which armies may refer to the great numbers of its hosts or its spiritual armaments and powers or perhaps something else besides. The revelation states that the Lord will cause his "army [to] become very great, and [to] be sanctified before me, that it may become fair as the sun, and clear as the moon, and that her banners may be terrible unto all nations; That the kingdoms of this world may be constrained to acknowledge that the kingdom of Zion is in very deed the kingdom of our God and his Christ" (D&C 105:31–32).

Matthew 13:32 *so that the birds of the air come and lodge in the branches thereof.*

The birds that will lodge in the tree's branches symbolize God's angels. Joseph Smith gave us this clear meaning when he taught, "The Kingdom of Heaven is like a grain of mustard seed. The mustard seed is small, but brings forth a large tree, and the fowls lodge in the branches. The fowls are the angels. Thus angels come down, combine together to gather their children, and gather them."[5] On another occasion the Prophet taught, concerning the parable of the mustard seed, that "God is sending down His powers, gifts and angels, to lodge in the branches thereof."[6] A representation of a bird in Facsimile 1 of the book of Abraham is another example of a bird representing an angel.

Personal Application

Those of us living today did not personally witness the very small beginnings of the Church in the early years of this dispensation. At first the Church membership consisted of a tiny mustard seed, or a single individual, the Prophet Joseph Smith. The Church then grew to a handful, then a few hundred, and later several thousand. Although we were not alive to witness this early period, all of us have witnessed, to some degree, the growth of the Church during the past few years or decades.

For instance, in 1930, the centennial year of the Church, there were 670,000 members. Twenty years later Church membership barely exceeded one million. But now, during the opening years of the twenty-first century, the Church has grown to more than twelve million members. And it will only continue to grow at an accelerating pace.

Elder Carl B. Pratt provides a perspective on the growth of the Church in recent decades: "My 'living' of [the parable of the mustard seed] began some 40 years ago with my service as a full-time missionary in Argentina. In the course of traveling home to Arizona, I passed through several South American countries. In many of those countries I found no missionaries, no members, not even the slightest trace of the presence of the restored Church of Jesus Christ. Even though missionary work in South America had begun in 1925, 37 years later the

Church existed in only a few of the countries there, with just seven missions. There were no high priests or patriarchs because there were no stakes, and the nearest temple was thousands of miles away in Mesa, Arizona. . . .

"Since my mission I have had the privilege of living and working in South America for 19 years. With amazement and fascination I have watched and had a small part in the astounding growth of the Church there. It has been particularly impressive to me to watch the crucial role of the Book of Mormon in this growth. Today the Church is firmly established in every nation on that continent. There are more than 550 stakes, 13 temples, 69 missions, and millions of Latter-day Saints. Truly the 'least of all seeds' has become the 'greatest among herbs' and is a tree into which God is sending down His powers, gifts, and angels. And the strength of the Church in South America is but a part of what is happening throughout the world as the kingdom rolls forth in 'God-like majesty.'"[7]

Latter-day Saints in these last days have the blessing and opportunity of participating in the impressive growth of the kingdom. We can establish families of faith, building the kingdom from within. And we can open our mouths and speak words of truth, testimony, encouragement, and comfort to those around us. As we go forth as member missionaries, on the Lord's errand, his angels will accompany and attend us:

"And any man that shall go and preach this gospel of the kingdom, and fail not to continue faithful in all things, shall not be weary in mind, neither darkened, neither in body, limb, nor joint; and a hair of his head shall not fall to the ground unnoticed. And they shall not go hungry, neither athirst. . . .

"Behold, I send you out to reprove the world of all their unrighteous deeds, and to teach them of a judgment which is to come. And whoso receiveth you, there I will be also, for I will go before your face. I will be on your right hand and on your left, and my Spirit shall be in your hearts, and mine angels round about you, to bear you up" (D&C 84:80, 87–88).

CHAPTER 5

The Leaven

Matthew 13:33

Another parable spake he unto them; The kingdom of heaven is like unto leaven, which a woman took, and hid in three measures of meal, till the whole was leavened.

The parable of the leaven forms a pair with the parable of the mustard seed. The mustard seed parable demonstrates the outward, visible manifestations of the growth of the Lord's Church. In contrast, the parable of the leaven shows how the Lord's kingdom will gradually and inexorably move with power throughout the world, invisibly influencing the whole. The first parable was drawn from the world of what was then men's work (sowing), while the second was drawn from traditional women's work (cooking). Interestingly, in both parables the thing described is living: a seed must be alive to sprout, and leaven contains living fungi that cause the fermentation and rising process in the dough.

Elder James E. Talmage, both an apostle and a scientist, wrote: "Yeast is no less truly a living organism than a mustard seed. As the microscopic yeast plant develops and multiplies within the dough, its myriad living cells permeate the lump, and every bit of the leavened mass is capable of affecting likewise another batch of properly prepared meal. The process of leavening, or causing dough 'to rise,' by the fermentation of the yeast placed in the mass, is a slow one, and moreover as quiet and seemingly secret as that of the planted seed growing without the sower's further attention or concern."[1]

Leaven was familiar to all of those who listened to Jesus. Bread was one of the basic foods of the time—typically made from wheat or barley flour—and leaven was the agent that caused the loaves of bread to rise. Leaven had power to permeate the entire lump of dough; through a chemical process it would affect every portion of the dough in which it had been placed. In the same way, through the processes of the Spirit, the lives and influence of the righteous Saints of God will affect the entirety of the world.

The prophet Daniel saw in vision how in the latter days God's kingdom would expand from a very small thing until it filled the world. It would start as small as a pebble. But in time it would roll forth until it "filled the whole earth" (Daniel 2:35). The kingdom will grow as a mustard seed grows into a great tree, or as the ferment of leaven spreads through an entire loaf of bread.

Commentary

Matthew 13:33 *Another parable spake he unto them; The kingdom of heaven*

As in other parables, the kingdom of heaven represents the Church and kingdom of God on the earth.

Matthew 13:33 *is like unto leaven,*

People who cook bread today typically use yeast, which can be packaged and stored for a time, particularly if kept refrigerated. Leaven, on the other hand, was created by letting barley and water ferment together or by mixing wine with bran. Once the fermented formula was ready, the baker could put it in the dough being prepared for bread. After it had risen, the baker would save a portion of the dough for the next batch, sometimes adding some juices to promote additional fermentation. When that dough was mixed with new dough, it would ferment (or leaven) the new batch and cause it to rise.

Matthew 13:33 *which a woman took, and hid in three measures of meal, till the whole was leavened.*

Leaven was always "hidden" in dough; that is, it was mixed in and quickly became invisible. Three measures of meal was a large amount, estimated to be about fifty pounds. The resulting bread would be enough to feed a hundred or more people. The exact amount of meal isn't the point of the parable. What matters is that a little leaven had a remarkable effect on a large amount of bread dough.

Paul spoke of the power of leaven when he wrote: "Know ye not that a little leaven leaveneth the whole lump? Purge out therefore the old leaven, that ye may be a new lump" (1 Corinthians 5:6–7). And Jesus warned, "Take heed, beware of the leaven of the Pharisees, and of the leaven of Herod" (Mark 8:15).

Jesus and Paul were using the power of leaven to warn against following the ways of sin and apostasy. But the same image can be used to encourage righteousness.

In this parable, the leaven symbolizes the righteous Saints in the world. As the kingdom goes forth, the Saints will mix and intermingle with the people of the world. As they do, they will have a powerful effect on those around them, even as a little leaven causes the entire loaf to rise.

Joseph Smith gave us an additional interpretation of this parable. After quoting the parable as found in Matthew, the Prophet said: "It may be understood that the Church of the Latter-day Saints has taken its rise from a little leaven that was put into three witnesses. Behold, how much this is like the parable! It is fast leavening the lump, and will soon leaven the whole."[2]

Joseph Smith never intended to imply that this was the only application of the parable. But it is important to understand what he was teaching. Truly the Book of Mormon, introduced by the testimony of the three witnesses, has gone forth to the whole earth, and has served to influence and bless the world, as leaven would do in a loaf.

Later in the same message the Prophet broadened the interpretation. Referring back to this parable, he said, "See the Book of Mormon coming forth out of the treasure of the heart. Also the covenants given to the Latter-day Saints, also the translation of the Bible—thus bringing forth out of the heart things new and old, thus answering to three measures of meal undergoing the purifying touch by a revelation of Jesus Christ, and the ministering of angels, who have already commenced this work in the last days, which will answer to the leaven which leavened the whole lump."[3] The three measures in this example are the Book of Mormon, the covenants of God, and the Joseph Smith Translation of the Bible.

Personal Application

There are two ways we can apply this parable: we can receive the leaven of the gospel into our own hearts, and we can be a leaven in the world.

When a baker wants to make bread, he or she must start with flour. To properly mix in the eggs and the water and the oil and the leaven, or yeast, the grain must be ground into powder.

So it must be with our hearts. If we hope to receive the leaven of the gospel, we must let our hearts be soft and broken. As long as we are hard in our hearts, the leaven can't be mixed in us.

Once we have received the leaven into ourselves, we are expected to be a leavening influence in the world—just as a lump of previously leavened dough is used to influence new dough.

The Lord repeatedly taught the idea that his Saints are to have a powerful effect on the world. We are to be the salt of the earth, lending savor to the whole. We are to be the light of the world. And we are to be the leaven in the loaf.

As we do so, we will help to fulfill the prophetic vision of Joseph Smith:

"The Standard of Truth has been erected; no unhallowed hand can stop the work from progressing; persecutions may rage, mobs may combine, armies may assemble, calumny may defame, but the truth of God will go forth boldly, nobly, and independent, till it has penetrated every continent, visited every clime, swept every country, and sounded in every ear, till the purposes of God shall be accomplished, and the Great Jehovah shall say the work is done."[4]

CHAPTER 6

The Hidden Treasure

Matthew 13:44

Again, the kingdom of heaven is like unto treasure hid in a field; the which when a man hath found, he hideth, and for joy thereof goeth and selleth all that he hath, and buyeth that field.

This parable was delivered in a house located near the Sea of Galilee. Jesus had presented a number of parables to a great multitude that had gathered on the shore while he sat on a ship anchored nearby. After Jesus "sent the multitude away" and went into a private residence, "his disciples came unto him" (Matthew 13:36), and he gave additional parables, including the parable of the hidden treasure. The house was probably in Capernaum, a coastal city located north of the sea.

The parable of the hidden treasure is comparable to the parable of the pearl of great price (Matthew 13:45–46). Both parables open with the words "the kingdom of heaven is like," an expression that we have already seen used in several other parables (see Matthew 13:24–30, 31–32, 33–35, 47–48; 20:1–16; 22:1–14). Both refer to something of great value (a treasure and a pearl); both have the man selling all that he possessed in order to obtain the item of value (he "selleth all that he hath" and he "sold all that he had"); and both have the man purchasing the precious item with the proceeds of his sale (he "buyeth" and he "bought"). In fact, Jesus presents the two parables back to back in order to emphasize the great value of the gospel. The major difference between the two parables is that the man in the parable of the hidden treasure appears to have found the treasure accidentally, while the other sought for the pearl intentionally, until he eventually located it.

Commentary

> ***Matthew 13:44*** *Again, the kingdom of heaven is like unto treasure hid in a field;*

The opening word of several parables in this chapter, *Again,* ties them together. The kingdom of heaven is the Church of Jesus Christ, or the gospel of Jesus Christ, with its spiritual blessings and gifts, teachings of salvation, powers, and saving ordinances. Jesus compares the Church to a treasure, which emphasizes the immense value of the gospel. Those who fully comprehend the significance of the gospel regard it as more important than all of earth's riches and treasures combined.

The central feature of the parable is something of great value, a "treasure," which may refer to coins, gems, pearls, diamonds, nuggets of gold, or other valuables—or the treasure may refer to a gold or silver mine in a field, waiting to be worked. Lacking the protective bank vaults or safety deposit boxes that exist in modern times, it was common for people in ancient Palestine to hide their treasures.

Treasures and riches in the scriptures represent both spiritual and temporal blessings. For example, speaking of the treasures of temporal blessings, God said to Moses:

"The Lord shall command the blessing upon thee in thy storehouses, and in all that thou settest thine hand unto; and he shall bless thee in the land which the Lord thy God giveth thee. The Lord shall establish thee an holy people unto himself, as he hath sworn unto thee, if thou shalt keep the commandments of the Lord thy God, and walk in his ways. . . . And the Lord shall make thee plenteous in goods, in the fruit of thy body, and in the fruit of thy cattle, and in the fruit of thy ground, in the land which the Lord sware unto thy fathers to give thee. The Lord shall open unto thee his good treasure, the heaven to give the rain unto thy land in his season, and to bless all the work of thine hand" (Deuteronomy 28:8–9, 11–12; see Proverbs 15:6; 21:20).

On another occasion God revealed that members of the house of Israel, if they remain faithful, are God's treasure: "If ye will obey my voice indeed, and keep my covenant, then ye shall be a peculiar treasure unto me above all people" (Exodus 19:5; see 1 Peter 2:9).

Two passages from the Doctrine and Covenants connect the gospel's blessings with spiritual treasures and riches: "If ye seek the riches which it is the will of the Father to give unto you, ye shall be the richest of all people, for ye shall have the riches of eternity" (D&C 38:39). Also: "Seek not for riches but for wisdom, and behold, the mysteries of God shall be unfolded unto you, and then shall you be made rich. Behold, he that hath eternal life is rich" (D&C 6:7). All of these blessings, of course, originate with God, for in him "are hid all the treasures of wisdom and knowledge" (Colossians 2:3).

Matthew 13:44 *the which when a man hath found,*

The man that found the treasure represents every individual who has discovered the gospel.[1] No matter how the discovery is made, this individual finds the gospel treasure, then investigates, and eventually gains faith in Jesus Christ and his restored gospel.

Although modern treasure seekers and others have located treasure caches throughout the Holy Land, many of the discoveries occurred through pure luck. Locating hidden treasure by chance is such a rare event that one scholar has estimated that it would happen only once in a thousand lifetimes.[2] This rarity may be the very reason that Jesus compared the discovery of treasure to finding the gospel treasure. Most people find the gospel through other means—they are born into the Church, the missionaries find them, or neighbors or loved ones introduce them to the Church—all different from those people stumbling by chance upon the gospel.

Still, some do come across the truth as the man in the parable came across his treasure. When that happens, even though the gospel discovery may appear to be purely coincidental, in reality the blessing has more likely come because divine Providence has guided the person to locate the treasure.

Matthew 13:44 *he hideth, and for joy thereof goeth and selleth all that he hath, and buyeth that field.*

The Joseph Smith Translation changes "he hideth" to "he secureth it" (JST, Matthew 13:46). The man who found the treasure did not hide it, but secured it, or obtained it and then made it safe so that he would not lose it. After securing the treasure, the man sold all of his possessions in order to purchase the field. According to the Rabbinic law of the time, if one finds a treasure on another's property, he cannot take it on the spot but must purchase the land in order to obtain the treasure.[3] This man, then, purchased the field and obtained title to the land. In other words, he did not receive the gospel outside the covenant; instead, he became a legal member of the Church.

Joy is an important word in the parable's closing statement, for it demonstrates the emotion the man felt when he discovered the gospel of Jesus Christ. In fact, it was joy that motivated him to sacrifice all that he had in order to claim the blessings of the gospel. A Book of Mormon passage similarly connects joy and sacrificing all for the gospel's sake. A certain king stated, "I will give up all that I possess, yea, I will forsake my kingdom, that I may receive this great joy" (Alma 22:15). This king had found the hidden treasure and sacrificed everything he had to obtain joy.

Although the parable explicitly identifies a single individual as the one who found the hidden treasure, Joseph Smith quoted the parable of the hidden treasure and then compared it to the kingdom of heaven, or the Church: "To illustrate more clearly this gathering: We have another parable—'Again, the Kingdom of Heaven is like a treasure hid in a field, the which, when a man hath found, he hideth, and for joy thereof, goeth and selleth all that he hath, and buyeth that field!' The Saints work after this pattern. See the Church of the Latter-day Saints, selling all that they have, and gathering themselves together unto a place that they may purchase for an inheritance, that they may be together and bear each other's afflictions in the day of calamity."[4]

Personal Application

Those reading this book have most likely found the treasure in the field. We have discovered the joy and blessing of the gospel of Christ. We have received the gift of the Holy Ghost and some of the attendant gifts of the Spirit. We have come to a measure of peace in life, comfort in trial, and guidance through daily difficulties. But finding the treasure, and even partaking of a portion of it, is not enough. As the parable demonstrates, for us to fully receive the treasure we need to sacrifice all we have for it. If we want to receive all the *Father* has, we must give all *we* have. Then, even though our offering is a mere pittance compared to God's, we will receive his great treasures for eternity.

President Spencer W. Kimball cited the parables of the hidden treasure and the pearl of great price in association with a beautiful story of a husband and wife he knew. Although these two were Church members, for a period they did not fully have in their possession the gospel's hidden treasure. Perhaps their experience is not unique; portions of the story may apply to each of us.

President Kimball wrote: "I have always loved the parables of the Master, particularly two that focus on our brothers and sisters who have temporarily lost their way. . . . I remember a couple who promised themselves that when they were married they would get their house in order and go to the temple and have their marriage eternalized. They loved each other very much, and they had some faith in the strength of the marriage covenant made under the binding power of the priesthood. But there were some reasons, they felt, why they could not attend diligently to these matters."

As time passed the wife grew more anxious to go to the temple with her husband, but his interest diminished. He found other things to do on Sunday, and eventually, "she felt that it was more peaceful to be with her husband on Sunday." So the years passed.

"One sad day it all came to an end. The family was off on a Sunday picnic and activity. There was an automobile accident and Jennie and one of the couple's children died.

"After the funeral, this man found life limited and lonely. The house seemed empty without his wife. His days were barren and life seemed desolate. Although he devoted himself to his work and to his remaining children, his suffering did not cease. His thoughts were constantly of Jennie, his companion. Neither solace nor peace came upon him, and he remembered that he had solace no priesthood sealing that would hold him to Jennie and Jennie to him throughout eternity. His tears and deep pain and anxiety went unrelieved."

One night the man had a dream. He thought of it all the next day. It felt particularly significant. In the dream, it seemed like he was somewhere he didn't recognize. He was looking through a gate that was open wide, and through the gate he saw a woman and a young girl.

"Suddenly, he became conscious of their identity and he felt a warm glow. Jennie was even more lovely than before. Then to his great joy, his loved ones saw him. They beckoned him to come through the gate. They seemed so anxious to be with him. But it was clear to him that it was his effort that was needed. He tried to move in his dream, but he seemed to have no power. Then, as he struggled ever more strenuously, the great gates began to close. . . .

"Both he and Jennie knew that he must urgently act. He looked again at Jennie, a final glimpse. He saw the terror in her face as she realized that the gates might close without her dear husband inside."

Then he awoke. "He felt that he would give his life, give anything he possessed if he could be with his wife and with his dear children, if he could have the full blessings of those who receive eternal life and all that it means."

He feared that he had lost his chance—and felt he needed to respond quickly.

President Kimball continued: "The Lord knows the power of righteous motivations, the power that can come to us when we learn the truths about the purpose of earth life and about conditions beyond the veil. Thus, he gave two other parables, trying to impress his message indelibly upon the hearts of those who cared enough to listen and ponder:

"'Again, the kingdom of heaven is like unto treasure hid in a field; the which when a man hath found, he hideth, and for joy thereof goeth and selleth all that he hath, and buyeth that field.

"'Again, the kingdom of heaven is like unto a merchant man, seeking goodly pearls: Who, when he had found one pearl of great price, went and sold all that he had, and bought it.' (Matthew 13:44–46.)

"Jennie's husband had come to recognize deeply the meaning of these parables. He would have sold everything he had for the peaceful assurance that he and Jennie would be together forever. Happily, he knew exactly what he needed to do and how he needed to live thereafter in order to bring it about. However, there are others of our brothers and sisters in need of these temple and other Church blessings who need our assistance to obtain the promises of the Lord."[5]

We can set aside the things of this world and choose the things of eternity, just as the man did who found the treasure in the field. And, as President Kimball suggested, we can help others find the same gift. When we do, we will experience the "joy thereof," and have cause to rejoice forever.

CHAPTER 7

The Pearl of Great Price

Matthew 13:45–46

Again, the kingdom of heaven is like unto a merchant man, seeking goodly pearls:

Who, when he had found one pearl of great price, went and sold all that he had, and bought it.

As we have already noted, after Jesus presented the parables of the sower, wheat and tares, mustard seed, and leaven near the northern shore of the Sea of Galilee, he "sent the multitude away" (Matthew 13:36) and went into a private residence. While he was in this setting, "his disciples came unto him, saying, Declare unto us the parable of the tares of the field" (Matthew 13:36). Jesus then delivered insights into the meaning of the parable of the wheat and tares, followed by the parables of the hidden treasure, the pearl of great price, and the gospel net.

As indicated earlier, the parable of the pearl of great price may be paired with the parable of the hidden treasure. Both are "kingdom of heaven" parables and pertain to the Church of Jesus Christ. Both deal with items of great value and both feature a person who sells all of his possessions in order to purchase those items. It seems likely that Jesus presented these two parables, one after the other, for the very purpose of emphasizing the immense, eternal worth of his gospel.

COMMENTARY

Matthew 13:45 *Again, the kingdom of heaven is like unto a merchant man, seeking goodly pearls:*

In the parable of the pearl of great price, Jesus compares his kingdom to something familiar to Palestinian life of the first century A.D. Here Jesus describes a common occupational pursuit: a merchant seeking fine pearls. Merchants have been part of the economic system in many ages of the world, allowing people to seek items of value and trade or sell those items to others for profit. Jesus' hearers would have related to both the merchant and the pearls, just as present-day readers of the parable appreciate high-quality pearls.

In this parable the kingdom of heaven represents Jesus' Church, the merchant symbolizes any person seeking the truth, and the "goodly pearls" signify the great treasures that are associated with the gospel or Church membership. These treasures include our living prophets and apostles, the gifts of the Spirit, the gospel ordinances, the scriptures (it is noteworthy that Franklin D. Richards gave to his collection of the Book of Moses, the Book of Abraham, and Joseph Smith's History the name, "The Pearl of Great Price"), and all of the blessings associated with the Atonement and the doctrines of the gospel. Elsewhere in scripture, goodly pearls are connected with such holy things as doctrines and gospel truths. For instance, in his Sermon on the Mount, Jesus taught: "Give not that which is holy unto the dogs, neither cast ye your pearls before swine, lest they trample them under their feet, and turn again and rend you" (Matthew 7:6).

Pearls are used elsewhere in scripture to represent something of great value. In the book of Revelation, John describes the beauty, splendor, and glory of the celestial city, the "great city, the holy Jerusalem" (Revelation 21:10). With regard to its twelve gates, each named after one of the twelve tribes of Israel (Revelation 21:12), John wrote, "And the twelve gates were twelve pearls; every several gate was of one pearl: and the street of the city was pure gold" (Revelation 21:21). This description of each gate consisting of a single huge pearl, together with the streets of pure gold, presents an image of incomparable magnificence. Contrast this with Babylon's unceasing attempt to counterfeit God's church and holy city, for "Babylon the great, the mother of harlots" uses pearls together with purple, scarlet, and precious stones to attract her many devotees (Revelation 17:4–5; 18:16).

Matthew 13:46 *Who, when he had found one pearl of great price, went and sold all that he had, and bought it.*

The merchant did not find a pearl of inferior quality, but one of great value. Pearls build personal wealth and were used by merchants to trade and purchase other items. This pearl was of such great value that the merchant sold all of his possessions—which presumably included his inventory of other pearls, gems, or precious stones—in order to purchase the one pearl. This discovery was a once-in-a-lifetime find, otherwise why would the merchant sell "all that he had" to gain possession of it? How many merchants do we hear about who have sold all their possessions to buy a single item? Certainly this pearl represents that which is to be desired above all other things.

Joseph Smith interpreted the parable of the pearl of great price by teaching that Zion is the goal of those seeking pearls of great price: "Again, the Kingdom of Heaven is like unto a merchantman seeking goodly pearls, who, when he had found one pearl of great price, went and sold all that he had, and bought it.' The Saints again work after this example. See men traveling to find places for Zion and her stakes or remnants, who, when they find the place for Zion, or the pearl of great price, straightway sell that they have, and buy it."[1]

Personal Application

Jesus' comparison of the pearl of great price with the gospel is fitting because the pearl and the gospel share a number of qualities. The merchant who sought for and located the pearl is comparable to all of us who search for and eventually locate the gospel. His selling all that he possessed in order to purchase the pearl is analogous to those who find the gospel and sacrifice all for the sake of obtaining it. This does not mean, of course, that we can purchase the gospel with money or that the gospel is available only to those who have money. It does mean that, regardless of economic status, we must sacrifice all for the Church.

There are additional parallels between the gospel and the pearl. The pearl has great monetary worth; in fact, pearls "were very highly valued in the ancient world, more so than gold."[2] The gospel, too, has great value—not of a monetary nature, but with regard to spiritual and eternal things. Many pearls are white, reflecting light as the gospel does. Both the gospel and the pearl have permanence, and both have features of beauty and loveliness. Further, the pearl is something its owner would want to share with others, that they also can have the joy of experiencing a beautiful thing. The same is true of God's kingdom: as with the light Christ gives us, when we have the gospel pearl we wish to share it, that others may also experience and enjoy its beauty and value.

The following true story is about a young man named Daniel,[3] who found a pearl of great value, or the gospel of Jesus Christ. The price he paid for that pearl was extreme: when he obtained the pearl his entire family—parents, siblings, grandparents, cousins, aunts, and uncles—forsook him, disowned him, and treated him as if he were dead. They vowed to never communicate with him again in any manner. And they have followed through on that threat. Over the years they have returned his letters unopened. When he has attempted to communicate with them by telephone, they've hung up on him as soon as he begins to speak. They refuse to welcome him into their homes or family gatherings. They have entirely renounced and disinherited him. To the family, he is dead. In fact, he is worse than dead, because if he had actually died they would have honored and remembered him with a funeral. After his conversion to the gospel of Jesus Christ, Daniel served a mission for the Church without receiving any financial, spiritual, or emotional support from his family. He received not one letter from his mother or father; nor was he privileged to speak via telephone with his family on Christmas or Mother's day, as other missionaries are.

With Daniel's permission, we share a portion of his story, though it has been shortened considerably. He tells the story in his own words.

"This is the story of how I found joy in my life. I was born in 1982. I was raised proudly in [a certain non-Christian religion] with my family. We were very religious, and we worshipped every week. Compared to the other families in our city we were very different. We never went to school parties or reunions if they were held on our Sabbath. I remember being invited to a birthday party of one of my friends on the Sabbath, and it was known that I would not attend. My school teacher also realized my devotion to my convictions and respectfully never suggested that I attend school activities on the Sabbath day. All the friends of my parents respected them because of their great faith and dedication to the Lord.

"One afternoon, I was sitting on my sister's front porch by myself, drawing, when I looked down the street and saw two young men dressed in white shirts and ties. Figuring that they were Americans, I decided to go after them and chat. I asked them if they had a minute. They replied, 'We have five!' I began to interrogate them as to where they were from and what they were doing in my area. I had thought that they were from the Peace Corps or the bank because of the way they dressed. They replied, 'No, we're missionaries from The Church of Jesus Christ of Latter-day Saints' and I thought to myself, 'Oh great, how do I get rid of them now?'

"They asked politely if they could come to my house to share a very important message. I didn't really want them to come, but I thought of my father's admonition to always be polite to everybody, regardless of their situation. At that time, nobody was home at my house, so I knew that I would be able to let them in. (My parents' home and my sister's home were very close to each other.) We walked into my house into the living room, and the TV was tuned to an American football game. I supposed they would be glued to the television, and I would be able to bypass their invitation to hear their message. Amazingly, they asked me if they could turn the television off to sing a hymn. Afterwards, they asked if they could offer a prayer. They then started talking about Jesus Christ, the restoration of the gospel, Joseph Smith, and the Book of Mormon. I had no clue what they were talking about. I didn't understand. I had never even heard of Joseph Smith before, or even the term *Mormon*. When I was growing up my family never really talked much about Jesus Christ. After the lesson, the missionaries left me with the Book of Mormon and asked if I would read and pray about it. I told them that I would, but I really did not want to. After a prayer, they quickly left because of another appointment they had."

Days and weeks passed. Daniel inadvertently found himself in an institute of religion building of The Church of Jesus Christ of Latter-day Saints, and he befriended two other youth from the Church. Later, two other missionaries taught him the missionary lessons.

Daniel continues his story: "As I was studying both the New Testament and the Book of Mormon, I realized that the New Testament fulfilled many of the prophecies that were given in the Old Testament, but I still wondered whether the New Testament had been put together by an Old Testament scholar who made up the story of Jesus Christ and matched all of the prophecies together. The missionaries asked me if I had prayed about Jesus Christ to find out if he was really the Messiah. The answer was obviously no. They then taught me how to pray by using my own words. I had thought that praying with our own words was disrespectful to God. In my faith, we recite prayers. So praying from my heart was very different from what I had been taught from my childhood. Nonetheless, the lesson made sense. I decided to pray and ask God to show the missionaries that they were wrong. The whole time that I was meeting with the missionaries, I kept it a secret from my parents."

As Daniel began to feel the truth of the missionaries' message, he became increasingly concerned about the idea of being baptized—he had great love and respect for his parents and his family and their religious beliefs, and he did not want to offend or hurt them.

"I talked with my Heavenly Father and asked him to show me what to do. I told him that if I needed to be baptized I would do it; he would just have to let me know. After I was finished praying I turned to the New Testament to read. The first thing that I turned to was Matthew 10:37–39. It said, 'He who loveth father or mother more than me is not worthy of me; and he that loveth son or daughter more than me is not worthy of me. And he that taketh not his cross, and followeth after me, is not worthy of me. He that findeth his life shall lose it: and he that loseth his life for my sake shall find it.' I knew that that was the answer to what I was looking for, and I knew exactly what I had to do. I felt somewhat like Joseph Smith when he read James 1:5.

The scripture 'seemed to enter with great force into every feeling of my heart.'"

Daniel determined to join the Church, knowing that it would be a considerable sacrifice because of his family's religious tradition. He was baptized on June 8, 2000.

"Now that I was a member of the Church, I knew it was going to be difficult to remain active. In order for me to go to church, I had to hide my church clothes in my backpack and tell my parents that I was going to a friend's house or to play basketball or something like that. I would then go to church and change into my church clothes and prepare myself for the Sabbath day. I also received the calling as activities coordinator. Most of the activities were on Friday or Saturday night. In order for me to fulfill my calling, I would pretend I was going to bed and then sneak out of the house. Or I would tell my parents I would be right back and not come back for two or three hours.

"I knew I could not continue to live like this. I felt as though I was obeying one commandment but disobeying another. This brought me to the conclusion that I must leave my home.

"In process of time I felt I should attend Brigham Young University in Provo, Utah. I felt if I attended that school I would be able to practice my new faith without any guilt. I told my father that I wanted to go to school at BYU. At first he did not like the idea because of the distance from the family, but he later decided that it would be the best thing for me. He liked the high standards of moral ethics that the students were required to obey. He also enjoyed the fact that BYU was recognized worldwide for its educational programs. He did not know that the school was owned by the Mormon Church.

"On August 30, the day before I flew to Utah, my dad brought me to his office. He sat me down and began to tell me how proud he was of me and what I was becoming. He began to cry. I had never seen my dad cry in his life. Even when his father died he never shed a tear. After he expressed his love and emotions for me, he told me to remember only one thing: remember who we are; never forget our faith; and do not let anybody try to change me. As he told me this my heart sank. I knew I had made the right decision, but I also knew that I had let my dad down. I felt, though, it wasn't time to tell him. I needed to go and be on my own for a time. The next day I flew to Utah. . . . It was a huge difference to go from an LDS branch of thirty to forty people to a singles ward of about 270 students. During the school year I received much support from friends and members of the Church.

"In April of 2001, I received a phone call from my father. He had found out about me joining the Church from a person who I knew back home. He only wanted to know one thing and that was if what he had heard was true. I knew then that I had to tell the truth. I told him I had joined the Church, but that is all he would allow me to say. He told me I had to come home right then and there. I told him I was the middle of finals and that I couldn't. He then told me to come home 'now or never.' That was the last time that I ever talked to my parents."

Daniel later served a full-time mission for the Church and, afterwards, returned to complete his education at Brigham Young University. He concludes his story with these words: "Sometimes over the years I have wondered why I had to go through the things that I did. Why couldn't I have a normal story to share? Regardless of the answer, I know that Christ is our Savior and Redeemer. He is the Messiah I had been looking for; He was prophesied from the prophets of old. I know that He lives and that He will come again. I can truly say today that I know what true happiness is. I know that somewhere down the line my family and the generations to come will appreciate what I have done."

CHAPTER 8

THE GOSPEL NET

Matthew 13:47–50

Again, the kingdom of heaven is like unto a net, that was cast into the sea, and gathered of every kind:

Which, when it was full, they drew to shore, and sat down, and gathered the good into vessels, but cast the bad away.

So shall it be at the end of the world: the angels shall come forth, and sever the wicked from among the just,

And shall cast them into the furnace of fire: there shall be wailing and gnashing of teeth.

Earlier on the same day that Jesus uttered this parable, he had sat in a fishing boat and delivered a number of parables to a great multitude. Then he moved with a few disciples to the privacy of a home, which itself may have been a stone's throw from the sea. As Jesus spoke this parable in that setting, the scene of the fishing boat and nets would have remained vivid in the minds of Jesus' hearers. Further, many of Jesus' disciples were by occupation fishermen. The images used in this parable would therefore have been well known to them. Jesus himself was familiar with the Sea of Galilee, for he walked on its waters (Matthew 14:25), calmed a storm that passed over it (Matthew 8:24–27), traveled past it as he journeyed and ministered to the inhabitants of Galilee (Matthew 15:29; Mark 7:31; John 6:1), sat on its shore (Matthew 13:1), walked its shores (Matthew 4:18), and sat in a ship that was anchored near the shore while teaching the multitude (Matthew 13:2). Additionally, he had lived in Capernaum, a town that was located on the northern shore of the Sea of Galilee (Matthew 4:13). In all of these associations with the Sea of Galilee, Jesus would have gained much exposure to the fishing industry.

The parable of the gospel net has in it themes that are similar to the parable of the wheat and tares. Both parables deal with foodstuffs—edible (wheat and good fish) and inedible substances (tares and bad fish); both share the theme of the separation of the righteous from the wicked, with angels serving as the agents of separation; and both involve the burning of that which is inedible.

Commentary

Matthew 13:47 *Again, the kingdom of heaven is like unto a net, that was cast into the sea, and gathered of every kind:*

Jesus compared the kingdom of heaven, or the Lord's Church, to a simple fishing net that, when cast into the sea, gathers all kinds of fish. Generally, the fishing nets of Jesus' day (see, for example, Matthew 4:18–21; Mark 1:16–19) were either dragged between two boats or between a boat located offshore and workers standing on the shore. The net had weights or sinkers on one side to pull it down into the water and floats on the other side to keep it on the water's surface while it was being dragged. Such a large net was designed to pull in a multitude of fish and, in doing so, would have collected both edible as well as trash fish. Some two dozen fish species inhabit the Sea of Galilee, and the fishermen were required to know the good from the bad so that once the fish were drawn to shore, the fishermen could sort them out, keeping the good and throwing out the bad.

Jesus called a number of fishermen to be apostles. Matthew recorded the following: "And Jesus, walking by the sea of Galilee, saw two brethren, Simon called Peter, and Andrew his brother, casting a net into the sea: for they were fishers. And he saith unto them, Follow me, and I will make you fishers of men. And they straightway left their nets, and followed him. And going on from thence, he saw other two brethren, James the son of Zebedee, and John his brother, in a ship with Zebedee their father, mending their nets; and he called them. And they immediately left the ship and their father, and followed him" (Matthew 4:18–22; see Luke 5:1–11). Such apostles and other disciples who were involved in the local fishing industry would have related easily to the elements of the story. As they sought to understand its meaning, they would have made mental comparisons between the parable of the gospel net and their own understanding of the local fishing industry.

The Lord does not explicitly mention fishermen or the word *fish* in the parable, but both are understood to belong to it. The fishermen are those who cast the net into the sea and draw it into the shore, full of fish. The fish thus caught are of every kind, and the fishermen separate them, placing the good into containers and throwing the trash fish away. The parable's fishermen represent God's servants—apostles, missionaries, and all who preach the gospel—whoever casts the fishing net into the sea and draws it to shore. Jesus declared unto those he called into his service, "Follow me, and I will make you fishers of men" (Matthew 4:19). The apostles transitioned from their temporal duties as fishers of food to a spiritual responsibility of becoming fishers of God's children, working to pull individuals into the gospel net.

If the fishermen of the parable represent God's missionaries, then the fish symbolize people. Old Testament imagery also makes comparisons between people and fish. For example, Ezekiel compared the Pharaoh of Egypt to a whale ("thou art as a whale in the seas," Ezekiel 32:2). And the writer of Ecclesiastes compared men to fishes when he wrote, "as the fishes that are taken in an evil net . . . so are the sons of men snared in an evil time" (Ecclesiastes 9:12). Further, speaking through Jeremiah, the Lord used imagery from the fishing industry in a prophecy about the gathering of Israel. The fishermen symbolize the Lord's authorized servants who are involved in the gathering and the fish symbolize those who are gathered: "Behold, I will send for many fishers, saith the Lord, and they shall fish them; and after will I send for many hunters, and they shall hunt them from every mountain, and from every hill, and out of the holes of the rocks" (Jeremiah 16:16).

Joseph Smith understood the plain meaning of the parable and likened it to missionary work and the gathering of modern-day Israel to Zion. Those who are of "seed of Joseph" are the fisherman or the missionaries. The Prophet wrote:

"'The Kingdom of Heaven is like unto a net that was cast into the sea, and gathered of every kind, which when it was full they drew to shore, and sat down, and gathered the good into vessels, but cast the bad away.' For the work of this pattern, behold the seed of Joseph, spreading forth the Gospel net upon the face of the earth, gathering of every kind, that the good may be saved in vessels prepared for that purpose, and the angels will take care of the bad. So shall it be at the end of the world—the angels shall come forth and sever the wicked from among the just, and cast them into the furnace of fire, and there shall be wailing and gnashing of teeth."[1]

> ***Matthew 13:48*** *Which, when it was full, they drew to shore, and sat down, and gathered the good into vessels, but cast the bad away.*

Fish are symbolic of people. Just as the parable identifies "good" and "bad" fish, even so there are a variety of people who are gathered by the gospel net. On the one hand, there are those who continually repent, who pray and worship regularly, who have love for God and humankind in their hearts, and who desire to obey God's commandments. On the other hand, there are those who carry hidden sins, who cannot give up bad habits, who have a selfish agenda, or who do not have the spiritual power to endure to the end. Some people join the Church for the wrong reasons. Perhaps they join under the pressure of a loved one, or they become members in order to receive welfare support. Jesus' expression "cast the bad away" has two applications: Church members who disobey certain Church commandments and rules may be "cast away" during mortality through excommunication, or, at the great and last judgment, they will be cast away from God's presence forever. But those who are good are "gathered . . . into vessels," which may be symbolic of God's protective care.

Jesus may have wished for his hearers to make an additional connection between the parable's good and bad fish and the law of Moses, which distinguished between clean and unclean animals, including fish. A passage in Leviticus reads: "For I am the Lord your God: ye shall therefore sanctify yourselves, and ye shall be holy; for I am holy. . . . This is the law of the beasts, and of the fowl, and of every living creature that moveth in the waters, and of every creature that creepeth upon the earth: To make a difference between the unclean and the clean, and between the beast that may be eaten and the beast that may not be eaten" (Leviticus 11:44, 46–47). With regard specifically to sea creatures (or, "all that are in the waters"), the Lord differentiated between the clean (which may be eaten) and the unclean (which may not be eaten). Those that lacked fins and scales may not be eaten, and those with fins and scales may be eaten (Leviticus 11:9–12; Deuteronomy 14:9–10). The bad fish of Jesus' parable may be comparable to the unclean animals of the Mosaic law, and the good may be likened to the clean.

> ***Matthew 13:49–50*** *So shall it be at the end of the world: the angels shall come forth, and sever the wicked from among the just, And shall cast them into the furnace of fire: there shall be wailing and gnashing of teeth.*

The Joseph Smith Translation adds an additional verse following verse 49 that reads, "And the world is the children of the wicked." This phrase clarifies that "the end of the world" refers to the destruction of "the children of the wicked." Their destruction is detailed in the verse that follows, which describes them being cast into the furnace.

Not all of Jesus' parables include interpretations or explanations. The parable of the gospel net, however, does include an interpretation, which pertains to the great judgment that will take place at the world's end. At that time the angels will serve as God's agents and will separate the righteous from the wicked. In the language of the parable, they will place the good fish in vessels and cast away the bad.

During our probationary period on the earth, the wicked and the righteous more or less dwell together in the same communities. But at the time of judgment the angels will remove the wicked and cast them out, just as fishermen separate good from bad fish. They will "sever" (a powerful word) the wicked from the righteous. These angels will then cast the wicked into a "furnace of fire," a symbol of the punishment of unrepentant sinners. In that state, the wicked will dwell in utter misery, with "wailing and gnashing of teeth."

Personal Application

This parable pertains to the gathering of Israel (*gathered* is used twice in the parable), the eventual separation of the good and the bad, and the judgment at the end of the world. The gathering is presently taking place throughout most parts of the world. A large force of full-time missionaries is daily casting out their nets in order to gather the Lord's children into the Church. An even larger force of member missionaries ("every member a missionary") serves in this same effort.

The gospel net has gathered all varieties of people into The Church of Jesus Christ of Latter-day Saints. They have diverse spiritual and temporal gifts, inclinations, expectations, skills, and occupational strengths. They are gathered into the gospel net from a variety of religious traditions, dissimilar social customs, and different political perspectives. Though most join the Church for righteous motives, some become members for a wrong reason. And while most probably fully repent of their sins before entering baptism's waters, some retain bad habits and addictions. Some want to look like good fish, but they eventually show, through their actions and attitudes, that their hearts are not pure. In the end, if they do not repent and change, they will be cast off.

All of us need to examine our hearts and our motives to make sure we are becoming what God would want us to be. We can be "good fish" in his kingdom, blessing others, contributing to the work, and developing a Christlike character. If we do, we will be received into vessels of honor and glory at the last day.

CHAPTER 9

The Lost Sheep

Luke 15:3–7

And he spake this parable unto them, saying,

What man of you, having an hundred sheep, if he lose one of them, doth not leave the ninety and nine in the wilderness, and go after that which is lost, until he find it?

And when he hath found it, he layeth it on his shoulders, rejoicing.

And when he cometh home, he calleth together his friends and neighbours, saying unto them, Rejoice with me; for I have found my sheep which was lost.

I say unto you, that likewise joy shall be in heaven over one sinner that repenteth, more than over ninety and nine just persons, which need no repentance.

Before Jesus uttered this parable, "all the publicans and sinners" drew near to hear him (Luke 15:1). Perhaps there was something in the power and comfort of his message that appealed to them and they were intrigued. A publican was a tax collector (sometimes a Jew) for the Roman government, which not only occupied the land of Palestine but was also sometimes oppressive. Those who collected taxes for the government were regarded by many as traitors to their own nation and people. Some scholars have suggested that the sinners mentioned here were more than people who had committed known sins—their sins may well have so grievous that they had been excommunicated and cast out of the Jewish synagogues.[1]

Not everyone was happy to have Jesus reach out to those who had been rejected by church and society. When the Pharisees and scribes saw him associating with the publicans and sinners, they "murmured, saying, This man receiveth sinners, and eateth with them" (Luke 15:2).

The Pharisees were a group of ultra-orthodox Jews who held to the strictest interpretation of the law of Moses. They were self-righteous, judgmental of others, and observed their religion at least partly to be seen of men. The scribes were men who were trained in the interpretation of the law. At one point in his ministry the Lord spoke with great plainness against both the scribes and the Pharisees. He called them "blind guides" and "whited sepulchres" and a "generation of vipers"; he accused them of being "full of extortion and excess," of being "full of hypocrisy and iniquity," and of being "the children of them which killed the prophets" (see Matthew 23:23–33).

It was these same Pharisees and scribes who criticized Jesus for associating with groups they found objectionable. In response, he told them a parable about a man with many sheep—a flock of one hundred. But when one was lost, he went out into the wilderness in search of it. When he found it, there was much rejoicing.

The application was plain. As it has been said in modern times, the Church is not a country club for the righteous. It is a hospital for sinners. If publicans and sinners were those in spiritual trouble, then Jesus had all the more reason to reach out to them, to seek for them, and to rejoice in those who returned to his fold.

This parable is also found in the Gospel of Matthew, where Jesus preceded it with the words, "For the Son of man is come to save that which was lost, and to call sinners to repentance" (JST, Matthew 18:11). The parable in Matthew was given in Capernaum. The parable in Luke was given more than a year later in Perea.

Commentary

Luke 15:3–4 *And he spake this parable unto them, saying, What man of you, having an hundred sheep, if he lose one of them, doth not leave the ninety and nine in the wilderness, and go after that which is lost, until he find it?*

Jesus personalizes this parable by asking them a rhetorical question that could lead to only one answer. If one of your sheep is lost, even if you have ninety-nine more, wouldn't you go out looking for the lost one? Some readers have wondered that the shepherd would leave the ninety-nine defenseless in the wilderness. Joseph Smith clarified this issue in the Joseph Smith Translation. There, Jesus observes that the shepherd would "leave the ninety and nine, and go into the wilderness" (JST, Luke 15:4). Thus, the sheep are not left in the wilderness; they are surely left in the care of another shepherd or perhaps secured in a sheepfold. Then the shepherd himself goes into the wilderness looking for his lost sheep. (The account in Matthew 18:12 has the shepherd searching in the mountains.)

How long does he search? "Until he find it."

The metaphor of people as sheep and God as the shepherd would have been familiar to the people. It had been used earlier by Ezekiel: "Thus saith the Lord God; Behold, I, even I, will both search my sheep, and seek them out. As a shepherd seeketh out his flock in the day that he is among his sheep that are scattered; so will I seek out my sheep, and will deliver them out of all places where they have been scattered in the cloudy and dark day. . . . I will seek that which was lost, and bring again that which was driven away" (Ezekiel 34:11–12, 16). Christ's listeners would have also known the beautiful psalm, "The Lord is my shepherd; I shall not want. He maketh me to lie down in green pastures: he leadeth me beside the still waters. He restoreth my soul." Twice the Psalmist says, "he leadeth me." And he says of the shepherd, "thou art with me" (Psalm 23:1–4).

A flock of one hundred sheep would have been considered to be a large one. Economically, the loss of one would not have been that serious. Yet, in his love, the shepherd regards each of his sheep as important, and he is not willing to lose even one.

> ***Luke 15:5–6*** *And when he hath found it, he layeth it on his shoulders, rejoicing. And when he cometh home, he calleth together his friends and neighbours, saying unto them, Rejoice with me; for I have found my sheep which was lost.*

There are two reasons why a shepherd would carry the lost sheep. First, the sheep would likely have been weary from its wandering. Second, it would have been frightened from having been separated from the rest of the flock. As a practical matter, carrying the sheep would be the quickest way to return with it to the flock. We can picture the sheep with its legs dangling against the shepherd's chest and with the shepherd holding the legs with his hands.

But the parable isn't only about sheep and a mortal shepherd. It is also about the Good Shepherd—or one of his helpers. Such a shepherd would have feelings of genuine love for all his sheep and would want to show that love and concern for the sheep that was lost.

Isaiah wrote of the tender love of the Lord, who is our Shepherd. He said, "He shall feed his flock like a shepherd: he shall gather the lambs with his arm, and carry them in his bosom, and gently lead those that are with young" (Isaiah 40:11). In the same way that the shepherd "layeth it on his shoulders," our Savior carries us in his arms when we have been lost and are found.

When the shepherd finds the sheep, he isn't simply satisfied—he *rejoices*. And he calls together his friends and neighbors and invites them to share with him in his great joy. The same invitation is issued by the woman who recovers her lost coin and the father of the returning prodigal son. In each instance, finding that which is lost occasions joy in the whole community when it is found.

> ***Luke 15:7*** *I say unto you, that likewise joy shall be in heaven over one sinner that repenteth, more than over ninety and nine just persons, which need no repentance.*

The Pharisees and scribes would have understood a shepherd's happiness over finding a lost sheep. But their attitude appears to have been different toward finding a lost soul. In fact, there was a rabbinic saying that claimed, "There is joy before God when those who provoke him perish from the world."[2] This stood in great contrast to the Lord's joy in finding and recovering those who had provoked God.

Even though we understand that there is great joy in heaven over the repentant sinner, it is difficult to understand that heaven's joy is *greater* than over those who "need no repentance." Elder James E.

Talmage explained this concept by saying, "Many have marveled that there should be greater rejoicing over the recovery of one stray sheep, or the saving of a soul that had been as one lost, than over the many who have not been in such jeopardy. In the safe-folded ninety and nine the shepherd had continued joy; but to him came a new accession of happiness, brighter and stronger because of his recent grief, when the lost was brought back into the fold."[3]

There is another possible interpretation. The Lord speaks of the joy in heaven over the sinner that repents—more than those who need no repentance. The truth is that every individual on the earth (except Jesus himself) is in need of repentance. "All have sinned, and come short of the glory of God" (Romans 3:23). "There is none that doeth good, no, not one" (Psalm 14:3). The scribes and Pharisees, in their self-righteousness, did not recognize their need for repentance. They would have counted themselves among the ninety and nine. But every individual in their number was indeed in need of repentance. And thus the heavens would have rejoiced over each one when they came to an understanding of their true state before God and began to seek to make things right again.

We have a similar teaching in latter-day revelation. "How great is his joy in the soul that repenteth!" the Lord said, speaking of his own joy. "Wherefore, you are called to cry repentance unto this people. And if it so be that you should labor all your days in crying repentance unto this people, and bring, save it be one soul unto me, how great shall be your joy with him in the kingdom of my Father!" (D&C 18:13–15).

Personal Application

As we apply this parable to our own lives, we can consider that each of us, at times, is the lost sheep, and each of us can be a shepherd.

Isaiah wrote with prophetic insight, "All we like sheep have gone astray; we have turned every one to his own way" (Isaiah 53:6).

Bruce Hafen wrote with powerful insight: "The lost sheep are not just the people who don't come to church. . . . The lost sheep is a mother who goes down into the valley of the dark shadows to bring forth children. The lost sheep is a young person, far away from home and faced with loneliness and temptation. The lost sheep is a person who has just lost a critically needed job; a business person in financial distress; a new missionary in a foreign culture; a man just called to be bishop; a married couple who are misunderstanding each other; a grandmother whose children are forgetting her. I am the lost sheep. You are the lost sheep. '*All* we like sheep have gone astray.' (Isaiah 53:6; emphasis added.)"[4]

Jesus himself often sought out the lost sheep, reaching out to those in need of blessing, help, or repentance. The Gospel of Luke alone records many instances of his selfless ministry (see, for example, Luke 5:29–32; 7:36–50; 17:11–19; 19:1–9). And even now he reaches out to each one of us, never failing in his desire to bless and help each one of us.

When we hearken to his voice and turn more fully to him, we can be the fulfillment of what Peter said: "Ye were as sheep going astray; but are now returned unto the Shepherd and Bishop of your souls" (1 Peter 2:25).

In the Gospel of John, Jesus teaches us more about the love of the Good Shepherd for his flock. "I am the good shepherd," he said. "The good shepherd giveth his life for the sheep."

The hireling, by contrast, will run away when the wolf comes, leaving the sheep to fend for themselves. The hireling cares more about himself than the sheep.

"I am the good shepherd," Jesus repeated, "and know my sheep, and am known of mine. . . . And I lay down my life for the sheep" (John 10:11–15).

If we are the true flock of Christ, we will know him. We will "follow him," and we will "know his voice" (John 10:4). We will seek with all our hearts to be with him, to set aside our sins and weaknesses, to love him with our whole souls.

Then, as members of the true flock, we will seek to assist him in his work. In addition to being lost sheep, at times we are shepherds seeking those sheep. President Spencer W. Kimball said, "This parable of the Lord is an assignment of love for us to search out and rescue individuals in need—particularly in this instance, those who have strayed from the fold."[5]

President James E. Faust told a heart-wrenching story of an experience he had as a shepherd when he was a very young boy. His father found a lamb that had been abandoned in the desert. If he had left it there it would have died of starvation—or fallen victim to the coyotes. "My father gave the lamb to me and I became its shepherd."

Young Jim fed the lamb with a baby's bottle for weeks. "We became fast friends. I called him Nigh—why I don't remember. It began to grow. My lamb and I would play on the lawn. Sometimes we would lie together on the grass and I would lay my head on its soft, woolly side and look up at the blue sky and the white billowing clouds. I did not lock my lamb up during the day. It would not run away. It soon learned to eat grass. I could call my lamb from anywhere in the yard by just imitating as best I could the bleating sound of a sheep: *Baa. Baa.*

"One night there came a terrible storm. I forgot to put my lamb in the barn that night as I should have done. I went to bed. My little friend was frightened in the storm, and I could hear it bleating. I knew that I should help my pet, but I wanted to stay safe, warm, and dry in my bed. I didn't get up as I should have done. The next morning I went out to find my lamb dead. A dog had also heard its bleating cry and killed it. My heart was broken. I had not been a good shepherd or steward of that which my father had entrusted to me. My father said, 'Son, couldn't I trust you to take care of just one lamb?' My father's remark hurt me more than losing my woolly friend. I resolved that day, as a little boy, that I would try never again to neglect my stewardship as a shepherd if I were ever placed in that position again."

Some years later he was called to be a junior companion to a home teacher. There were times when he didn't want to go do his duty—instead, he wanted "to stay home and be comfortable, but in my mind's ear I could hear my little lamb bleating, and I knew I needed to be a good shepherd and go with my senior companion. In all those many years, whenever I have had a desire to shirk my duties, there would come to me a remembrance of how sorry I was that night so many years ago when I had not been a good shepherd. I have not always done everything I should have, but I have tried."[6]

The Good Shepherd has called each one of us to be an "under shepherd," to represent and assist him in our small area of the fold. As we do, we can follow the example of our leader. As he sacrificed in giving his life for the sheep, so also can we sacrifice as we seek ways to bless those we have been called to serve.

The Lord will guide us in our service. If we do indeed know his voice, he will direct us in how to live our lives—and how to more fully bless others. We must not be hirelings, who serve because they are assigned or called, but do not do so out of love. We can truly love the sheep, and, in doing so, we will be able to be inspired and empowered agents of God in their lives.

CHAPTER 10

The Lost Coin

Luke 15:8–10

Either what woman having ten pieces of silver, if she lose one piece, doth not light a candle, and sweep the house, and seek diligently till she find it?

And when she hath found it, she calleth her friends and her neighbours together, saying, Rejoice with me; for I have found the piece which I had lost.

Likewise, I say unto you, there is joy in the presence of the angels of God over one sinner that repenteth.

The parable of the lost coin may be paired with the parable of the lost sheep (Luke 15:3–7), which immediately precedes it in Jesus' teachings. There are many parallels between the two parables. Both describe a lost soul who repents and returns to the faith and both refer to the quality of joy ("joy" and "rejoiceth") at the repentant soul. Both mention something that is lost—a sheep in the first parable and a coin in the second. In both parables there is a single thing that is lost, *one* lamb and *one* coin. The lost sheep parable features a man who is comparatively rich; the parable of the lost coin presents a woman who is relatively poor. The parable about the sheep uses the numeral *one hundred;* the other parable employs the numeral *ten*. Both demonstrate God's keen interest in the sinner and his or her subsequent repentance. God plays a significant role in both parables; he is called "Father" in the parable of the lost sheep and "God" in the parable of the lost coin.

There is an important difference in the manner in which the

coin and the sheep became lost. In the parable of the lost sheep, the sheep became lost when it wandered from the fold, perhaps looking for greener pasture. This sheep may symbolize any individual who exercises his moral agency to leave the fold (the gospel and its teachings) and its shepherds (parents, leaders, teachers). Perhaps the sheep demonstrated willful disobedience. By contrast, the coin was lost because of the carelessness of its owner or another person; its loss apparently did not result from the volition of the coin itself.

COMMENTARY

Luke 15:8 *Either what woman having ten pieces of silver,*

A woman takes the chief position in the parable of the lost coin, where she owns ten pieces of silver. Women also have prominent roles in the parables of the leaven (Matthew 13:33), importunate widow and unjust judge (Luke 18:1–8), and ten virgins (Matthew 25:1–13). The woman who loses the coin represents anyone who is given stewardship and care over precious souls (pieces of silver). The woman may also symbolize the Church (see, for example, Isaiah 54:1–6; Matthew 25:1–13; Ephesians 5:27; Revelation 21:2, 9, 27; D&C 109:73–74) or its leaders, who are overseers. The coin (or Church member) is lost through neglect, some form of carelessness, or lack of proper loving care.

The ten pieces of silver are ten coins. Coins, with an image or seal indicating its value or weight, had been in usage for centuries before Jesus' mortality and ministry. Most coins existed in one of four metals—gold, silver, copper, or bronze. Money was coined by a government entity or a localized ruling power.

The woman's ten pieces of silver, or ten *drachmas* (*drachma* is a Greek word translated as "piece of silver" in the King James Version) were not of great value. Each *drachma* weighed about an eighth of an ounce; one may compare this to Judas' thirty silver shekels, received to betray Jesus Christ (Matthew 26:15), each of which weighed approximately a half an ounce. Each of the woman's ten pieces of silver was equivalent in value to the Roman penny (Greek *denarion,* which was much different in value from the copper penny in the United States). A penny was a day's payment for work by a Roman soldier or a common laborer in Palestine. The woman's ten pieces of silver, then, were equivalent in value to a worker's payment for ten days of labor. One New Testament scholar showed the relative value of the *drachma* when he wrote that "soldiers of Mark Antony looked on a gift of a hundred drachmas each as a token of stinginess," although "there was a time when its [one hundred *drachmas'*] purchasing power was considerable, enough to buy a sheep."[1] The fact that the woman swept her house without using a servant indicates that she was relatively poor and that the lost coin had true value to her.

The number *ten* used in this parable likely has symbolic significance. E. W. Bullinger provides several biblical examples wherein *ten* is used, including the ten nations (Genesis 15:19–21), the tithes, the ten plagues (Exodus 9:14), the ten commandments (Exodus 20:1–17), the ten *gerahs* of the redemption money (Exodus 30:12–16), the "tenth generation" prohibition against Ammonites and Moabites entering the Lord's congregation (Deuteronomy 23:3–5), ten pounds (Luke 19:12–27), and the ten virgins (Matthew 25:1–14). Bullinger concludes that the number ten "signifies the perfection of Divine order" and "completeness of order."[2]

With Bullinger's interpretation in mind, the ten pieces of silver may refer to any group of souls within the Church—a family unit, a youth group, a priesthood quorum. When the lost piece of silver is found, or when the sinning person repents, then the unit or group becomes complete again. At the time that the person repents, then the woman rejoices with her friends and neighbors; this joy, in fact, extends well beyond earthly quarters, for God's angels also share in the joy.

Luke 15:8 *if she lose one piece, doth not light a candle, and sweep the house, and seek diligently till she find it?*

The lost piece of silver signifies a sinner, a wayward child, a rebellious man or woman, or any spiritually lost soul. The woman performs three acts to locate the lost coin. She lights a candle so that she can peer into the corners of her house where the natural light of the windows cannot reach; she sweeps the house hoping to uncover the coin; and she seeks diligently, conducting a careful and thorough search for the coin. These three acts symbolize our efforts to recover a lost soul. We should provide light to the lost soul or provide opportunities for them to feel the light of the Holy Ghost. We should "sweep until a treasured possession or lost soul is found and returned to a rejoicing home."[3] And we should "diligently" seek for the lost soul until he or she is found and reclaimed.

Unlike the lost sheep, which wandered from the care of the shepherd, the coin was lost as a result of the woman's lack of attention. President David O. McKay explained: "In this case the thing lost was not in itself responsible. The one who had been trusted with that coin had, through carelessness or neglect, mislaid it or dropped it. . . . Our charge is not only coins, but living souls or children, youth, and adults. . . . Someone may be wandering because of the careless remark of a girl of her age in Mutual (and I have in mind a case), and the president of the Mutual lets her go, fails to follow her next Tuesday night and invite her to come. Another may be lost because of the inactivity of the Sunday School teacher, or the indifference of the Sunday School teacher who is satisfied with the fifteen people there that morning, instead of thinking of the fifteen who are wandering because of neglect."[4]

> ***Luke 15:9*** *And when she hath found it, she calleth her friends and her neighbours together, saying, Rejoice with me; for I have found the piece which I had lost.*

The "how much more so" principle is being used in this parable. Upon locating the lost piece of silver, the woman feels to share her good fortune with both neighbors and friends. "Rejoice with me," she tells them. If the woman has such cause to rejoice for locating a small coin that weighs about an eighth of an ounce and is worth about a day's payment for a common laborer, how much more so should we rejoice at the repentance of a sinner? Certainly one's soul is worth far more than a small silver coin.

"Remember the worth of souls is great in the sight of God," the Lord said in a revelation to Joseph Smith. "For, behold, the Lord your

Redeemer suffered death in the flesh; wherefore he suffered the pain of all men, that all men might repent and come unto him. . . . And how great is his joy in the soul that repenteth!" (D&C 18:10–11, 13).

> ***Luke 15:10*** *Likewise, I say unto you, there is joy in the presence of the angels of God over one sinner that repenteth.*

In the parable of the lost coin, Jesus first delivers the parable (Luke 15:8–9) and then provides the interpretation (Luke 15:10). The interpretation, introduced with the word "likewise," is straightforward. The lost coin represents the one who is lost from God, or the sinner. When found, the coin refers to the "sinner that repenteth." The woman's invitation to her friends and neighbors to "rejoice" at finding the lost coin parallels the "joy" that is experienced among God's angels when the sinner repents. The angels' joy teaches an important principle—heavenly beings are fully aware of us on the earth, and they are attentive to us when we repent. In fact, the angels of God experience an emotional response at our repentance, and that response is joy.

Personal Application

Although one searching for a lost coin must "seek diligently" to locate it, finding it does not require a series of complicated and difficult actions. The parable mentions three activities: lighting a candle, sweeping the house, and seeking diligently. Just as locating and retrieving a lost coin is uncomplicated, finding a lost soul may be equally uncomplicated. The seeker of a lost coin need not be a trained professional, one who has received university degrees in searching for lost coins. Coin seeking is not an activity reserved for adults only; a young child may participate. Seekers of a lost coin may include one person, an entire family, or an unrelated group effort. It may take minutes to find it, several hours, days, or even longer.

The lost coin represents each of us who needs to repent. It also represents those who have not yet found the gospel and wayward family members or unrepentant individuals from our ward or branch. The seeker of a lost soul need not be a philosopher, theologian, clinical psychologist, or counselor. Each of us can participate, individually or as a group. Any of us, regardless of our social or occupational status, may seek diligently and find a lost soul.

Virtually every one of us has someone in our circle of responsibility or influence who has become lost in one way or another. It is both our opportunity and obligation to search as the woman did—diligently, until we find and then recover the soul who is lost.

The following two brief stories feature two individuals who found the gospel. These people may be likened unto lost coins who were found, meaning they repented of their ways in order to receive the gospel. Elder J. Richard Clarke, who shared these stories, points out the simplicity of it all. "It was all so simple, so genuine," he writes.

"Yes, the Spirit giveth light in this church. I am thinking of a wonderful new convert in England. In response to my asking, he told me about his conversion. He explained how he was kneeling at his flower bed on a Saturday morning preparing the soil for spring planting. All of a sudden an unseen voice from behind asked the simple question, 'Sir, do you love the Lord?'

"He said that he turned around, fully expecting to see an angel standing there; instead there were two angels, two Mormon missionaries. And his response was, 'Of course I love the Lord. Please come in the house so we can talk about it.' It was all so simple, so genuine. It was an approach that the Savior might have used. . . .

"Not long ago a young American woman living in Taiwan felt that her taxi driver was taking her the long way around in order to increase the fare. She was in the process of venting her feelings in unmistakable terms when the young Chinese driver, obviously hurt by the accusation, stopped the cab, turned off the ignition, then turned around and said simply, 'I would not do that. I am a Mormon.' Calmed down and totally disarmed by the sincerity of his statement, she then asked what a Mormon was. She obviously found out, as she joined the Church just three weeks later. It all happens so simply when the honest in heart are involved."[5]

CHAPTER 11

THE PRODIGAL SON

Luke 15:11–32

And he said, A certain man had two sons:

And the younger of them said to his father, Father, give me the portion of goods that falleth to me. And he divided unto them his living.

And not many days after the younger son gathered all together, and took his journey into a far country, and there wasted his substance with riotous living.

And when he had spent all, there arose a mighty famine in that land; and he began to be in want.

And he went and joined himself to a citizen of that country; and he sent him into his fields to feed swine.

And he would fain have filled his belly with the husks that the swine did eat: and no man gave unto him.

And when he came to himself, he said, How many hired servants of my father's have bread enough and to spare, and I perish with hunger!

I will arise and go to my father, and will say unto him, Father, I have sinned against heaven, and before thee,

And am no more worthy to be called thy son: make me as one of thy hired servants.

And he arose, and came to his father. But when he was yet a great way off, his father saw him, and had compassion, and ran, and fell on his neck, and kissed him.

And the son said unto him, Father, I have sinned against heaven, and in thy sight, and am no more worthy to be called thy son.

But the father said to his servants, Bring forth the best robe, and put it on him; and put a ring on his hand, and shoes on his feet:

And bring hither the fatted calf, and kill it; and let us eat, and be merry:

For this my son was dead, and is alive again; he was lost, and is found. And they began to be merry.

Now his elder son was in the field: and as he came and drew nigh to the house, he heard musick and dancing.

And he called one of the servants, and asked what these things meant.

And he said unto him, Thy brother is come; and thy father hath killed the fatted calf, because he hath received him safe and sound.

And he was angry, and would not go in: therefore came his father out, and intreated him.

And he answering said to his father, Lo, these many years do I serve thee, neither transgressed I at any time thy commandment: and yet thou never gavest me a kid, that I might make merry with my friends:

But as soon as this thy son was come, which hath devoured thy living with harlots, thou hast killed for him the fatted calf.

And he said unto him, Son, thou art ever with me, and all that I have is thine.

It was meet that we should make merry, and be glad: for this thy brother was dead, and is alive again; and was lost, and is found.

This parable has been called the gospel in the Gospel, the crown and pearl of all parables. It brings together principles pertaining to sin, repentance, confession, forgiveness, and (to a degree) restoration of blessings. Of this parable Elder Gordon B. Hinckley said, "I ask you to read that story. Every parent ought to read it again and again. It is large enough to encompass every household, and enough larger than that to encompass all mankind, for are we not all prodigal sons and daughters who need to repent and partake of the forgiving mercy of our Heavenly Father and then follow his example?"[1]

The parable of the prodigal son is part of a trilogy of parables Jesus spoke when the Pharisees and scribes murmured about Jesus mingling with publicans and sinners. In company with the parables of the lost sheep and the lost coin, this parable shows the great joy there is in heaven when those who are lost return.

Some have called this the parable of the two lost sons. The younger son was lost when he strayed from the path of righteousness, leaving his father and his home and wasting his substance with riotous living. In some respects, the older son may have been lost when he refused to forgive his younger brother and refused to rejoice in his repentance.

The father in the parable represents our Heavenly Father—as well as each of us when others offend us. The younger son represents each of us when we stray. The older son represents us when we need to accept the repentance of others, with joy.

God gives us agency, the power to choose what we will make of our lives. When the younger son determined that he wanted to take his inheritance early and go away from his home and family, the father agreed to it. Our Heavenly Father will plead with us through his Spirit in an effort to seek to encourage us to follow the right way, but in the end he will allow us to choose, just as the father in the parable did.

Unfortunately, the departing son discovered what each of us eventually learns: "that to depart from Him is not to throw off the yoke, but to exchange a light yoke for a heavy one, and one gracious Master for a thousand imperious tyrants and lords."[2]

Commentary

Luke 15:11–12 *And he said, A certain man had two sons: And the younger of them said to his father, Father, give me the* *portion of goods that falleth to me. And he divided unto them his living.*

According to Mosaic law, the division would not have been equal. The elder son would have received two-thirds of the inheritance, while the younger son would have received one-third. With his extra portion, the elder son would have been responsible to care for family members who did not have means to care for themselves (see Deuteronomy 21:15–17).

The last part of this verse suggests that the father gave the allotted portions to each of his sons: "And he *divided unto them* his living." Yet, according to custom, the father continued to remain in control of the estate, which he would have done until he died.

Luke 15:13 *And not many days after the younger son gathered all together, and took his journey into a far country, and there wasted his substance with riotous living.*

Some of the younger son's share of the estate would likely have been in real property, which he would have had to convert into cash by selling it. Thus, the son would have broken off a major piece of the estate and sold it outside the family, something that would have gone contrary to both wisdom and tradition.

We can read the "journey into a far country" literally in the story, as well as figuratively—he went far from his father and his God. In the literal sense, the far country would have been a land of Gentiles, where the people of Israel would likely be scarce.

It would be bad enough for the younger son to have taken his inheritance prematurely and spent it wisely. Even then his decision to receive his share of the estate early would have been offensive to his father and his family. But the younger son did something much worse: he "wasted" his inheritance with "riotous living." That last expression suggests drinking, gambling, bad friends—and perhaps worse.

Further, by taking his inheritance and leaving, the younger son turned away from his duty to honor his father and his mother, one of the essential commandments of God. That responsibility was left solely to the older son.

Elder Neal A. Maxwell spoke of how we often go into far countries ourselves: "Like the prodigal son, we too can go to 'a far country,' which may be no farther away than a vile rock concert. The distance to 'a far country' is not to be measured by miles but by how far our hearts and minds are from Jesus! (see Mosiah 5:13). Fidelity, not geography, really determines the distance!"[3]

Luke 15:14 *And when he had spent all, there arose a mighty famine in that land; and he began to be in want.*

Famines were common in the ancient world, and the land of Palestine had its share (for one New Testament example, see Acts 11:27–30).

Two kinds of famines are recorded in the scriptures, and this young man seemed to experience both: a physical famine, where there was insufficient food for the people, and a spiritual famine, where the young man divorced himself from the Spirit and the word of God.

Luke 15:15 *And he went and joined himself to a citizen of that country; and he sent him into his fields to feed swine.*

Here the story takes a turn wherein the young man does some of the worst work imaginable. Pigs were considered unclean animals under the law of Moses (see Leviticus 11:7; Deuteronomy 14:8), and caring for pigs—in service to a Gentile!—was absolutely degrading. Such work would also make one ritually unclean.

Farmers of that day had three types of workers: the lowest on the scale, in terms of security and ability to meet one's needs, were day laborers, who may or may not have work on a given day. We would call day laborers "temporary help." Next came the lower class of man servants and maidservants (see Luke 12:45), who had regular jobs but were far down on the economic and social scale. Those in the best position were the bondservants, who had absolute security and who also enjoyed some of the privileges of family members.

In his employment for the pig farmer, the younger son's status appears to have been that of a manservant. He had a regular job, much better than a day laborer, but he also would not have had the status or privileges of a bondservant.

> ***Luke 15:16*** *And he would fain have filled his belly with the husks that the swine did eat: and no man gave unto him.*

The young man was starving because of the famine and because he had wasted his money. No one would give him any food, so he was forced to make do with the only thing he could find: the carob beans he fed to the swine. Bible scholars are unsure whether these "husks" were the fruit of the *Ceratonia siliqua,* which was edible, or the berries of the wild carob, which were bitter and unpleasant to the taste. Either way, the food the young man had available was unsatisfying and, as his sole source of nutrition, not particularly healthy. Further, the story indicates that his hunger was so great that he wanted to eat the husks, but he was unable even to have that.

> ***Luke 15:17*** *And when he came to himself, he said, How many hired servants of my father's have bread enough and to spare, and I perish with hunger!*

The Greek word used for *servants* here refers to day laborers, those who would have been hired on a day-by-day basis, the lowest on the scale of economic security. The son was willing to take a step down from his steady employment with the pig farmer in the expectation that even as a day laborer for his father he would have more to eat.

> ***Luke 15:18–19*** *I will arise and go to my father, and will say unto him, Father, I have sinned against heaven, and before thee, and am no more worthy to be called thy son: make me as one of thy hired servants.*

The son here took the first steps to returning to his father and his God: he resolved to go back, and in the going back, he decided to confess his sinfulness. His expression of lack of worthiness is a mark of humility.

His specific sins are not enumerated. We can tell from the story that he was guilty of not honoring his father and mother. He was guilty of leaving the covenant and going to live with unbelieving Gentiles. He had wasted the family holdings. He had herded swine. He had given himself to "riotous living." He had shamed his family.

Regardless of the sins he had committed, he was now ready to acknowledge them before his father and his God, to take the steps he could to return to the household of his birth.

Luke 15:20 *And he arose, and came to his father.*

With an attitude of faith and a desire to repent, he returned to his father and his true home.

The words "he arose" have a scriptural resonance. The Lord often asks his children, as part of their repentance, to arise and move forward in a new life. Through Isaiah he said, "Shake thyself from the dust; *arise,* and sit down, O Jerusalem: loose thyself from the bands of thy neck, O captive daughter of Zion" (Isaiah 52:2; emphasis added). Lehi uttered the same plea to his children: "O that ye would awake; awake from a deep sleep, yea, even from the sleep of hell, and shake off the awful chains by which ye are bound, which are the chains which bind the children of men, that they are carried away captive down to the eternal gulf of misery and woe. Awake! and *arise* from the dust, . . . And now that my soul might have joy in you, . . . *arise* from the dust, my sons, and be men. . . . Shake off the chains with which ye are bound, and come forth out of obscurity, and *arise* from the dust" (2 Nephi 1:13–14, 21, 23; emphasis added).

Luke 15:20 *But when he was yet a great way off, his father saw him, and had compassion, and ran, and fell on his neck, and kissed him.*

It seems apparent from the account that the father was watching for the son's return—it's unlikely that he saw his son at a great distance simply by chance. When the father saw the son, he did something that would have been viewed as undignified and uncharacteristic for a respectable Middle Eastern man: he ran. We can picture him lifting his long robes, exposing his lower legs (another undignified action), and running as fast as he could to reach and embrace his long-lost son.

The father ran because of the feelings of his heart: he had compassion on his son. The Greek word for *compassion* used here occurs rarely in the New Testament, and then only in the Gospels. That term is found in two other parables. It expresses the feelings of the king who forgave the unmerciful servant (before that servant then lost his blessings through lack of compassion himself); and it describes the reaction of the Samaritan to the wounded man on the road. With these parables as exceptions, the word always applies specifically to the love of Christ—and, by interpretation, the word applies with the same meaning in these parables.

The father didn't wait for the son to speak. Instead he immediately "fell on his neck, and kissed him." The idiom "fell on his neck" does not refer to a mere perfunctory embrace, but implies an embrace that is born of joy and truly comes from the heart (see Genesis 33:4; 45:14; 46:29; Acts 20:37). Each instance of that idiom in the Bible refers to an incident where the person giving the embrace has a deep desire to demonstrate love in a greeting to someone else.

The embrace and the kiss signified that the father still considered the son to be part of his family. He accepted him, he loved him, and he rejoiced in his return.

> ***Luke 15:21–23*** *And the son said unto him, Father, I have sinned against heaven, and in thy sight, and am no more worthy to be called thy son. But the father said to his servants, Bring forth the best robe, and put it on him; and put a ring on his hand, and shoes on his feet: And bring hither the fatted calf, and kill it; and let us eat, and be merry:*

The son's statement included three important concessions: he had sinned against heaven, he had sinned against his father, and he was not worthy any longer to be considered a member of the family.

These statements were not hyperbole. His lifestyle was indeed sinful and offensive to both his Heavenly Father and his earthly father. In our modern Western culture, a person's unworthiness does not generally result in a loss of place in the family. But that was not true in the ancient Middle East. An individual could indeed lose position in a family through bad behavior; if one was unworthy of being called a son, he might indeed be disowned by the family.

The son had a speech prepared, and it wasn't from a lack of sincerity (as some commentators have suggested) that he failed to finish that speech. Instead, the father seemed to interrupt him; once the basic confession was made, the father was moved to respond with a generous demonstration of love. It would have been inappropriate and ungrateful for the son to continue with what he had thought to say.

The son may not have been worthy to be part of the family, but the father did not respond to the issue of worthiness. The father's desire was not that justice be done, but that mercy be offered and received. The son received a position back as a member of the family not through his merit but through the father's mercy.

The best robe may have been the father's own robe, which he would have worn on special occasions. We have earlier scriptural examples of someone receiving a robe of honor—Jacob received such a robe from Rebekah, a robe that had belonged to Esau (see Genesis 27:15). Pharaoh put such a robe on Joseph (see Genesis 41:42). In a spiritual sense, the best robe can also represent the white robe of righteousness through Christ, or the robes of the priesthood.

The ring, likely a signet ring, was a sign of authority. Again, Pharaoh gave a ring of authority to Joseph (see Genesis 41:42) and in the book of Esther, the king gave his ring to the man to whom he also gave authority (see Esther 3:10; 8:2).

Shoes, or sandals, indicated that the wearer was a free man. Slaves did not wear shoes. (The fact that the son came home barefoot is another mark of how destitute he was.) The servants undoubtedly cleansed the young man's feet before they shod them.

Together, the robe, the ring, and the shoes stood as clear symbols of the young man's restored position.

Further, the father instructed his own servants to clothe his son, sending the signal that the son was to be considered their master.

The fatted calf would have been an animal that was being prepared for a special occasion, readied for a big feast. A goat would have been enough to feed the man and his household, but a calf implies a larger group. Perhaps the father planned to host a feast for the village.

The son came home asking only to be received as a lowly servant. In response, the father accepted him fully as a son, even treating him as an honored guest and bestowing tokens of significant authority.

> ***Luke 15:24*** *For this my son was dead, and is alive again; he was lost, and is found. And they began to be merry.*

Obviously the son was not physically dead, but he had become dead to Christ. Paul used this figure when he wrote to the Ephesians, "And you hath he quickened, who were dead in trespasses and sins. . . . Even when we were dead in sins, [God] hath quickened us together with Christ, . . . and hath raised us up together" (Ephesians 2:1, 5–6).

Paul is saying here that when we sin, we become dead in the ways that matter most—for the dead in the body can still live in God, but the spiritually dead remain so regardless of what sphere they dwell in. But when we repent, we are renewed and revitalized. It is as though we were raised from the dead, resurrected in our spiritual being.

The father of the prodigal son understood these things, and he rejoiced that the son who was dead had come to an awareness of his sins and, repentant, had come home, not only to the father's estate but also to God.

The expression about the lost being found links this parable to those of the lost sheep and the lost coin, with the same exclamation being found in each parable (see Luke 15:6, 9).

The banquet and merrymaking are not to be considered an entertainment for the returning son; rather, it was an opportunity for the father and his friends to rejoice together. The idea of making merry is an idiom that means they joined together in a meal of rejoicing (see Deuteronomy 14:26; 27:7; Ecclesiastes 8:15; Luke 12:19; 16:19), combined with the music and dancing that often accompany a celebration.

> ***Luke 15:25–27*** *Now his elder son was in the field: and as he came and drew nigh to the house, he heard musick and dancing. And he called one of the servants, and asked what these things meant. And he said unto him, Thy brother is come; and*

thy father hath killed the fatted calf, because he hath received him safe and sound.

The fact that the elder son was out working in the field indicates that he was dependable and doing his duty. We're not told in the parable why no one went into the field to find the elder son and tell him the good news; rather, he was forced to find out about his brother's return in an awkward way from a servant. The fact that the elder son was the last to know probably added to his injured feelings. Not only had the younger son wasted his inheritance, and not only had the father thrown that son a big party when he returned, but the older son, the faithful one, hadn't even been invited to that party!

Luke 15:28 *And he was angry, and would not go in: therefore came his father out, and intreated him.*

The younger son insulted the father by taking his inheritance and wasting it. Now the older son insults the father by refusing to join in the rejoicing the father has organized.

Earlier the father had reached out to the younger son. Now he reaches out to his older son, pleading with him to join the group in their rejoicing over the recovery of the wayward son. For the father to reach out in this way goes contrary to Middle Eastern traditions. It was viewed to be beneath a father's dignity to go out after a son; the son should respond to a father's request to come. But the father, in love and patience, went out to talk to his son. The word *intreated* (now spelled "entreated") indicates that the father did not command his son to come in to the party but instead tried to persuade him. Again the father is demonstrating a spirit of forgiveness and love.

President Joseph F. Smith gave this representation of what the father may have said to his son: "Now we may suppose the father reasoned with him somewhat in this wise: 'My son, I am surprised at your short sightedness; you should not be jealous of your poor, unfortunate brother, for he is to be pitied; he has squandered his substance, and I thought he was lost forever, that he was as good as dead to me, and hope for his restoration to us had fled. But he has returned in sorrow for his follies, in abject poverty, penitent and humble, freely confessing that he has sinned against heaven and in my sight, and that he is unworthy to be my son or your brother, and would become our servant forever. Shall we not have compassion upon him, shall we utterly banish him from us, since he has returned so humble and repentant? I love him as my son, but with my love for him is mingled sorrow, pity, chagrin, and commiseration. You have been faithful to me all the while, and in you I have exceeding great joy. I love you with all the affection of my soul, and in you I have perfect confidence, for you have never betrayed it. Beside all this, you have forfeited nothing nor lost anything. . . . Can we not well afford to be charitable and forgiving?' "[4]

> ***Luke 15:29*** *And he answering said to his father, Lo, these many years do I serve thee, neither transgressed I at any time thy commandment: and yet thou never gavest me a kid, that I might make merry with my friends:*

The elder son makes three separate claims: (1) he has served the father many years; (2) he has never failed to do anything the father has asked; (3) the father has never rewarded him by preparing a celebration in his behalf (implying the father has not been appreciative or grateful).

The first claim is somewhat just and true. He did indeed stay on the farm while his younger brother went off to have a good time. However, he had been viewing himself as a servant rather than as a son. He had not recognized the truth of his position with the father, even though the father had always treated him as a son.

Even though there was partial truth in his first claim, his next claim was most likely not true. When he says "neither transgressed I at any time thy commandment," he is claiming to have been perfect in his work. But who can make such a claim? And, as we then translate the parable into spiritual terms, we have to ask, Who is wholly without sin? Who can honestly say that they have never transgressed any commandment of the Father?

The third claim is also untrue and unfair. The son is saying heatedly that his father has not rewarded him for his service. It likely is accurate that the father never threw a special party for this son; he never slew the fatted calf or even a goat, which would have been much smaller and cheaper. Goats were much more common than cows and calves, and goats cost only a tenth as much as cows. To serve goat meat would have been fairly common at mealtimes, though the fatted calf would be reserved for special occasions.

But even though the father had not given such a party for his older son, at the same time the father had provided generously for him (as he did even for his servants!). He surely rewarded the son with love and affection, for the father was clearly that sort of man. And, in the end, the son would have a double portion of the estate, if he had not already received it.

The truth is that the elder son was jealous and prideful. He was upset that his profligate brother was the guest of honor at a party when he (the elder son) had not even been invited. And, based on the tone and content of his words, it appears that that elder son had not been serving the father out of love or respect or desire to bless, but primarily out of duty, worried about what he was not receiving from that service.

Earlier, the younger son demanded what he perceived were his rights: to receive a portion of the inheritance. Now the older son is demanding his rights: to have a party like his young brother is receiving—or, perhaps more accurately, to get the father to agree that it was wrong to give the younger son a party because he was wasteful and sinful and because the older brother, who was faithful, never received such a party.

It is also important to note that the younger son began his speech by addressing his father by his kinship name, "Father," but the older son did not show that mark of respect. The father, however, began his response to the older son by using a word that denotes not only kinship but affection, calling him "Son" or, as is found in some translations, "Dear son."

> ***Luke 15:30*** *But as soon as this thy son was come, which hath devoured thy living with harlots, thou hast killed for him the fatted calf.*

The elder brother is both envious and judgmental. There is no evidence in the story that the younger son had been spending his time with harlots. Yes, he had been engaged in "riotous living," and this may have included sexual sin—but not necessarily so. Could the older brother be guilty of assuming to assign transgression where there may have been none?

Sadly, the older brother doesn't even refer to his sibling by his kinship name or his given name. Instead of saying, "As soon as this *my brother* was come," he says "As soon as this *thy son* was come." He is disowning his brother by his language and his attitude.

When we consider Jesus' teachings about forgiving others if we hope to be forgiven, we realize that unless the elder brother can forgive and welcome his brother, he (the elder brother) has now become, at least to a degree, the lost son.

Even though the older son demonstrated weakness and a lack of a pure heart, we should be cautious in comparing the sin of the two sons. As Elder James E. Talmage expressed it: "We are not justified in extolling the virtue of repentance on the part of the prodigal above the faithful, plodding service of his brother, who had remained at home, true to the duties required of him. The devoted son was the heir; the father did not disparage his worth, nor deny his deserts. His displeasure over the rejoicing incident to the return of his wayward brother was an exhibition of illiberality and narrowness; but of the two brothers the elder was the more faithful, whatever his minor defects may have been. The particular point emphasized in the Lord's lesson, however, had to do with his uncharitable and selfish weaknesses."[5]

***Luke 15:31** And he said unto him, Son, thou art ever with me, and all that I have is thine.*

The father affirms that the elder son had continued faithfully to be with him and that that son was indeed the major heir of the father's estate.

The promise found in the oath and covenant of the priesthood has an echo from this parable. To those who are "faithful," receiving the priesthood, God's servants, and the Savior, the promise is given, "He that receiveth me receiveth my Father; and he that receiveth my Father receiveth my Father's kingdom; therefore all that my Father hath shall be given unto him" (D&C 84:33–38).

Certainly outward obedience is not enough to inherit the supreme blessings of exaltation. But if we are faithful with all our hearts, repenting when we fail—as the elder son may have done—we can indeed, through the power of the Atonement, receive "all that [the] Father hath."

> ***Luke 15:32*** *It was meet that we should make merry, and be glad: for this thy brother was dead, and is alive again; and was lost, and is found.*

The parable ends with the father repeating words he had expressed earlier to his household. The younger boy "was dead, and is alive again; and was lost, and is found." These two expressions are identical, with one significant difference. The first time the father says, "this my *son* was dead"; the second time he says, "this thy *brother* was dead."

The difference between those two expressions contains much meaning. When we lose a son or daughter, and that child returns, we can rejoice. Likewise, when *anyone* (a brother or sister in the broad sense) becomes lost and then returns, we can equally rejoice. There is much joy in heaven when a sinner repents and returns. And there is likewise an opportunity for much joy in our hearts at such repentance in anyone we know, regardless of how terrible their lives might have become before they turned and experienced a change of heart.

The parable ends with this expression. But Elder Bruce R. McConkie sees the best possible ending to the story, believing that the elder son must at that point have repented of his disrespect for the father and bad feelings toward his brother: "We may suppose that the elder son, accustomed as he was to obeying the will of his father, then went in to the feast, welcomed his wayward brother in a compassionate manner, and rejoiced along with the father because the spiritually dead was born again, because he who was lost to the kingdom had been reclaimed."[6]

Some may foolishly take license from this parable, thinking that they can sin, repent, and suffer no loss. The truth is that there is always loss from sin—loss either to us as sinners or to our Savior, who suffered deeply to cleanse and sanctify us. It is a serious mistake to sin with the premeditated intention of repenting later. But when we do sin, it also is a great comfort to know that when we repent with all our hearts we can partake of the powers and blessings of the Atonement, and we can once again be received back into our Father's house.

PERSONAL APPLICATION

The parable can properly be interpreted on two levels: that of our interaction with one another, and that of God's interaction with us.

The father is a wonderful example of how we should treat one another, including those who have offended us (or "sinned against" us).

Although the two sons' lifestyle choices are very different from each other, in one essential way they are the same: both are disrespectful of their father, even treating him with contempt.

On the other hand, the father is consistent in his response to both of his boys. As one commentator wrote, "The attitude of the father toward his sons is not determined by their character, but his."[7] He exemplifies the principles of Christlike loving described in latter-day revelation: "No power or influence can or ought to be maintained by virtue of the priesthood," the Lord says, or, to paraphrase, "No power or influence can or ought to be maintained by virtue of one's position in the Church or in the family." If our priesthood or position is not to be used to influence others, how are we to do it? The Lord explains that we can and should obtain power and influence "only by persuasion, by long-suffering, by gentleness and meekness, and by love unfeigned; by kindness, and pure knowledge" (D&C 121:41–42). These principles were an essential part of the make-up of the father, and through telling us this parable, the Savior sets up the father's behavior as an example for all of us.

The father's response to his son's appearance on the horizon is also a manifestation of grace, demonstrating in the story the grace of God toward us. He waits and watches as we walk a path of sin, yearning for us to return. When we do, he sees us even when we are a long ways off, and he meets us with an embrace of pure love.

The scriptures refer repeatedly to this precious embrace. Lehi said, "I am encircled about eternally in the arms of his love" (2 Nephi 1:15).

And Mormon added his testimony that the righteous will be "clasped in the arms of Jesus" (Mormon 5:11).

This parable, in company with the two that precede it, emphasizes the joy experienced by God and all the heavenly hosts—as well as the righteous on earth—when a sinner repents and returns to the path of righteousness. Some individuals are like the sheep, that wanders off from the flock, not because the shepherd was careless and seemingly not because the sheep was being willful, but perhaps it was inattentive. Some are like the coin that is lost through the neglect of its caretaker. And some are like the prodigal son, who leaves home in a spirit of disobedience. In all cases, God feels the loss very deeply, and when that which is lost is found, he and those who are of one heart with him join together in great joy and rejoicing.

CHAPTER 12

The Unmerciful Servant

Matthew 18:23–35

Therefore is the kingdom of heaven likened unto a certain king, which would take account of his servants.

And when he had begun to reckon, one was brought unto him, which owed him ten thousand talents.

But forasmuch as he had not to pay, his lord commanded him to be sold, and his wife, and children, and all that he had, and payment to be made.

The servant therefore fell down, and worshipped him, saying, Lord, have patience with me, and I will pay thee all.

Then the lord of that servant was moved with compassion, and loosed him, and forgave him the debt.

But the same servant went out, and found one of his fellowservants, which owed him an hundred pence: and he laid hands on him, and took him by the throat, saying, Pay me that thou owest.

And his fellowservant fell down at his feet, and besought him, saying, Have patience with me, and I will pay thee all.

And he would not: but went and cast him into prison, till he should pay the debt.

So when his fellowservants saw what was done, they were very sorry, and came and told unto their lord all that was done.

Then his lord, after that he had called him, said unto him, O thou wicked servant, I forgave thee all that debt, because thou desiredst me:

Shouldest not thou also have had compassion on thy fellowservant, even as I had pity on thee?

And his lord was wroth, and delivered him to the tormentors, till he should pay all that was due unto him.

So likewise shall my heavenly Father do also unto you, if ye from your hearts forgive not every one his brother their trespasses.

Some parables are given to us without any clear context. This is not the case with the parable of the unmerciful servant.

At one point Jesus taught his disciples essential principles concerning handling offenses and offering forgiveness. "If thy brother shall trespass against thee," he said, don't let it fester and don't gossip about it. Instead, "go and tell him his fault between thee and him alone: if he shall hear thee, thou hast gained thy brother" (Matthew 18:15).

Shortly after receiving this instruction, Peter approached Jesus and asked, "Lord, how oft shall my brother sin against me, and I forgive him? till seven times?" (Matthew 18:21).

Peter no doubt thought he was being generous. The rabbis prescribed forgiveness for the first, second, and third offenses only.

But Jesus had a higher standard in mind. "I say not unto thee, Until seven times: but, Until seventy times seven" (Matthew 18:21–22).

This may hearken back to Lamech's terrible statement in Genesis 4:24, after he has taken revenge on his enemy: "If Cain shall be avenged seven-fold, truly Lamech seventy and sevenfold." Lamech wanted unlimited vengeance. But the Savior tells us to grant unto one another unlimited forgiveness.

The numbers seven and ten are both symbolic of completion. Seven times ten times seven (or "seventy times seven") seems to symbolize a perfection of completion, or an infinity thereof. God's goodness and forgiveness are infinite, and we ever seek to be like him.

This parable tells a simple, yet incredible, story. A man owes a tremendous sum of money to his king and hasn't paid it in a timely manner. The king nearly sells the man and his family into slavery in an attempt to recoup part of the money. But when the man pleads for more time, the king instead forgives him the entire debt.

Much relieved, the man leaves the presence of the king. Not long after he searches out a "fellowservant" who owed him a relatively small amount of money. The first man literally attacks the second man, taking him by the throat and demanding immediate payment. When the second man pleads for more time, his creditor refuses and has him thrown into prison.

When the king finds out what his servant has done, refusing to grant a small mercy when such a great mercy was offered to him, he revokes his previous magnanimous offer and has the servant also thrown into prison.

This is a principle that governs the Lord's kingdom, Jesus taught. We must forgive one another from our very hearts if we hope to be forgiven by our Heavenly Father.

Commentary

Matthew 18:23 *Therefore is the kingdom of heaven likened unto a certain king, which would take account of his servants.*

The kingdom of heaven in this parable is the Lord's kingdom on the earth. The Lord wants us to learn from the parable one or more lessons about how his kingdom works—and how we should behave as members of that kingdom. The king of the kingdom, of course, is God himself. The servants are those who owe allegiance to the king, God's children on the earth. It is a common practice for a leader to require an accounting of those who work or serve under him. So it is here—the king desires to know how his servants are doing with the stewardships that are given them.

Matthew 18:24 *And when he had begun to reckon, one was brought unto him, which owed him ten thousand talents.*

As the king proceeds with the accountability process, the servant who is the focus of the parable is brought to him. The amount of money owed suggests that this should not be regarded as a menial or household servant; the man referred to seems to be a high official under the king. It is important to note that the servant may not have come of his own accord. He "was brought" or summoned. Perhaps he was hesitant to step forward because of what he owed. The sum of 10,000 talents was nothing less than astronomical. In fact, the number 10,000 and the measure of a talent were "the highest magnitudes in use"—"10,000 is the highest number used in reckoning, and the talent is the largest currency unit in the whole of the Near East."[1] In other words, the Lord was using figures specifically designed to emphasize the outrageous magnitude of the debt.

A talent represented a particular weight in gold or silver, rather than a denomination of money. That weight could equal different values at different times. However, during the first century A.D., it is estimated that 10,000 talents equaled 100,000,000 denarii. One denarius was a typical day's wage for a common laborer. If that laborer worked three hundred days a year, it would take about 33 years for him to be able to purchase *one* talent. And it would take over 300,000 years to earn 10,000 talents, the sum of the servant's debt.

To give it another perspective, Josephus recorded that a year's combined taxes for all of Judea, Idumea, Samaria, Galilee, and Perea at the time of the death of Herod the Great (4 B.C.) came to only 800 talents.

How could the servant have accumulated so much debt? The answer is that it would not be possible—if we are talking about worldly debt. But the Lord intended us to see beyond the earthly example to the heavenly truth. Given all we owe him, our debt to God is beyond measure and really beyond all reckoning.

Matthew 18:25 *But forasmuch as he had not to pay, his lord commanded him to be sold, and his wife, and children, and all that he had, and payment to be made.*

The law of Moses required that a man pay that which he owed—or suffer (see Exodus 22:3; Leviticus 25:39, 47).

Certainly there were slaves in the Middle East, and even Jews owned slaves. Slaves were not obtained by kidnapping (the common practice with American slavery during the pre-Civil War period) but were typically one of the spoils of war. A slave would often be given common household duties; a male slave might work with his master in the master's occupation. Slaves had opportunity to earn their freedom, and, according to the law of Moses, all slaves were to be set free in the jubilee year, which fell every fiftieth year (see Leviticus 25:8–16, 23–55; 27:16–25).

It was not acceptable practice among Jews to sell a debtor and his family for failure to pay the debt, although it did happen in the Gentile world. Nevertheless, Jesus' listeners would have been familiar with the practice. If the man and his family all were sold as slaves, the amount gained would fall far short of the amount owed on the debt—a slave could be sold for 500 to 2,000 denarii. The sale of the whole family would therefore have brought the king less than one talent. Obviously, the king's purpose was not to regain his lost money but to punish the servant.

> ***Matthew 18:26*** *The servant therefore fell down, and worshipped him, saying, Lord, have patience with me, and I will pay thee all.*

This is a brash promise, one that could never be fulfilled. The servant simply asks for more time and he will repay "all" the debt. But even if he earned one hundred times more than the common laborer, he still would earn only three talents a year. At that rate, even if he used none of his earnings for living expenses, it would take him three thousand years to repay what he owed. Clearly, this is a debt beyond repayment.

In the Joseph Smith Translation, the first part of this verse replaces the phrase "therefore fell down, and worshipped" with "besought": "And the servant besought him, saying . . ." (JST, Matthew 18:26).

> ***Matthew 18:27*** *Then the lord of that servant was moved with compassion, and loosed him, and forgave him the debt.*

Here the story takes a surprising turn. The servant owes a sum that is impossible to pay. The king is ready to sell him and his family and all he owns in an attempt to recoup at least a tiny portion of his losses. But when the servant pleads for more time to pay, promising to pay the debt in its entirety, the king does the unexpected: rather than have mercy and accept the servant's offer, he has boundless mercy and forgives him everything he owes. Once the king made his decree that the servant was to be sold, the servant must have immediately been put under arrest, or at least in bonds. But now the king looses him and sets him free without even the debt hanging over his head.

The Greek term from which the word *compassion* was translated is found a dozen times in the New Testament, all of them in the Gospels. With three exceptions, it is used to express the divine compassion of God. Those three exceptions are all found in parables: the unmerciful servant, the good Samaritan, and the prodigal son. In each of these parables, the compassion denoted is godly compassion expressed in a human heart.

In his infinite love, our Heavenly Father is like the king in the parable. When we plead unto him, asking for mercy, he is "moved with compassion." He looses us from the bonds that hold us down and forgives us our great debt.

In the Joseph Smith Translation, the first part of verse 26 ("The servant therefore fell down, and worshipped him") is moved to the end of verse 27; hence, the falling down and worshipping occurs *after* the debt is forgiven.

> ***Matthew 18:28*** *But the same servant went out, and found one of his fellowservants, which owed him an hundred pence: and he laid hands on him, and took him by the throat, saying, Pay me that thou owest.*

Here, again, the story takes a surprising twist. Once the first servant is free, both physically and from the bondage of his debt, he goes out looking for a fellowservant who owes him money. He takes the second servant by the throat and demands payment.

Whereas the amount the first servant owed the king was impossibly large, the amount owed by the second servant was relatively small: one hundred pence, or a hundred denarii. As noted above, one denarius was a day's wages for a common laborer. It would take about four months to earn a hundred denarii. Even though that would be considered a significant amount of money, it was about a million times less than the amount the first servant had owed.

> ***Matthew 18:29*** *And his fellowservant fell down at his feet, and besought him, saying, Have patience with me, and I will pay thee all.*

Now the earlier scene is repeated with the first servant acting the role of the creditor, the one who has power to show mercy. His fellowservant fell down at his feet, as the first servant had done with the king, and pleads in language that is identical to that used by the first servant: "Have patience with me, and I will pay thee all."

Surely, when we consider how the king forgave the first servant's debt, we could expect that servant to forgive his fellow. In fact, the first servant had no possible expectation of being able to fulfill his promise, while the second servant's promise is very realistic. But the story has yet another surprising twist.

> ***Matthew 18:30*** *And he would not: but went and cast him into prison, till he should pay the debt.*

In every way the first servant responded in a way that was opposite to the magnanimous king: he refused to give his fellowservant extra time, he cast him into prison, and he still required him to pay the entire debt.

> ***Matthew 18:31*** *So when his fellowservants saw what was done, they were very sorry, and came and told unto their lord all that was done.*

When we see our brethren and sisters in trouble, it is most appropriate, even pleasing to God, that we should take up their cause in prayer to him as the Heavenly King. We should pray and plead in their behalf, and then seek to do what we can to bless them.

Matthew 18:32–34 *Then his lord, after that he had called him, said unto him, O thou wicked servant, I forgave thee all that debt, because thou desiredst me: Shouldest not thou also have had compassion on thy fellowservant, even as I had pity on thee? And his lord was wroth, and delivered him to the tormentors, till he should pay all that was due unto him.*

God, our king, does not take it lightly when we fail to forgive others. In the parable, the king "was wroth," which indicates he was angry to the core. He not only delivered the man to prison, but to torture in prison.

How long would he stay in that condition? Until he paid all of his debt to the king. But the debt was so great he could never pay it—and while he remained in prison he could not earn money to pay a single pence. His only hope for deliverance was the mercy of the king, but that mercy was no longer available to him.

If we come unto Christ with all our hearts; if we repent, receive the ordinances, and keep our covenants; and if we forgive others of their offenses against us, we place ourselves into the hands of Jesus Christ. We thereby come unto the "throne of grace" (Hebrews 4:16) and receive the gifts and blessings of the Atonement. Christ then pays "all that [is] due" on our account. But if we reject Christ and his commandments, and if we refuse to grant mercy to others around us, we are denied the blessings that could have been ours. As the Lord said through Joseph Smith, "Every man must repent or suffer. . . . Wherefore, I revoke not the judgments which I shall pass, but woes shall go forth, weeping, wailing, and gnashing of teeth. . . . If they would not repent they must suffer even as I" (D&C 19:4–5, 17).

Matthew 18:35 *So likewise shall my heavenly Father do also unto you, if ye from your hearts forgive not every one his brother their trespasses.*

The moral to this story is a sobering one. "So likewise shall my heavenly Father do also unto you, if . . ." We can avoid the punishment if we will forgive others their trespasses with all our hearts. But if we fail to so forgive, "so likewise" shall God do to us. He will be angry, and he will deliver us to torment. As James said, "He shall have judgment without mercy, that hath shewed no mercy" (James 2:13). And Jesus said very plainly, after teaching the Lord's Prayer, "If ye forgive men their trespasses, your heavenly Father will also forgive you; but if ye forgive not men their trespasses, neither will your Father forgive your trespasses" (Matthew 6:14–15).

When we enter into a covenant relationship with God, wherein we partake of the blessings of Christ's atonement, he requires us to enter into a new relationship with our fellowman. As he has demonstrated great love, compassion, and mercy to us, so must we do to others.

Personal Application

Jesus has commanded us to love one another—even as he has loved us (see John 15:12). We are not to love as those who know not God, as those who are unaware of his bounteous goodness. We are to love freely and in a godly way.

An essential part of such love is to forgive. In the Lord's Prayer we are taught to beg the Lord to forgive us our trespasses—but in the very same sentence we are informed that in order to be forgiven we must also forgive those who have trespassed against us (Matthew 6:12). Jesus taught the same principle in another setting: "When ye stand praying, forgive, if ye have ought against any; that your Father also which is in heaven may forgive you your trespasses" (Mark 11:25). And he said, "With what measure ye mete [or use], it shall be measured to you again" (Matthew 7:2).

This parable teaches in a powerful way the goodness of God. We owe him everything we are, everything we have, and everything we ever hope to be. King Benjamin put this beautifully: "In the first place, he hath created you, and granted unto you your lives, for which ye are indebted unto him. And secondly, he doth require that ye should do as he hath commanded you; for which if ye do, he doth immediately bless you; and therefore he hath paid you. And ye are still indebted unto him, and are, and will be, forever and ever" (Mosiah 2:23–24).

But beyond our temporal existence, we owe him our spiritual lives. Our Savior made the ultimate sacrifice to enable us to repent and be cleansed of our sins. When he forgives us of our wrongdoing, it is not a light thing for him. He paid a terrible price to redeem us. Yet he still forgives us freely when we repent with honest hearts. His forgiveness comes again and again. We sin daily, and still he reaches out to us—seven times, seventy times, seventy times seven, an infinity of goodness. The Psalmist said, "If you, Lord, kept a record of sins, O Lord, who could stand? But with you there is forgiveness; therefore you are feared. . . . O Israel, put your hope in the Lord, for with the Lord is unfailing love and with him is full redemption" (NIV, Psalm 130:3–4, 7).

When we sin against God and then repent, he forgives us—and remembers the sin no more. Should we do less for those who have hurt or offended us?

Yes, some may have deeply wronged us. But we have wronged our God even more. The debt others owe us is like pennies compared to the millions we owe God.

Corrie Ten Boom, a devout Christian woman, was arrested during World War II for concealing Jews in Nazi-occupied Holland. She was taken to a concentration camp, where she suffered brutality, abuse, and daily horror. Her sister Betsie, who also had been captured, died in the camp.

Years later, Corrie was speaking in a church service about her experience—and about the need to forgive. After the meeting she recognized one of the S.S. guards from the prison camp. "And suddenly it was all there," she recalled, "the roomful of mocking men, the heaps of clothing, Betsie's pain-blanched face."

The man approached her "as the church was emptying, beaming and bowing. 'How grateful I am for your message, Fraulein,' he said. 'To think that, as you say, He has washed my sins away!'

"His hand was thrust out to shake mine. And I, who had preached so often to the people of Bloemendaal the need to forgive, kept my hand at my side.

"Even as the angry, vengeful thoughts boiled through me, I saw the sin of them. Jesus Christ had died for this man; was I going to ask for more? Lord Jesus, I prayed, forgive me and help me to forgive him.

"I tried to smile, I struggled to raise my hand. I could not. I felt nothing, not the slightest spark of warmth or charity. And so again I breathed a silent prayer. Jesus, I cannot forgive him. Give me Your forgiveness.

"As I took his hand the most incredible thing happened. From my shoulder along my arm and through my hand a current seemed to pass from me to him, while into my heart sprang a love for this stranger that almost overwhelmed me.

"And so I discovered that it is not on our forgiveness any more than on our goodness that the world's healing hinges, but on His. When He tells us to love our enemies, He gives, along with the command, the love itself."[2]

CHAPTER 13

The Good Samaritan

Luke 10:30–37

A certain man went down from Jerusalem to Jericho, and fell among thieves, which stripped him of his raiment, and wounded him, and departed, leaving him half dead.

And by chance there came down a certain priest that way: and when he saw him, he passed by on the other side.

And likewise a Levite, when he was at the place, came and looked on him, and passed by on the other side.

But a certain Samaritan, as he journeyed, came where he was: and when he saw him, he had compassion on him,

And went to him, and bound up his wounds, pouring in oil and wine, and set him on his own beast, and brought him to an inn, and took care of him.

And on the morrow when he departed, he took out two pence, and gave them to the host, and said unto him, Take care of him; and whatsoever thou spendest more, when I come again, I will repay thee.

Which now of these three, thinkest thou, was neighbour unto him that fell among the thieves?

And he said, He that shewed mercy on him. Then said Jesus unto him, Go, and do thou likewise.

This is at once one of the sweetest and most troubling stories in all scripture. It tells of a man in dire trouble who is ignored and abandoned by those who should have been willing to assist him. And of another man who, by definition, might have been considered the injured man's enemy. But that "enemy" instead treated the man in need as a dear friend.

Jesus was often tested by the scribes, the Pharisees, those schooled in the law. Their motives may have varied, but the desire was the same: to try to prove to Jesus' followers that his understandings of Jewish doctrine and practice were flawed and inferior.

Invariably Jesus' opponents were disappointed. With all the wisdom given him by his Father, with all the spiritual depth he brought with him from premortality, he was in every case able to teach deep truth about complicated issues.

Such was the case with this parable. A lawyer stood and tempted him, or tested him, asking for a brief summation of the requirements of eternal life. "Master, what shall I do to inherit eternal life?" he asked (Luke 10:25). This was not a lawyer like those we see in our culture today. Very likely his specialty was the Mosaic law. Rather than answer directly, Jesus asked, "What is written in the law? how readest thou?" It was the response of a master teacher. Sometimes a student asks a question the answer to which he already knows.

The lawyer had a ready and a correct answer, quoting from the Lord's words to Moses: "Thou shalt love the Lord thy God with all thy heart, and with all thy soul, and with all thy strength, and with all thy mind; and thy neighbor as thyself" (Luke 10:27; see Deuteronomy 6:5; Leviticus 19:18).

Jesus commended him for his answer. "Thou hast answered right: this do, and thou shalt live," meaning, obey the law of love, and you will have eternal life (Luke 10:28).

But the lawyer wasn't willing to conclude the interchange on that note. Perhaps desiring to limit his responsibility ("willing to justify himself" the account says), the lawyer asked, "And who is my neighbor?" As Elder James E. Talmage wrote, "If he had to love his neighbors as he loved himself, he wanted to have as few neighbors as possible."[1]

The lawyer may have been small-hearted, but we can be very grateful that he asked the question. The result was the marvelous parable of the good Samaritan.

The lawyer, who almost certainly was well schooled in the minutia of the law and the prophets, may have heard in the parable echoes from a story recorded in 2 Chronicles. During the reign of King Ahab, the people of the northern kingdom of Israel rose up in war against the people of Judah. Israel prevailed and took many thousands captive into Samaria. But in Samaria a prophet rose up and commanded the captors to let the people of Judah go free.

Then the people of Israel "took the captives, and with the spoil clothed all that were naked among them, and arrayed them, and shod them, and gave them to eat and to drink, and anointed them, and carried all the feeble of them upon asses, and brought them to Jericho, the city of palm trees, to their brethren: then they returned to Samaria" (2 Chronicles 28:15).

This parable of the good Samaritan reinforces the great lesson that Paul taught: "[God] hath made of one blood all nations of men" (Acts 17:26).

Commentary

Luke 10:30 *A certain man went down from Jerusalem to Jericho, and fell among thieves, which stripped him of his raiment, and wounded him, and departed, leaving him half dead.*

It would have come as no surprise to Jesus' listeners that there was peril on the road to Jericho. Because of thieves, it was a dangerous and uninviting road—but a necessary route for those who had to travel from Jerusalem to Jericho. It was commonly traveled both by pilgrims to Jerusalem and commercial caravans. Because of the dangers, people often traveled in groups for protection. But in this instance the man is said to be traveling alone.

The road is about eighteen miles long and often quite steep; it drops some 3,500 feet, ending in one of the lowest areas on earth. It is a barren, desert area. In biblical times it was called "the path of blood," or the "bloody way," probably because of the bandits and robbers that lay in wait in its many hiding places in the limestone hills.

Luke 10:31–32 *And by chance there came down a certain priest that way: and when he saw him, he passed by on the* *other side. And likewise a Levite, when he was at the place, came and looked on him, and passed by on the other side.*

It is likely that both the priest and the Levite were traveling home after having performed their temple service in Jerusalem. The priests and Levites, of course, were those who were appointed to officiate in the temple and perform the sacrifices that were part of the worship services. These, therefore, weren't ordinary Jews; they were those with a special assignment to serve their fellowmen. They would have been considered holy men—in great contrast to the Samaritan, who would have been viewed as unholy.

Perhaps they were fearful of being attacked themselves. Perhaps they were prideful and wouldn't stoop to get their hands or robes dirty to help a man lying in the dirt. Perhaps they considered that since the road was heavily traveled, someone else would soon come along to help.

Priests and Levites also had unique complicating factors that may have contributed to their response. The law of Moses specified that priests were not to touch a corpse, except for a family member—and even then they would be ritually unclean for a week (see Leviticus 21:1–2; Numbers 19:11; Ezekiel 44:25–27). Likewise, the Levite would be limited in his ability to serve in the temple if he were to touch a dead person. He also would be considered unclean for seven days (see Numbers 5:2; 19:11–13).

The fact is, however, that the man was not dead, and if the priest and Levite had drawn close enough, that would have been obvious. Further, every priest and Levite would have understood that saving another person's life overrode any other consideration of the law. According to the law, even a beast, including the beast of an enemy, was to receive care in time of need (see Deuteronomy 22:4; Exodus 23:4–5).

Further, the priest and the Levite were supposed to be holy—servants of God and servants of others.

Nevertheless, the priest and Levite might have supposed that the wounded man was a Gentile (which would have been pure supposition, since the man was stripped of his identifying clothes). If that were the case, as Elder David B. Haight said, "To the Jews in Jesus' day this unconcern for the victim in the parable was considered appropriate religious behavior. Their rabbinical teaching declared, 'We are not to contrive the death of the Gentiles, but if they are in any danger of death we are not bound to deliver them, . . . for such a one is not thy neighbour.'"[2]

The Joseph Smith Translation indicates that the priest passed by "on the other side of the way," adding to the symbolism, suggesting that the priest moved off the correct path when he refused to help the stricken man. It also makes an important addition to the end of verse 32, indicating that the Levite also passed by "on the other side of the way; for they desired in their hearts that it might not be known that they had seen him."

Luke 10:33 *But a certain Samaritan, as he journeyed, came where he was:*

Those listening to the parable at this point may have expected the teacher to make the point that the priest had failed the test, as had the Levite. Perhaps an ordinary Jew would be the hero.

But the story turned in a different direction, one that likely no one anticipated. The hero was a Samaritan!

The Samaritans were a hated race. The land of Samaria had once been occupied by Israelites, but many of the land's inhabitants had been transported from the land by the Assyrians in the eighth century B.C. The Assyrian conquerors had then resettled the area with people from other lands. Over time, those new settlers had intermarried with Israelites, but they were not regarded as part of the "pure" race of God's chosen people.

Many of the Samaritans converted to the worship of the true God, but their worship also wasn't regarded as pure. They accepted only the first five books of the Old Testament as scripture. They built their own temple on Mount Gezirim, which the Jews considered to be an abomination. In 128 B.C. the Jews attacked Samaria, destroying their temple and their city.

In about A.D. 6, some Samaritans sneaked into the Jerusalem temple by night, during Passover, and polluted it by scattering human bones around the Temple Mount.

The animosity was so great between the Jews and Samaritans that Jews typically skirted Samaria when traveling from Galilee to Judea, even though the roundabout route was much longer. Not only did the Jews desire to avoid contact with their enemies, it was unsafe for a Jew to take the direct route.

Luke 10:33 *and when he saw him, he had compassion on him,*

As mentioned previously, the Greek word translated *compassion* here is the same word used to describe the feelings of the king in the parable of the unmerciful servant and the father in the parable of the prodigal son. It is the word used to refer to divine or godly compassion. The Samaritan felt deeply in behalf of the wounded man, desiring from the depths of his heart to help him.

Luke 10:34–35 *And went to him, and bound up his wounds, pouring in oil and wine, and set him on his own beast, and brought him to an inn, and took care of him. And on the morrow when he departed, he took out two pence, and gave them to the host, and said unto him, Take care of him; and whatsoever thou spendest more, when I come again, I will repay thee.*

The Samaritan not only felt deeply for the injured man, but he acted on it. Each of his actions was exemplary:

1. He went to him. Unlike the others, who passed by on the other side, he sacrificed both time and safety to go to this man who lay helpless and half dead on or beside the road.

2. He bound up his wounds. What did the Samaritan use for bandages? Surely he didn't carry ready-made bandages with him. Might he have taken of his own clothing, perhaps part of his own robe, to help the man?

3. He administered oil and wine to the man's wounds. Wine would have been used as a mild disinfectant, and oil would have been a soothing ointment.

4. He set him on his own donkey. Most likely the Samaritan had been riding that donkey himself. But now, with real sacrifice, he chose to walk, allowing the wounded man to ride.

5. He took him to an inn where the man could recover in safety and in at least a little comfort. Inns in ancient Palestine were not the type of roadside inn we picture from European medieval times. Instead, an inn was typically a "walled-off area with an open space in the centre for travellers' animals and porticoes round the sides under which visitors would sleep on the ground."[3]

6. He didn't just drop the man off at the inn. He took further care of him there. In the compassion of his heart, he apparently sought to do all he could to make sure the man would recover from his wounds.

7. The next day, when he finally left to continue on his journey, he gave money out of his own pocket to the host of the inn. The two pence (or denarii, which were silver coins) were the equivalent of two days' wages for a common laborer. We can't tell if it would have been used to pay for lodging, food, or the attention of the innkeeper (there is some evidence that a stay at an inn in ancient Palestine was free; the innkeeper made his money from the food he served). We do know that two denarii would pay for a month's worth of food for an adult.[4]

8. He promised to cover the bill for the injured man, whatever it came to. In essence, the Samaritan was giving the innkeeper a blank check to make sure that the other man was cared for and able to fully recover.

Each of these is analogous to a way in which Christ blesses us. In one interpretation of the parable, each of us is the man traveling from Jerusalem to Jericho. The symbolism may be stated as follows:

- Jerusalem, the holy city, represents the place of holiness, or the innocence and purity we had before coming to earth.
- The journey down to Jericho represents the fall each of us experiences as we come to earth and makes wrong choices and commits sin.
- The robbers are the spiritual enemies we encounter on earth.
- The wounds are the real spiritual wounds we receive through sin and mortal adversity.
- The priest and Levite are those who could and should help us but fail to do so.
- The good Samaritan is our Savior, who administers wine

(representing the blood of his atoning sacrifice) and oil (symbolic of the Holy Ghost). He binds up our wounds and carries us on his own beast.

- The inn represents the Church, the place of safety and healing where the Lord takes us and stays with us as we begin our recovery.
- The innkeeper can symbolize the leaders of the Church who represent Christ when he is gone, ministering to those in need.
- The two pence (and more, if needed) represent the cost of returning us to spiritual health. The Lord pays the full price that is required.[5]

Thus, in the parable we can see our Savior as the Samaritan. And we can see ourselves, following His perfect example.

> ***Luke 10:36–37*** *Which now of these three, thinkest thou, was neighbour unto him that fell among the thieves? And he said, He that shewed mercy on him. Then said Jesus unto him, Go, and do thou likewise.*

When Jesus asked the lawyer to identify the neighbor in the story, the answer was plain. It seems that the lawyer must have choked on the word *Samaritan,* refusing to say it, responding instead, "He that shewed mercy on him." Still, he understood correctly how to identify one who exemplifies the essence of godly neighborliness: by showing mercy to others.

As President Howard W. Hunter taught: "We need to remember that though we make our friends, God has made our neighbors—everywhere. Love should have no boundary; we should have no narrow loyalties. Christ said, 'For if ye love them which love you, what reward have ye? do not even the publicans the same?' (Matthew 5:46)."[6]

The conclusion to this story teaches an important truth. In answer to the question, "Who is my neighbor?" Jesus answered with another question, asking in essence, How can we be a neighbor to others? How can we reach out to others in their time of need and bless them, even in sacrifice?

Even as we saw the Samaritan do, so should we likewise do.

Personal Application

This parable puts into wonderful story form the timeless principle Jesus taught earlier, known as the golden rule: "As ye would that men should do to you, do ye also to them likewise" (Luke 6:31).

As this parable demonstrates, our neighbor isn't always the nice friend in the nice house next door. Our neighbor isn't always the person who is easy to love, or even to approach. The neighbor to the priest, Levite, and Samaritan was a man who was bloody, dirty, half-naked, and hurt. He was a person with a great need who was unable to reciprocate to the least degree. He was someone who would take time and money and effort to care for. And so it is with us.

Jesus taught in direct precept the ideas conveyed through example in the story of the good Samaritan. In the Sermon on the Mount he said: "Ye have heard that it hath been said, Thou shalt love thy neighbour, and hate thine enemy. But I say unto you, Love your enemies, bless them that curse you, do good to them that hate you, and pray for them which despitefully use you, and persecute you; that ye may be the children of your Father which is in heaven" (Matthew 5:43–45).

The Samaritan was a man who obeyed this command. He didn't separate his world into friend (neighbor) and enemy (non-neighbor). Instead, he regarded everyone as his neighbor, and he did what he could to bless them.

At the end of the parable, Jesus said, "Go, and do thou likewise." As James, the Apostle and half-brother of Jesus, taught in his epistle, "Be ye doers of the word, and not hearers only, deceiving your own selves" (James 1:22). If we listen to impressive sermons or lessons or read scripture or conference reports and don't act on them, we are cheating ourselves. If we *know* and fail to *do,* we are forgetting what Paul taught so eloquently: "Though I . . . understand all mysteries, and all knowledge; . . . and have not charity, I am nothing" (1 Corinthians 13:2).

Joseph Smith taught: "Love is one of the chief characteristics of Deity, and ought to be manifested by those who aspire to be the sons of God. A man filled with the love of God, is not content with blessing his family alone, but ranges through the whole world, anxious to bless the whole human race."[7]

This is underscored in latter-day revelation, where the Lord declared, "Let every man esteem his brother as himself" (D&C 38:24).

Of course, in this as in all things, Jesus is our great Exemplar. He dedicated his life to helping others. He went out of his way to bless. He gave little regard to his own comfort and needs. As one early Christian exclaimed, "He hungered, but He fed thousands; He was weary, but He is the Rest of the weary; He is saluted 'Samaritan' and 'Demoniac,' but He saved him that went down from Jerusalem and fell among thieves."[8]

President Thomas S. Monson asked some very timely questions about how we can apply this parable in our lives. "Each of us, in the journey through mortality, will travel his own Jericho Road," he said. "What will be your experience? What will be mine? Will I fail to notice him who has fallen among thieves and requires my help? Will you? Will I be one who sees the injured and hears his plea, yet crosses to the other side? Will you? Or will I be one who sees, who hears, who pauses, and who helps? Will you?

"Jesus provided our watchword: 'Go, and do thou likewise.' When we obey that declaration, there opens to our view a vista of joy seldom equaled and never surpassed.

"Now the Jericho Road may not be clearly marked. Neither may the injured cry out, that we may hear. But when we walk in the steps of that good Samaritan, we walk the pathway that leads to perfection."[9]

CHAPTER 14

The Friend at Midnight

Luke 11:5–8

And he said unto them, Which of you shall have a friend, and shall go unto him at midnight, and say unto him, Friend, lend me three loaves;

For a friend of mine in his journey is come to me, and I have nothing to set before him?

And he from within shall answer and say, Trouble me not: the door is now shut, and my children are with me in bed; I cannot rise and give thee.

I say unto you, Though he will not rise and give him, because he is his friend, yet because of his importunity he will rise and give him as many as he needeth.

This parable is about approaching God in prayer with confidence. The parable is set in the context of other teachings on prayer, underscoring the doctrine that God our Father hears and answers our prayers. In the verses preceding the parable (Luke 11:1–4), Jesus "was praying in a certain place, when he ceased, one of his disciples said unto him, Lord, teach us to pray" (Luke 11:1). Then the Lord presented what has been become known as the Lord's Prayer. Luke's version of the Lord's Prayer is less well-known than Matthew's, which is more often quoted in lessons and gospel teaching.

After teaching the Lord's Prayer, Jesus gave the parable of the friend at midnight.

The verses that follow the parable also pertain to prayer, with a focus on asking, seeking, and knocking. The Lord taught, "Ask, and it shall be given you; seek, and ye shall find; knock, and it shall be opened" (Luke 11:9–10). Then follow verses 11–13, which pertain to the Father's wisdom in giving gifts to us, his children. The parable itself, sandwiched between these teachings on prayer, features the petitioner who prays, represented by one who visits his friend at midnight and asks for three loaves of bread.

The parable of the importunate widow and unjust judge (Luke 18:1–8), which will be discussed later, shares parallel themes and concepts with the friend at midnight. Both parables address the concept of prayer; both deal with a human character who seeks for and receives help from a "friend" or from a "judge"; and both present phrases that are conceptually similar: "trouble me not" and "because this widow troubleth me." Jesus probably repeated many of his teachings to different people at different times, and sometimes he seems to have adapted the precise mode of teaching to his specific audience at the time. These two parables are a likely example of that practice.

Commentary

Luke 11:5 *And he said unto them, Which of you shall have a friend,*

Friend is a significant word in this parable, appearing four times. All three of the parable's principal characters are called "friend." *Friend* refers to the hosting man who at midnight goes to the householder to ask for three loaves; *friend* designates the journeying man who needs the bread; and *friend* twice refers to the householder who tells the midnight visitor, "Trouble me not: the door is now shut, and my children are with me in bed." In this parable Jesus, then, emphasizes friendship and connects it to prayer, which is the parable's chief focus.

What is the connection between the three friends and prayer? Friend 1, the man who hosts the midnight visitor, arises at a late hour and leaves his own home in order to borrow bread for his midnight guest (Friend 2). While standing outside the door of Friend 3, he persists (the parable mentions "his importunity") until his friend arises and gives him the three loaves. Then he returns home to share with the midnight visitor. He does all of this without complaint, protest, or grumbling.

Friend 2, the journeying man who visits Friend 1 at a very late hour, serves as a symbol of each of us. We are journeying through mortality and at odd times we seek for bread or subsistence to supply our bodies with nourishment. We also seek for spiritual bread, the sort that gives us eternal life. Friend 2 asks Friend 1 for bread, although the hour is late, and receives according to his request. Perhaps the central lesson to be learned here is that we may approach God with our needs at any time, and he will respond by providing us with temporal and spiritual bread.

Friend 3, the householder who is in bed when Friend 1 calls upon him at midnight, mildly protests at being inconvenienced. "Trouble me not," he says, "I cannot arise and give thee." His excuse is that the door is locked and the children are asleep. And yet, in the end, he does arise and give to his friend according to his request. In one sense, Friend 3 is likened unto God, who hearkens to us when we go to him repeatedly. God, of course, does not respond to us just so that we will stop annoying him, as Friend 3 does when his neighbor knocks on the door. In this parable the "how much more so" principle is in effect. In this setting, this principle teaches us that while a human friend will provide for the needs of another friend (despite the inconvenience), how much more so will God with his perfect love and his perfect capability provide for the needs of each of us.

Luke 11:5 *and shall go unto him at midnight,*

The parable does not explain why the traveler was out at such a late hour. Perhaps he was trying to avoid journeying during the heat of the day, or maybe he was traveling in haste to fulfill a business obligation. It is possible, also, that the traveler was not journeying late—maybe he arrived earlier in the evening, and he and his friend had visited for several hours. Then, hungry, they desired something to eat and discovered there was no bread. So the host went to the neighbor and asked for help. The parable's emphasis is on prayer, and midnight is mentioned because it shows that God, similar to the man who hosted the midnight visitor, is available at any time and under any circumstance, to respond to our earnest petitions. He will do what is necessary to help us, when we go to him with honest and sincere hearts, even if we have put off or delayed approaching him, as the host may have done in going to his neighbor.

The hour of midnight is also distinguished in another parable. In the parable of the ten virgins (Matthew 25:1–13), midnight is the hour when Jesus returns, when the cry is made, "Behold, the bridegroom cometh; go ye out to meet him" (Matthew 25:6). In another scriptural passage about the Second Coming, Jesus compared himself to the master of the house who took a long journey. Before his departure he gave assignments to his servants and staff and commanded them to be prepared at all times for his return, whether it be in the evening, at midnight, when the rooster crows, or in the morning (see Mark 13:34–37). Midnight could be symbolic of the final hour or the last chance.

Luke 11:5 *and say unto him, Friend, lend me three loaves;*

Bread is not mentioned explicitly in this parable, but it is understood from the context that "lend me three loaves" denotes three loaves of bread. The parable's host wishes to supply his guest with bread, which is symbolic not only of hospitality but of manna and the bread of life.

The same is supplied to those who approach God in prayer. The Lord serves as the perfect host and a chief example of hospitality. He provided bread (manna; see Exodus 16:31–35; Numbers 11:7–9) and water (see Exodus 15:24–25, 27; 17:1–7) to his people as they sojourned in the wilderness. During mortality, Jesus appeared to serve as part of the host family at the wedding at Cana (see John 2:1–11; it was the duty of the host to provide the food and drink). He also broke bread with his apostles during his final meal as a mortal. As a resurrected being, he broke and served bread to the disciples he had met on the road to Emmaus.

Luke 11:6 *For a friend of mine in his journey is come to me, and I have nothing to set before him?*

The journeying man went to his friend, in part, because hotels and inns were scarce, especially in sparsely populated areas. The rules of hospitality at the time of Christ required the homeowner to welcome guests, provide them with food, and on occasion provide them with lodging (see 1 Timothy 3:2; Titus 1:8). This was not only a privilege but a duty. Both bishops and Christians in general were required to be "given to hospitality" (Romans 12:13; 1 Timothy 3:2; see Titus 1:8). As Peter wrote, "Use hospitality one to another without grudging" (1 Peter 4:9). Some Saints hosted and entertained strangers and were wholly unaware that they were in fact hosting angels (see Hebrews 13:2). Jesus taught that when we feed the hungry and clothe the naked and provide drink to the thirsty, it is the same as providing these things to the Lord himself. Such will be blessed and will "inherit the kingdom prepared for [them] from the foundation of the world" (Matthew 25:31–46).

Through his Apostle John, Jesus revealed that he will become our guest if we will but hear his voice: "Behold, I stand at the door, and knock: if any man hear my voice, and open the door, I will come in to him, and will sup with him, and he with me" (Revelation 3:20).

The rules of hospitality at Jesus' time had their roots in the Old Testament. The Mosaic law required that the Israelites extend hospitality to the fatherless, widows, strangers (see Leviticus 19:33–34; Deuteronomy 10:18–19; 24:17–22), and slaves who had escaped their masters (see Deuteronomy 23:15–16). Specifically, the Israelites were commanded to love the stranger and to provide him with food and clothing because, as the Lord explains, the Israelites too were once strangers, "strangers in the land of Egypt" (Deuteronomy 10:19). The minimum that one was required to give his or her guest was bread and water (see 1 Kings 17:10–11).

Judgment and disaster sometimes came to those who ignored the rules of hospitality. For example, neither Ammonite nor Moabite was allowed to enter "into the congregation of the Lord; even to their tenth generation" because they failed to provide the Israelites "with bread and with water in the way, when [they] came forth out of Egypt" (Deuteronomy 23:3–4). Several centuries later, Nabal, a very wealthy man, refused to provide King David and his army with food (see 1 Samuel 25). This refusal, together with other iniquities that Nabal committed, resulted in his death: "The Lord smote Nabal, that he died. And when David heard that Nabal was dead, he said, Blessed be the Lord, that hath pleaded the cause of my reproach from the hand of Nabal . . . for the Lord hath returned the wickedness of Nabal upon his own head" (1 Samuel 25:38–39). Another example is seen in the destruction that came to the men of Succoth because they refused to give bread unto Gideon and his army (see Judges 8:5–17).

> ***Luke 11:7*** *And he from within shall answer and say, Trouble me not: the door is now shut, and my children are with me in bed; I cannot rise and give thee.*

The man's house would likely have been a simple one-room dwelling, which would explain why the parents and children were sleeping in the same room. Because household oil lamps did not provide sufficient light to continue with many of the day's activities, people in those days generally retired to bed soon after dark. The person who was awakened by his friend was therefore likely in a deep sleep at the midnight hour. It may have been for this reason that he called out, "Trouble me not: the door is now shut, and my children are with me in bed; I cannot rise and give thee."

> ***Luke 11:8*** *I say unto you, Though he will not rise and give him, because he is his friend, yet because of his importunity he will rise and give him as many as he needeth.*

At first the retired householder responded to the man at the door with the words, "Trouble me not: the door is now shut." After a moment, however, he reconsidered and arose to deliver the three loaves because of his friend's "importunity." Importunity describes the persistence and "boldness"[1] of the man at the door in getting the sleeper to arise from his bed.

Inasmuch as this parable is about prayer and receiving answers to prayer, some commentators have compared the man at the door to one who is praying and the householder to God, who responds to the man at the door. The comparison, of course, cannot be taken too far because God would never say "Trouble me not" to his children who seek him during prayer. The point of this part of the parable is that if the annoyed and hesitating mortal friend finally arises from the comfort of his bed to provide the three loaves, how much more so will God respond to one's prayers at all times, even during the late hours of the night. And God does so willingly, with perfect love, and with no hesitation or complaint.

Elder James E. Talmage explained: "The parable is regarded by some as a difficult one to apply. . . . The Lord's lesson was, that if man, with all his selfishness and disinclination to give, will nevertheless grant what his neighbor with proper purpose asks and continues to ask in spite of objection and temporary refusal, with assured certainty will God grant what is persistently asked in faith with righteous intent. No parallelism lies between man's selfish refusal and God's wise and beneficent waiting."[2]

Personal Application

The parable of the friend at midnight is set in the context of teachings about prayer, and the parable itself is also about prayer. Jesus spoke the parable after "one of his disciples said unto him, Lord, teach us to pray" (Luke 11:1). The parable has direct application to all of God's children because he desires for all of us to communicate with him. In connection with this, President Marion G. Romney said, "There isn't any commandment from the Lord that is repeated more often than the commandment to pray to the Lord."[3]

Certainly the command to pray is often repeated in the New Testament, as well as the other scriptures. In 3 Nephi 11–20 alone, approximately sixty verses are dedicated to the subject of prayer and some eleven prayers are mentioned. In this extended account of Jesus' visit to the Nephites, the resurrected Savior repeatedly taught and exemplified prayer to the Nephite multitude:

The parable of the friend at midnight applies to each of us. This parable should be placed in the context of all scriptures that teach us how, where, when, and what to pray and to whom to pray, giving us the testimony that our Father does indeed love us and will ever hear and answer the prayer of the honest in heart.

CHAPTER 15

THE FOOLISH RICH MAN

Luke 12:16–21

And he spake a parable unto them, saying, The ground of a certain rich man brought forth plentifully:

And he thought within himself, saying, What shall I do, because I have no room where to bestow my fruits?

And he said, This will I do: I will pull down my barns, and build greater; and there will I bestow all my fruits and my goods.

And I will say to my soul, Soul, thou hast much goods laid up for many years; take thine ease, eat, drink, and be merry.

But God said unto him, Thou fool, this night thy soul shall be required of thee: then whose shall those things be, which thou hast provided?

So is he that layeth up treasure for himself, and is not rich toward God.

When Jesus was teaching in Judea during the latter part of his ministry, "there were gathered together an innumerable multitude of people, insomuch that they trode upon one another" (Luke 12:1). But rather than try to teach the huge crowd, Jesus spoke more particularly to his disciples. He taught them some very important truths: that men's secrets would eventually be revealed to all, even "proclaimed upon the housetops"; that they should not fear man, even with his ability to kill, but they should instead fear Satan, with his ability to destroy the soul;

that the fact that God remembers the well-being of the sparrows teaches us about how much more he cares for his children; that they should beware the sin against the Holy Ghost; that when they were called to account before earthly powers for their beliefs and actions and testimonies, the Holy Ghost would help them know how to respond (see Luke 12:2–12).

During this significant discourse, one of the men present apparently had other things in mind than the words of eternal life. He was more concerned about the things of this world.

"Master," he said to Jesus, interrupting him, "speak to my brother, that he divide the inheritance with me" (Luke 12:13). The speaker obviously was referring to his older brother. According to Jewish tradition and law, the oldest son in a family received a double portion of the inheritance. With that extra portion, he was obligated to care for members of the family who were unable to care for themselves. Thus, if there were two brothers, the older would receive as an inheritance two-thirds of their father's wealth and holdings and the younger brother would receive one-third.

The man who interrupted Jesus appears to have wanted Jesus to convince his older brother that he should vary from tradition and law and divide the inheritance fifty-fifty.

Jesus always refused to become involved in matters of civil law, and this case was no exception. "Man," Jesus answered, "who made me a judge or a divider over you?" (Luke 12:14).

Then turning back to the group, Jesus said, "Take heed, and beware of covetousness: for a man's life consisteth not in the abundance of the things which he possesseth" (Luke 12:15).

This is a teaching he reiterated again and again. The purpose of our lives is not to please ourselves. We are not here to amass wealth, to become rich in worldly things. We are not to look at what others have and wish it were our own. The meaning of life is not to possess an abundance of things. Rather it is, as Jesus said at the end of the parable he then gave, to be "rich toward God" (Luke 12:21).

Commentary

> **Luke 12:16–18** *And he spake a parable unto them, saying, The ground of a certain rich man brought forth plentifully: And he thought within himself, saying, What shall I do, because I have no room where to bestow my fruits? And he said, This will I do: I will pull down my barns, and build greater; and there will I bestow all my fruits and my goods.*

There is no indication in this parable that the rich man was dishonest or lazy. He may have worked hard for that which he had attained. Yet nowhere in his success did he acknowledge the goodness of God toward him. It was *the ground* that brought forth plentifully; soil that had been freely given to him by God. And the seed, the water, the sun—all these likewise are obviously necessary for success in farming; if we lack any one of these four ingredients, we will fail if we hope to grow crops. And all these come from God.

Yes, we must be industrious. We need to prepare the ground, plant the seed, irrigate with the water, keep weeds and animals and grasshoppers out, and harvest the crop. But many seeds will grow and bear fruit without any involvement of man—while no seeds will grow without the involvement and contribution of God.

Thus, when the man's farm "brought forth plentifully," he may have done his part to help it do so. But he utterly failed to acknowledge how absolutely essential God's part in the process was.

So it was that when he looked at his success, he was very much focused on *himself:* "What shall *I* do, because *I* have no room where to bestow *my* fruits? And he said, This will *I* do: *I* will pull down *my* barns, and build greater; and there will *I* bestow all *my* fruits and *my* goods. And *I* will say to *my* soul . . ." In that short passage, we find a first-person singular pronoun repeated eleven times! In other words, the man was saying, "[I will make] provision for the flesh, to fulfill the lusts thereof" (Romans 13:14).

On the surface, it may seem that the man was simply exercising good management. But the reality was that he was solely laying in store for the future, instead of acknowledging two truths: (1) We have no control over the future, despite our best efforts; and (2) there are many in the world who need our help now. We are not here only to care for ourselves and watch out for our own needs—although we do have a responsibility to do both. But as we see in the parable of another rich man, the one who spurned the beggar named Lazarus, we also have a responsibility to look after the poor who are around every one of us.

> ***Luke 12:19*** *And I will say to my soul, Soul, thou hast much goods laid up for many years; take thine ease, eat, drink, and be merry.*

Certainly it is appropriate to retire from our daily labors when we reach a certain age, should we have the financial capacity to do so. It is wise to lay aside money for the purpose of being self-sufficient in our old age. But even though the rich man thought himself wise to prepare for the future—and many today would agree with his seeming wisdom, later the Lord calls him a fool. Why?

First, he misunderstands what is most important in life. He says to his soul, "Soul, thou hast much goods laid up for many years." As Jesus taught later that same day, our lives consist of more than just meat and raiment (see Luke 12:23). Our souls also need spiritual food and drink, the bread of life, the living water that is Christ. If we are pleased with our temporal preparations and feel they are sufficient, we are missing one of the great lessons of life: "Man shall not live by bread alone, but by every word that proceedeth out of the mouth of God" (Matthew 4:4).

Second, he is living for himself. He is not taking thought for his neighbor but only for his own comfort and pleasure. He is concerned with his ease, his food and drink, his enjoyment of life. Meanwhile, there are people around who need financial help, who need an offering of time and energy. There is Church service to be given and full-time missions to be served. If we "take [our] ease, eat, drink, and be merry" we will perhaps take pleasure in the moment, but we will at the same time lose our opportunity for greater joy and blessings.

Those who make these two fundamental mistakes receive the epithet the Lord gave to the rich man: "Thou fool."

Luke 12:20 *But God said unto him, Thou fool, this night thy soul shall be required of thee: then whose shall those things be, which thou hast provided?*

Earlier the man was concerned about the comfort of his soul. But here the Lord tells him that his soul, or spirit, will be taken from the mortal world that very night. When that happened, what would become of the wealth he had accumulated? It would go to his heirs (if he had any), who, in turn, would be equally unable to take it with *them*. Down through the generations, people would have use of that land and the things it would produce, but none of the rich man's successors would be able to enjoy it for more than a brief season. In every case their souls would ultimately "be required" of them by God, and they would leave all their earthly possessions behind.

God is the master of the earth. He is the master of each individual on the earth. He gives us the breath we need to live, and he decides the length of our days. It may be possible that God will allow a person's life to seemingly be cut short through their own or another's misuse of agency; He may allow sickness or accident or war or natural disaster to take some at a time that seems to be too soon. If so, God in his goodness will provide that they will suffer no loss in this mortal experience; through grace they will receive all the blessings and growth that are their portion. But even though some lives might seem to be cut short, it is a fact of the universe that no earthly soul can lengthen his or her days beyond God's appointed allotment.

Since God is in charge, and since he decides when we are born and when we die, we are fools if we suppose we can control the number of days or length of years, and we are likewise fools if we think we can take any of our temporal gains with us into the next world.

Luke 12:21 *So is he that layeth up treasure for himself, and is not rich toward God.*

The rich fool spent his years accumulating wealth. He had so much he couldn't hold it in the storage buildings he owned, so he planned to tear down those buildings and build bigger and better ones.

He was laying up treasure for himself. But he was not rich toward God.

He was like the person today who spends a lifetime chasing fame, fortune, or pleasure. Some people are consumed with worldly things. But in the end all such things will remain here on earth when each such person dies.

When we die we will take with us our character, our knowledge and understandings, our talents, and our relationships (if those are sealed by priesthood power). We will also take the intangibles of the Spirit. Those who are "rich toward God" will take with them those things of righteousness they spent their lives seeking. As Elder Bruce R. McConkie put it, they are "rich in the currency negotiable in the courts above; rich in eternal things; rich in the knowledge of the truth, in the possession of intelligence, in obedience to gospel law, in the possession of the characteristics and attributes of Deity, in all of the things which will continue to be enjoyed in eternity."[1]

The Lord summed it up in a revelation given through the Prophet Joseph Smith: "Behold, he that hath eternal life is rich" (D&C 6:7).

Personal Application

The Apostle John taught a great truth when he said, "Love not the world, neither the things that are in the world. If any man love the world, the love of the Father is not in him. For all that is in the world, the lust of the flesh, and the lust of the eyes, and the pride of life, is not of the Father, but is of the world. And the world passeth away, and the lust thereof: but he that doeth the will of God abideth for ever" (1 John 2:15–17).

President Spencer W. Kimball told of an experience he had with a wealthy man he knew, a man who did love the world. They traveled in the man's expensive new car to see his ranch. When they arrived, the friend said, "with no little pride, 'This is my home.'" They stood on a grassy knoll, where they could see the man's holdings. "From the clump of trees, to the lake, to the bluff, and to the ranch buildings and all between—all this is mine. And the dark specks in the meadow—those cattle also are mine."

President Kimball asked his friend how he got the land, and the friend said he purchased it with money.

"Where did you get the money?"

"My toil, my sweat, my labor, and my strength."

"Where did you get your strength to toil, your power to labor, your glands to sweat?"

The man answered that he received his strength from food.

"Where did the food originate?"

"From sun and atmosphere and soil and water."

"And who brought those elements here?"

The answer, of course, is God. Our ability to live and to do comes from God. The land comes from God. The sun and the rain come from God. The seeds come from God. In every way we are utterly dependent upon him.

President Kimball concluded the story by saying, "That was long years ago. I saw him lying in his death among luxurious furnishings in a palatial home. His had been a vast estate. . . . I spoke at his funeral, and I followed the cortege from the good piece of earth he had claimed to his grave, a tiny, oblong area the length of a tall man, the width of a heavy one."[2]

The Lord has commanded us to seek first the kingdom of God, and then the things of the temporal world will be added unto us (see Luke 12:31). That does not mean that we ignore our responsibility to provide for ourselves and our families. But the Lord is giving us a priority list: seek *first* the kingdom of God—meaning, let our first priority be to turn our hearts to God and to seek to build his kingdom. Then, as we do so, we are also obligated to seek to care for our temporal needs.

The law of riches was explained clearly by the prophet Jacob: "Think of your brethren like unto yourselves, and be familiar with all and free with your substance, that they may be rich like unto you. But before ye seek for riches, seek ye for the kingdom of God. And after ye have obtained a hope in Christ ye shall obtain riches, if ye seek them; and ye will seek them for the intent to do good—to clothe the naked, and to feed the hungry, and to liberate the captive, and administer relief to the sick and the afflicted" (Jacob 2:17–19).

The rich man was not a fool because he sought to prepare temporally for the future. He was a fool because he focused only on the temporal. If we set our hearts on the things of this world we will lose our souls. Death will come to all of us—absolutely no one will be excepted. What kind of life will we have in the eternal world? We get to choose. We can choose death by seeking first the things of the adversary and the things of the world. Or we can choose life through Jesus Christ, our Lord.

CHAPTER 16

THE BARREN FIG TREE

Luke 13:6–9

He spake also this parable; A certain man had a fig tree planted in his vineyard; and he came and sought fruit thereon, and found none.

Then said he unto the dresser of his vineyard, Behold, these three years I come seeking fruit on this fig tree, and find none: cut it down; why cumbereth it the ground?

And he answering said unto him, Lord, let it alone this year also, till I shall dig about it, and dung it:

And if it bear fruit, well: and if not, then after that thou shalt cut it down.

The five verses that precede the parable of the barren fig tree provide the setting for this parable. Certain people had informed Jesus that Pilate had slaughtered a group of Galileans, apparently while the Galileans were offering sacrifices (see Luke 13:1). Upon hearing this, Jesus responded by saying, "Suppose ye that these Galileans were sinners above all Galileans, because they suffered such things? I tell you, Nay: but, except ye repent, ye shall all likewise perish" (Luke 13:2–3). Jesus then related an event where eighteen people were killed when a tower in Siloam fell on them. Once more Jesus asked his audience, "Think ye that they were sinners above all men that dwelt in Jerusalem? I tell you, Nay: but, except ye repent, ye shall all likewise perish" (Luke 12:4–5). While speaking of both disasters—the Galilean slaughter and the deaths from the falling tower—Jesus repeated the same words: "except ye repent, ye shall all likewise perish." This repetition gives added emphasis to Jesus' message of repentance. Immediately following these words, Jesus presented the parable of the barren fig tree. This parable, then, is set in the context of Christ's admonition to repent—and his warning that if we fail to repent, we will perish.

The parable of the barren fig tree shares many similarities with Isaiah's Song of the Vineyard: "Now will I sing to my wellbeloved a song of my beloved touching his vineyard," the Lord said to Isaiah. "My wellbeloved hath a vineyard in a very fruitful hill: And he fenced it, and gathered out the stones thereof, and planted it with the choicest vine, and built a tower in the midst of it, and also made a winepress therein: and he looked that it should bring forth grapes, and it brought forth wild grapes.

"And now, O inhabitants of Jerusalem, and men of Judah, judge, I pray you, betwixt me and my vineyard. What could have been done more to my vineyard, that I have not done in it? wherefore, when I looked that it should bring forth grapes, brought it forth wild grapes?

"And now go to; I will tell you what I will do to my vineyard: I will take away the hedge thereof, and it shall be eaten up; and break down the wall thereof, and it shall be trodden down: And I will lay it waste: it shall not be pruned, nor digged; but there shall come up briers and thorns: I will also command the clouds that they rain no rain upon it. For the vineyard of the Lord of hosts is the house of Israel, and the men of Judah his pleasant plant: and he looked for judgment, but behold oppression; for righteousness, but behold a cry" (Isaiah 5:1–7).

Commentary

> ***Luke 13:6*** *He spake also this parable; A certain man had a fig tree planted in his vineyard; and he came and sought fruit thereon, and found none.*

The Joseph Smith Translation adds clarification to this parable because it reads "husbandman" in place of "man": "a certain *husbandman* had a fig tree." The husbandman symbolizes God, the owner of the vineyard. The vineyard represents the world. Several actions describe God's work with the fig tree—he had the fig tree planted in his vineyard; he came to the tree three years in a row (see verse 7); and he looked for figs but found none. Although God had a vineyard steward ("dresser of the vineyard"), he demonstrated personal care for and concern about the tree.

The barren fig tree has at least two levels of meaning:

First, the fig tree signifies the Jewish nation during the first century A.D., which God planted in his vineyard. The tree's barrenness symbolizes the Jews' failure to produce good works or their failure to accept Jesus Christ and his gospel. Elsewhere in the scriptures God's covenant people are likened to trees of various sorts (see, for example, Jeremiah 8:13; Hosea 2:12; 9:10; Amos 2:9; Micah 7:1). For instance, Judah is called "a green olive tree" (Jeremiah 11:16–19), and the Lord said that Israel's beauty "shall be as the olive tree" (Hosea 14:6). The Book of Mormon prophets also compared the house of Israel to an olive tree (1 Nephi 10:12–14; 15:7, 10–22).

In Isaiah's song, quoted above, the vineyard represents the house of Israel, and the kingdom of Judah symbolizes God's "pleasant plant." In the parable given by Jesus, the barren fig tree represents the Jewish nation. In the song, the Lord exerts great effort to care for his vineyard and fig tree so that they might produce much fruit. He builds a fence around it to keep out predators, he removes the stones, he plants his choicest vine, he builds a watchtower, and he makes a winepress in anticipation of a bounteous harvest. But after all that, the vineyard produces nothing but sour grapes. So, too, with the parable's fig tree: God takes special interest in it but in the end it fails to produce fruit.

Second, the parable's barren fig tree also symbolizes people from all ages who fail to bring forth righteousness or good works. Trees are used as symbols for men and women in numerous scriptural passages (see, for example, Judges 9:8–15; Psalm 52:5–8; Job 15:20–34; Matthew 7:16–20; Alma 5:52). Standing in contrast to the barren fig tree are symbolic trees that produce fruit. Jeremiah compared a righteous person to a tree that continually yields fruit. "Blessed is the man that trusteth in the Lord, and whose hope the Lord is," he wrote. "For he shall be as a tree planted by the waters, and that spreadeth out her roots by the river, and shall not see when heat cometh, but her leaf shall be green; and shall not be careful in the year of drought, neither shall cease from yielding fruit" (Jeremiah 17:7–8; see Psalm 52:8). Psalm 1:3, too, compares a righteous person to a "tree planted by the rivers of water, that bringeth forth his fruit in his season; his leaf also shall not wither; and whatsoever he doeth shall prosper."

> ***Luke 13:7*** *Then said he unto the dresser of his vineyard, Behold, these three years I come seeking fruit on this fig tree, and find none: cut it down; why cumbereth it the ground?*

God, the owner of the vineyard, provides sufficient time for the fig tree to mature. A fig tree grows slowly, taking several years to bear fruit. After the tree in the parable has grown to the point that it should have become a fruit-bearing tree, the owner of the vineyard gives it yet another three years to produce fruit, but it does not. He then speaks to his employee, the vineyard's dresser who is the day-to-day steward of the vineyard, and tells him, "Behold, these three years I come seeking fruit on this fig tree, and find none."

Following the symbolism of the parable, with God as the vineyard's owner and the fig tree as the Jewish nation, the parable suggests that vineyard's dresser was Jesus Christ. The three years corresponds to the time of Jesus' ministry, when he worked with the Jewish community and gave them time to repent. The vineyard's owner instructs the dresser to cut down the fig tree because it is taking up valuable space that could be occupied by a fruitful tree.

> ***Luke 13:8–9*** *And he answering said unto him, Lord, let it alone this year also, till I shall dig about it, and dung it: And if it bear fruit, well: and if not, then after that thou shalt cut it down.*

In verse 9, the Joseph Smith Translation makes a significant change, reading "And if it bear fruit, the tree is saved" in place of "well." Inasmuch as *saved* (and *salvation*) is a scriptural word that often pertains to people and not to trees, this textual change fits well the parable's context, that the barren fig tree refers to the Jewish nation at Jesus' time as well as to individuals of all ages. That is to say, if the

Jewish nation (or any nation or individual) bears fruit, then they will be saved in the Lord's kingdom.

The vineyard's dresser responds to the owner's command to "cut it down" by pleading, as an intercessor, "Lord, let it alone this year also." The dresser then proposes that he provide additional care and attention to the fig tree. He will loosen the soil around it, an action that allows moisture to more easily reach the tree's roots. He will also fertilize it with dung, hoping the additional nutrients will stimulate it to thrive. After he has done these things, if the tree bears fruit, "the tree is saved."

Just as God gives the tree a chance to bear fruit, he also gave the Jewish nation (and he gives individuals) a period to repent and to produce righteousness. This period of time (the parable mentions a "year") may speak of the time between the end of Jesus' ministry and A.D. 70, when the Romans destroyed Judea. During this period the Apostles, Seventies, and other Church officers taught the gospel of repentance and ministered among the people. Paul, in his epistle to the Ephesians, first listed the titles of the Church officers who continued the work of Jesus ministry and then he summarized their objectives: And Jesus Christ "gave some, apostles; and some, prophets; and some, evangelists; and some, pastors and teachers; for the perfecting of the saints, for the work of the ministry, for the edifying of the body of Christ: till we all come in the unity of the faith, and of the knowledge of the Son of God, unto a perfect man, unto the measure of the stature of the fulness of Christ" (Ephesians 4:11–13).

We recall that the five verses that preceded the parable of the barren fig tree provided the setting for this parable. These five verses related two different accounts of the destruction of people—the slaughtered Galileans and the individuals who were killed by a falling tower. Jesus spoke of these disasters and then warned his audience, "I tell you, . . . except ye repent, ye shall all likewise perish" (Luke 13:3, 5). He then related the parable, which also pertains to repentance and perishing, or being "cut down."

Historically, the greater Jewish community failed to hearken to Jesus' words and those of his servants, and thus was destroyed. The agent of destruction was the Roman army, which moved from village to village and from city to city until it had conquered all of Judea, including the great city of Jerusalem and the mighty fortress of Masada. In this way the parable—in the form of a prophecy—was fulfilled: the barren fig tree was indeed cut down.

Personal Application

The parable of the barren fig tree has many symbols and applications. One application involves comparing the fig tree to each of us, as individuals. If we serve and love others and obey God, we are as trees that are loaded with fruit that is of great value to humanity. We are "filled with the fruits of righteousness, which are by Jesus Christ" (Philippians 1:11). Some of these fruits are listed by Paul, who wrote that the "fruit of the Spirit is love, joy, peace, longsuffering, gentleness, goodness, faith, meekness, temperance" (Galatians 5:22–23). If we love and serve others, we will be like the trees depicted in Ezekiel's vision, "whose leaf shall not fade" and whose leaf will be used for medicine and to heal the nations (Ezekiel 47:12; see Revelation 22:2). Our fruits will grow in such abundance that we will bear fruit twelve months a year. Unlike the fruit tree of the typical orchard, which yields fruit only in its season, we will yield fruit every single month of the year (see Ezekiel 47:12; Revelation 22:2).

However, if we fail to serve and love others and to love and obey God, we are like a barren fruit tree that fails to yield produce that benefits others. Or, if we do yield fruit, it is "evil fruit." Jesus taught that "every good tree bringeth forth good fruit; but a corrupt tree bringeth forth evil fruit. A good tree cannot bring forth evil fruit, neither can a corrupt tree bring forth good fruit" (Matthew 7:17–18). The fruits generated by evil persons are "unfruitful works of darkness" (Ephesians 5:9, 11); and evil people are like "trees whose fruit withereth, without fruit, twice dead" (Jude 1:12; see Hosea 9:16). If we fail to bear fruit, just as the parable's fig tree failed, then we will be cut down. Or as Paul wrote, "The motions of sins . . . did work in our members to bring forth fruit unto death" (JST, Romans 7:5).

The following story illustrates the principle of bearing fruit. The story features two lovely sisters who blessed a third sister who dearly needed it. In fact the story, as told by J. Elaine Lattimore, is entitled, "Their Message Bore Fruit."

Sister Lattimore tells of how challenges in her life had left her bitter and inactive in the Church. She was resentful toward God, feeling that she had not received the heavenly support or blessings she so much needed in times of trial.

One March afternoon as she was planting strawberries in a field next to her house, trying to finish before a threatening storm arrived, she saw her visiting teachers coming across the field to see her.

"Although I had been inactive in the Church for nearly a year, I had always allowed the visiting teachers into my home. I must confess that often I considered them something of a nuisance, for though their manners were always kind and polite, their very presence reminded me that I was not living up to my beliefs."

Even though Sister Lattimore was often cold toward them, and sometimes made "biting remarks" about the Church, these sisters were the essence of faithfulness. They visited on the same day every month, bore their testimonies to her, and gave her words of encouragement. Frequently they brought a treat with them.

As she saw them arriving on this day, Sister Lattimore decided she would have to tell them she had no time for them. "But I was never to have that chance. Wearing their Sunday best, complete with nylon stockings, each of my visiting teachers got down on her knees in that strawberry patch. My mouth was still hanging open as Sister Batty began to read the monthly message while Sister Costner began planting strawberries beside me."

Before long a heavy rain began to fall. "Still we planted, and still Sister Batty read on. I don't remember what the official message was, but I was grateful that it was raining hard enough to hide the flood of tears that ran down my face as I received a message, not of word, but of deed—a message of love, unselfishness, and devotion. A message that would literally bear fruit."

By the time the planting was done they were soaked to the skin. She invited them in, but they had to leave, saying they had other appointments. "They then produced a fragrant loaf of banana bread from the back seat of their car and drove away, leaving me to marvel at their dauntless spirits."

Sister Lattimore concludes: "Years have passed since that blustery day in March. Those fine sisters do not know it, but their unfaltering love worked a miracle in my life. Through their example I was able to yield up my bitterness and again seek the blessings that come through active Church membership. I cannot eat a strawberry or hear the words 'visiting teaching' without thinking of those dear sisters on their knees in my garden. And I cannot examine my life without thanking my Heavenly Father for their faithfulness."[1]

We can be trees of righteousness, trees of service, trees of love, trees bearing the fruit of the gospel. As we do, we will truly bless the lives of those around us—and we will be greatly blessed in return by the owner of the vineyard, and by his holy Son, the vineyard's dresser.

CHAPTER 17

The Great Supper

Luke 14:16–24

Then said he unto him, A certain man made a great supper, and bade many:

And sent his servant at supper time to say to them that were bidden, Come; for all things are now ready.

And they all with one consent began to make excuse. The first said unto him, I have bought a piece of ground, and I must needs go and see it: I pray thee have me excused.

And another said, I have bought five yoke of oxen, and I go to prove them: I pray thee have me excused.

And another said, I have married a wife, and therefore I cannot come.

So that servant came, and shewed his lord these things. Then the master of the house being angry said to his servant, Go out quickly into the streets and lanes of the city, and bring in hither the poor, and the maimed, and the halt, and the blind.

And the servant said, Lord, it is done as thou hast commanded, and yet there is room.

And the lord said unto the servant, Go out into the highways and hedges, and compel them to come in, that my house may be filled.

For I say unto you, That none of those men which were bidden shall taste of my supper.

During the Old Testament era, banquets and feasts were an important part of social life. For example, a feast celebrated the covenant of peace made between Isaac and Abimelech (see Genesis 26:26–31). Feasts were part of wedding ceremonies, such as the feast prepared by Laban in honor of Jacob, his new son-in-law (see Genesis 29:20–22; see also Judges 14:10). On the occasion of the temple dedication, King Solomon, together with all of Israel, offered a great number of sacrifices, including 22,000 oxen and 120,000 sheep. "And at that time Solomon held a feast, and all Israel with him, a great congregation"; so great was that feast that it lasted fourteen days (1 Kings 8:62–66). Some feasts were no more than impressive parties. Such was the case with the banquet that King Belshazzar prepared for "a thousand of his lords," plus hundreds of others. During the feast the revelers drank wine from the temple vessels that Belshazzar's father had stolen from the Jerusalem temple (Daniel 5:1–4).

Great feasts accompanied Israelite festivals such as Passover (see Exodus 12:3–20), Pentecost (see Exodus 23:14–17; Numbers 28:26), the Feast of Tabernacles (see Leviticus 23:34; Numbers 29:12–38), and Purim (see Esther 9). These occasions were called "the feasts of the Lord" and were "holy convocations" (Leviticus 23:37). The Lord commanded the Israelites, "Thou shalt rejoice in thy feast, thou, and thy son, and thy daughter, and thy manservant, and thy maidservant, and the Levite, the stranger, and the fatherless, and the widow, that are within thy gates" (Deuteronomy 16:14).

The prophet Zechariah prophesied that in the Millennium the Feast of Tabernacles will be celebrated by all nations when they go to Jerusalem to worship the Lord. "And it shall come to pass, that every one that is left of all the nations which came against Jerusalem shall even go up from year to year to worship the King, the Lord of hosts, and to keep the feast of tabernacles" (Zechariah 14:16).

During the New Testament period, Jesus presented a number of lessons or sermons in the setting of a meal: in Bethany, at Simon the leper's home (see Mark 14:1–9); in the home of a Pharisee (see Luke 7:36–50); while eating with publicans and sinners (see Matthew 9:9–11); while enjoying supper with Mary, Martha, Lazarus, and others in Bethany (see John 12:1–8); and at the Passover meal when Jesus instituted the sacrament (see Matthew 26:19–29). Jesus also combined teaching and eating in the same setting when he "gave thanks" for "seven loaves and the fishes" and then he "brake them, and gave to his disciples, and the disciples to the multitude" (Matthew 15:36). Likewise, it was when Jesus "went into the house of one of the chief Pharisees to eat bread on the sabbath day" (Luke 14:1) that he presented two parables—the wedding guests (Luke 14:7–11) and the great supper (Luke 14:16–24). This last parable, which is now under discussion, was given in the context of eating bread.

Commentary

> ***Luke 14:16–17*** *Then said he unto him, A certain man made a great supper, and bade many: And sent his servant at supper time to say to them that were bidden, Come; for all things are now ready.*

The two main characters of this parable are "a certain man" and "his servant." The "certain man" represents God, who three times is called "lord" and once "master of the house." The servant refers to Jesus Christ,[1] who is referred to (as "servant") five times in the parable. (By extension it also refers to all of the Lord's servants—his apostles, faithful elders and sisters, and missionaries.) Together, God and the servant figure prominently in this parable, as God oversees the preparation of the great feast and the servant manages the invitations and the bidding of the guests. God "bade many," or sent out invitations for guests to attend the feast. Similarly, in the parable of the royal marriage feast (or marriage of the king's son), the king sent out invitations to attend a feast held in honor of his son's marriage (see Matthew 22:1–14). Beyond God and the servant, the parable's main theme is the great supper, which symbolizes the gospel and all of its blessings.

By teaching the gospel to the earth's inhabitants, our missionaries invite people to come to this feast, also called "the supper of the Lord" (D&C 58:11), the "supper of the house of the Lord" (D&C 58:9), and the "marriage supper of the Lamb" (Revelation 19:9). "All nations" are invited—"first, the rich and the learned, the wise and the noble"—

but when these reject the invitation to the feast, the Lord's representatives will invite the poor and the humble (see D&C 58:9, 10).

> ***Luke 14:18–20*** *And they all with one consent began to make excuse. The first said unto him, I have bought a piece of ground, and I must needs go and see it: I pray thee have me excused. And another said, I have bought five yoke of oxen, and I go to prove them: I pray thee have me excused. And another said, I have married a wife, and therefore I cannot come.*

The supper has been prepared and it is now time for the guests to arrive, so the master sends his servant to inform the invited guests to "come; for all things are now ready." All of the invitees are too involved with temporal or domestic matters, and they make excuses "all with one consent." The phrase "all with one consent" suggests that all of the invitees are united in their excuses as to why they will not go to the great feast.

The parable presents four groups of people. The initial invitees represent the first two groups, the wealthy and those occupied with familial concerns.

Group 1, the wealthy. These are represented by the one person who purchased real estate and by another who bought ten oxen. The two purchases indicate the status of those who made the purchases, because in Jesus' day only the rich could afford such things. By rejecting the invitation to attend the feast, both owners presumably are fulfilling their temporal responsibilities and giving attention to them while neglecting weightier concerns, particularly the Lord's invitation to join with him in a blessed experience.

Group 2, those occupied with familial concerns. The man who makes the excuse "I have married a wife, and therefore I cannot come" symbolizes people who are too occupied with family to attend the feast. Such make their family a higher priority than God and his gospel. In an effort to place God and family in the proper perspective, Jesus taught, "If any man come to me, and hate not his father, and mother, and wife, and children, and brethren, and sisters, or husband, yea and his own life also; or in other words, is afraid to lay down his life for my sake; he cannot be my disciple" (JST, Luke 14:26). Certainly we are not to *hate* our family members. But neither are we to place them before God. In a translation that may be more accurate, we read that Jesus also taught, "He that loveth father or mother more than me is not worthy of me: and he that loveth son or daughter more than me is not worthy of me. And he that taketh not his cross, and followeth after me, is not worthy of me" (Matthew 10:37–38).

> ***Luke 14:21–22*** *So that servant came, and shewed his lord these things. Then the master of the house being angry said to his servant, Go out quickly into the streets and lanes of the city, and bring in hither the poor, and the maimed, and the halt, and the blind. And the servant said, Lord, it is done as thou hast commanded, and yet there is room.*

Group 3, the poor and the humble. The servant returns to his master and informs him that the original invitees refused to come to the great feast. This report angers the master, who then commands his servant to "go out quickly into the streets and lanes of the city" and invite the third group to the feast: the poor, the maimed (or crippled), halt (or lame), and blind. The city refers to Jerusalem and its Jewish inhabitants. The poor are situated in contrast to the wealthy, those who were first invited to the feast. The crippled, lame, and blind symbolize society's humble people, those (in that era) who were unable to care for themselves. "Streets and lanes" seem to pertain to the dire circumstances of the poor, crippled, lame, and blind, meaning, they are homeless and living in the streets or they sit in the streets while begging for sustenance.

In this parable, the city Jerusalem is symbolic of the entire Jewish nation, wherever they lived.

> ***Luke 14:23–24*** *And the lord said unto the servant, Go out into the highways and hedges, and compel them to come in, that my house may be filled. For I say unto you, That none of those men which were bidden shall taste of my supper.*

Group 4, the Gentiles. The servant invites the poor and afflicted to the feast, according to his master's instructions, and determines that "yet there is room" for additional guests. His master then commands him to "go out into the highways and hedges, and compel them to come, that my house may be filled." *Compel* here means to strongly encourage.

Those who are located in the highways and hedges constitute group 4, the Gentiles. "Highways" suggests major roads, which differ from the city's "streets and lanes," mentioned in verse 21. The Gentiles were those who lived outside of Jerusalem (the Jewish community). They lived in countries that surrounded the Holy Land, which countries were connected to one another with great highways. As one historian has written: "Romans were . . . good road builders. They realized the strategic importance of land highways for military, commercial, and other purposes. Their policy was to build and maintain good roads into every new area as the Empire expanded."[2] Although Jesus spoke of highways, this symbolically refers to those who lived near those highways. Isaiah and other prophets, too, referred to *highways, paths,* and *way* symbolically (see, for example, Isaiah 11:16; 35:8–10; 40:3; 42:16; 49:11; 57:14; 62:10).

"Hedges" suggests the interior of the country, the places off the great highways and roads. This would include villagers, farmers, and others. Anciently, farmers planted "hedges" or built stone fences to indicate the boundaries of their farms and also to discourage predators from eating their crops. The Lord's servant, then, invited all peoples, regardless of where they lived, to attend and partake of the supper.

The countries surrounding the Holy Land are symbolic of all the lands of the earth.

Historically, the Lord first invited the Jewish community to attend the great feast. Afterward, his apostles and missionaries took the gospel to the Gentiles. Luke recorded in the book of Acts: "There came many to [Paul] into his lodging; to whom he expounded and testified the kingdom of God, persuading them concerning Jesus, both out of the law of Moses, and out of the prophets, from morning till evening. And some believed the things which were spoken, and some believed not.

"And when they agreed not among themselves, they departed, after that Paul had [said], . . . Be it known therefore unto you, that the salvation of God is sent unto the Gentiles, and that they will hear it. And when he had said these words, the Jews departed, and had great reasoning among themselves" (Acts 28:23–29).

Personal Application

The parable of the great supper applies directly to each of us, whether or not we have been baptized members of The Church of Jesus Christ of Latter-day Saints. This parable applies to us if we are so occupied with the obtaining of wealth or with occupational pursuits that we fail to attend the Lord's great supper. This parable also applies to us if we are more concerned with family than with Jesus Christ, or if we make excuses so that we do not accept the Lord's invitation to enjoy his banquet.

Elder F. Melvin Hammond likened the parable of the great supper to us when he wrote: "We often must make significant changes in our lives in order to attend the feast at the table of the Lord. Too many of us put those changes off, thinking there is no urgency. Perhaps this parable could be called the 'don't bother me now, Lord' parable. We try to excuse ourselves in various ways. Each rationalization comes from selfishness and almost always relates to something temporal. For some it is the Word of Wisdom. For others it is the law of tithing. Perhaps it is a reluctance to live the law of chastity. Whatever the reason, we who reject or delay our response to the Savior's invitation show our lack of love for Him who is our King. . . .

"Some who have accepted the gospel by being baptized do not continue to enjoy the feast. Once we have come to the Lord's table, let us not leave too early!

"Continuing to feast on the good things of the gospel means we will keep the commandments, attend our meetings, and contribute to the happiness of those around us by being good neighbors and friends."[3]

For further insight on the great supper, see the discussion of the parable of the ten virgins (pages 238–53).

CHAPTER 18

The Unrighteous Steward

Luke 16:1–8

And he said also unto his disciples, There was a certain rich man, which had a steward; and the same was accused unto him that he had wasted his goods.

And he called him, and said unto him, How is it that I hear this of thee? give an account of thy stewardship; for thou mayest be no longer steward.

Then the steward said within himself, What shall I do? for my lord taketh away from me the stewardship: I cannot dig; to beg I am ashamed.

I am resolved what to do, that, when I am put out of the stewardship, they may receive me into their houses.

So he called every one of his lord's debtors unto him, and said unto the first, How much owest thou unto my lord?

And he said, An hundred measures of oil. And he said unto him, Take thy bill, and sit down quickly, and write fifty.

Then said he to another, And how much owest thou? And he said, An hundred measures of wheat. And he said unto him, Take thy bill, and write fourscore.

And the lord commended the unjust steward, because he had done wisely: for the children of this world are in their generation wiser than the children of light.

This parable was directed to the disciples and not to the public at large. The opening words are "And [Jesus] said also unto his disciples" (Luke 16:1). After giving the parable, the Lord gave the following important instructions:

"And I say unto you, Make to yourselves friends of the mammon of unrighteousness; that, when ye fail, they may receive you into everlasting habitations. He that is faithful in that which is least is faithful also in much: and he that is unjust in the least is unjust also in much. If therefore ye have not been faithful in the unrighteous mammon, who will commit to your trust the true riches? And if ye have not been faithful in that which is another man's, who shall give you that which is your own? No servant can serve two masters: for either he will hate the one, and love the other; or else he will hold to the one, and despise the other. Ye cannot serve God and mammon" (Luke 16:9–13).

Commentary

> ***Luke 16:1–2*** *And he said also unto his disciples, There was a certain rich man, which had a steward; and the same was accused unto him that he had wasted his goods. And he called him, and said unto him, How is it that I hear this of thee? give an account of thy stewardship; for thou mayest be no longer steward.*

A steward is a manager or administrator over his master's domestic or business affairs. He is not simply the head of the servants but is a trained and trusted agent of his employer's enterprises. He has authority (which his master has delegated to him) and is entrusted to make major decisions on behalf of his employer and to work with third parties, such as his master's debtors. In this parable the steward works for "a certain rich man." That the man is wealthy is shown by the fact that he has sufficient money to employ a steward and that there are debtors who owe him great amounts of goods, including nine hundred gallons of oil and a hundred bushels of wheat.

A third party informs the rich man that his steward had "wasted his goods." This third party is represented in the passive phrase "the same was accused unto him" and in the employer's question, "How is it that I hear this of thee?" The parable does not inform us how the steward wasted his employer's goods. Perhaps he was incompetent or careless. Or maybe he embezzled or misappropriated his employer's goods, money, or assets. In any case, when the employer discovers his steward's wastefulness, he instructs him to give him an accounting of his stewardship. This accounting may have included what the rich man's debtors owed him, the status of his present inventory of goods, and an accounting of recent transactions. The rich man needed the accounting so that he could determine if the steward really had wasted "his goods"—and perhaps to pass the reports on to a new steward.

> ***Luke 16:3*** *Then the steward said within himself, What shall I do? for my lord taketh away from me the stewardship: I cannot dig; to beg I am ashamed.*

Upon hearing that he would soon be left without employment, the steward asks himself, "What shall I do [for employment]? . . . I cannot dig." Digging here stands for any type of menial labor. Maybe the steward cannot dig because of his age and health; digging ditches or canals, foundations of buildings, roadways, walkways, or for other construction needs requires great physical strength and endurance. Or, more likely, he cannot dig because he is too proud to perform such unskilled labor. Further, digging was below his capability and would lower his occupational status, thus preventing him from obtaining another job as a steward.

"To beg I am ashamed," he added. While digging is conducted by unskilled and often uneducated laborers, still it is an occupationally honorable effort. In Jesus' society, begging was not considered an occupation, and most believed it to be less than honorable. Only in the most extreme circumstances would an honorable person resort to begging. The steward, for this reason, said within himself, "To beg I am ashamed."

> ***Luke 16:4–7*** *I am resolved what to do, that, when I am put out of the stewardship, they may receive me into their houses. So he called every one of his lord's debtors unto him, and said*

unto the first, How much owest thou unto my lord? And he said, An hundred measures of oil. And he said unto him, Take thy bill, and sit down quickly, and write fifty. Then said he to another, And how much owest thou? And he said, An hundred measures of wheat. And he said unto him, Take thy bill, and write fourscore.

After consideration, the steward determines what to do with his employment crisis. He says to himself, "I am resolved what to do, that . . . they may receive me into their houses." Or to put it another way, "That I may continue to be welcomed into the homes of my business associates and clients." The steward summons "every one" of his master's debtors. Although the rich man had more than two debtors, the parable gives but two representative examples, one debtor who owed "an hundred measures of oil" and another who owed "an hundred measures of wheat."

The steward sits down with the debtors, reviews the debt that is owed to his employer, and then cancels a portion of the debt. The first debtor owes a hundred measures of oil and the steward reduces the bill to fifty. The second debtor owes a hundred measures of wheat and the steward reduces the bill to eighty. What was the steward's objective in reducing the debts? (1) Perhaps the steward's employer had charged the debtors an exorbitant interest rate. Charging interest on borrowed money was contrary to the law of Moses (see Exodus 22:25; Leviticus 25:36; Deuteronomy 23:19), and it is possible that the steward was simply forgiving the amount of interest that had been charged. (2) One biblical scholar has suggested that the steward met with the debtors in order to forgive the portion of the debt that was his own commission. "This does not mean a cancellation of half the debt or falsification of accounts. . . . It means that the debtor actually owed the master only fifty jugs of oil, and that the other fifty were the steward's commission."[1]

Some have supposed that the steward was unethically and dishonestly reducing the debt at the rich man's expense to gain favor with those who owed the debt. But this interpretation doesn't make sense in the context of Jesus' teaching, wherein he encourages his followers to be wise in temporal things, as the steward was. Note that Jesus does not commend any malfeasance or bad judgment that may have led to the initial accusation against the steward. The Lord focuses on the steward's behavior after he was informed by the employer that he was going to be discharged.

By reducing the amount owed to his employer, the steward was demonstrating a spirit of generosity to the debtors and at the same time gaining support for possible future employment in an occupation similar to his office as steward. "The ancient world ran on the basis of a reciprocity ethic: good turns given and returned. The steward's move gave him a claim upon his master's debtors that was much more secure than any contract. Public honor required that they make some appropriate return to their benefactor. The steward had secured his future!"[2]

The debts owed to the rich man represent very large amounts. "An hundred measures of oil" reads literally "a hundred baths (a liquid measure from the Greek *batos* and Hebrew *bat*) of oil."[3] Each *bat* was equal to about nine gallons of oil; hence, a hundred *bats* would have been about nine hundred gallons of oil. "An hundred measures of wheat" literally reads "a hundred *kors*" (from Greek *koros* and Hebrew *kor*), a dry measure that "might actually be considerably more than 'a hundred bushels.'"[4] According to one biblical commentator, "The quantities involved are quite huge. The oil involved would represent the annual yield of a very large olive grove. Similarly the wheat debt 'would represent a half-share rent for almost 200 acres, which is perhaps twenty times the size of an average family plot.' . . . The master is dealing with large-scale business associates here, not with ordinary people and ordinary economic levels."[5]

> ***Luke 16:8*** *And the lord commended the unjust steward, because he had done wisely: for the children of this world are in their generation wiser than the children of light.*

Jesus tells the story of the unrighteous steward in the first eight and one-half verses (Luke 16:1–8a), concluding the story when the master commends his steward by stating that "he had done wisely." Then, in the remaining five and one-half verses of the account (Luke 16:8b–13) Jesus explains the meaning of the parable and provides three applications. The three applications are located in verses 9–13 and will be discussed later.

"Lord" here means "master" and refers to the rich man or employer. It is the master, not Jesus Christ, who commends his steward for doing wisely. The employer commends his steward not for dishonesty or misuse of his goods, but because he had acted shrewdly, possibly by donating his commission back to the debtors. "The children of this world" probably refers to those who pursue worldly concerns. They stand opposite the "children of light," or those who are Christ's faithful disciples (see John 12:36; Ephesians 5:8; 1 Thessalonians 5:5; D&C 106:5). The parable states that "the children of this world" are "wiser than the children of light." This is a difficult saying and could be misinterpreted by some. The word "wiser," according to the context of the parable, refers to temporal goods and the world's business, and certainly not to spiritual things. If one is to be a true disciple, one must know how to work faithfully with temporal affairs. Christ's disciples can learn much about dealing with temporal goods and wealth from those who are not of the faith. For example, disciples can learn to avoid receiving exorbitant profits from others; they can also learn to forgive debts or portions of debts and to be generous when working with others.

Personal Application

In Luke 16:9 Jesus provides the first of three lessons or applications to the parable. Jesus' words, as translated into archaic English phrases, are sometimes difficult to comprehend. For example the phrase, "Make to yourselves friends of the mammon of unrighteousness," has been rendered quite differently by modern biblical translations. For this phrase the Jerusalem Bible reads, "Use money, tainted as it is, to win friends" and the New International Version reads, "Use worldly wealth to gain friends for yourselves." There are two other difficult phrases in this verse: "When ye fail" means "when ye die,"[6] and "everlasting habitations" refers to heaven.

The verse under discussion, then, deals with how we should prudently use our temporal goods and wealth. One biblical interpreter captures the essence of the verse with this explanation: "Use [money] for the needs of the poor, and they will be there to welcome you into eternity."[7] Another explains, "When possible the righteous should be friends, not enemies, with people in positions of authority or wealth, for someday those friends may assist the righteous and the kingdom of God."[8] Renewing the instruction for our day, the Lord said through Joseph Smith in 1832: "And now, verily I say unto you, and this is wisdom, make unto yourselves friends with the mammon of unrighteousness, and they will not destroy you" (D&C 82:22).

In Luke 16:10–12, Jesus provides the second of three lessons in the parable: "He that is faithful in that which is least is faithful also in much: and he that is unjust in the least is unjust also in much. If therefore ye have not been faithful in the unrighteous mammon, who will commit to your trust the true riches? And if ye have not been faithful in that which is another man's, who shall give you that which is your own?"

This lesson may be summed up as follows: Inasmuch as the Lord's mortal saints are required to conduct business in a telestial world, with worldly people, Babylon's currency, and the world's system of economics, they must conduct such business with faithfulness and wisdom. If you are not faithful with your earthly stewardship and the temporal things that have been entrusted to you, you will be less likely to be faithful with regard to the "true riches." The true riches pertain to all things that are spiritual, including the gifts of the Spirit, Church callings and assignments, and all aspects of Jesus Christ's atonement.

The parable's steward had learned how to conduct business in a telestial world by demonstrating a spirit of generosity to the debtors and at the same time obtaining support for possible future employment opportunities. The lord commended him for his actions "because he had done wisely" (verse 6).

In Luke 16:13, Jesus gives the third of three lessons in the parable: "No servant can serve two masters: for either he will hate the one, and love the other; or else he will hold to the one, and despise the other. Ye cannot serve God and mammon."

Any servant that is ruled by two different masters will be troubled as to which of the two masters' commands to follow. Competing commands to a servant only confuse him and unduly test his loyalty. If he obeys one master he may have to disregard the other's commands, thereby dissatisfying the other master. An ancient apocryphal Christian text named the Gospel of Thomas attributes words to Jesus that explain the difficulty of serving two masters. "Jesus said, 'It is impossible for a man to mount two horses (or) to stretch two bows. And it is impossible for a servant to serve two masters—otherwise he will honor the one and contemn the other.'"[9]

The two masters, according to Jesus' explanation, are God and riches (mammon). If we apply this principle to our own lives, each of us is a servant, and we all have two masters that are seeking our services and attention—God and mammon (money). We cannot serve both of these masters; we can serve only one. If we serve the money master then we will hate the master God; and if we hold to, possess, or grip the money master, we will despise the master God.

President Spencer W. Kimball's story of how tenaciously monkeys hold on to their food provides a vivid metaphor of how desperately some individuals cling to and worship mammon:

"I am reminded of an article I read some years ago about a group of men who had gone to the jungles to capture monkeys. They tried a number of different things to catch the monkeys, including nets. But finding that the nets could injure such small creatures, they finally came upon an ingenious solution. They built a large number of small boxes, and in the top of each they bored a hole just large enough for a monkey to get his hand into. They then set these boxes out under the trees and in each one they put a nut that the monkeys were particularly fond of.

"When the men left, the monkeys began to come down from the trees and examine the boxes. Finding that there were nuts to be had, they reached into the boxes to get them. But when a monkey would try to withdraw his hand with the nut, he could not get his hand out of the box because his little fist, with the nut inside, was now too large.

"At about this time, the men would come out of the underbrush and converge on the monkeys. And here is the curious thing. When the monkeys saw the men coming, they would shriek and scramble about with the thought of escaping; but as easy as it would have been, they would not let go of the nut so that they could withdraw their hands from the boxes and thus escape. The men captured them easily.

"And so it often seems to be with people, having such a firm grasp on things of the world—that which is telestial—that no amount of urging and no degree of emergency can persuade them to let go in favor of that which is celestial. Satan gets them in his grip easily. If we insist on spending all our time and resources building up for ourselves a worldly kingdom, that is exactly what we will inherit."[10]

Jacob taught us the proper method of making God our master while at the same time obtaining riches for the purpose of helping others: "But before ye seek for riches, seek ye for the kingdom of God. And after ye have obtained a hope in Christ ye shall obtain riches, if ye seek them; and ye will seek them for the intent to do good—to clothe the naked, and to feed the hungry, and to liberate the captive, and administer relief to the sick and the afflicted" (Jacob 2:18–19).

Elder James E. Talmage summarized the lesson of this parable when he wrote: "Worldly-minded men do not neglect provision for their future years, . . . while the 'children of light,' or those who believe spiritual wealth to be above all earthly possessions, are less energetic, prudent, or wise. . . . Emulate the unjust steward and the lovers of mammon [money], not in their dishonesty, cupidity, and miserly hoarding of the wealth that is at best but transitory, but in their zeal, forethought, and provision for the future. . . . Take a lesson from even the dishonest and the evil; if they are so prudent as to provide for the only future they think of, how much more should you, who believe in an eternal future, provide therefore!"[11]

CHAPTER 19

Lazarus and the Rich Man

Luke 16:19–31

There was a certain rich man, which was clothed in purple and fine linen, and fared sumptuously every day:

And there was a certain beggar named Lazarus, which was laid at his gate, full of sores,

And desiring to be fed with the crumbs which fell from the rich man's table: moreover the dogs came and licked his sores.

And it came to pass, that the beggar died, and was carried by the angels into Abraham's bosom: the rich man also died, and was buried;

And in hell he lift up his eyes, being in torments, and seeth Abraham afar off, and Lazarus in his bosom.

And he cried and said, Father Abraham, have mercy on me, and send Lazarus, that he may dip the tip of his finger in water, and cool my tongue; for I am tormented in this flame.

But Abraham said, Son, remember that thou in thy lifetime receivedst thy good things, and likewise Lazarus evil things: but now he is comforted, and thou art tormented.

And beside all this, between us and you there is a great gulf fixed: so that they which would pass from hence to you cannot; neither can they pass to us, that would come from thence.

Then he said, I pray thee therefore, father, that thou wouldest send him to my father's house:

For I have five brethren; that he may testify unto them, lest they also come into this place of torment.

Abraham saith unto him, They have Moses and the prophets; let them hear them.

And he said, Nay, father Abraham: but if one went unto them from the dead, they will repent.

And he said unto him, If they hear not Moses and the prophets, neither will they be persuaded, though one rose from the dead.

This parable was given in the context of a discussion of the righteous and unrighteous uses of wealth. The chapter begins with the parable of the unjust steward, which Jesus spoke to his disciples. One point of that parable is that we should learn to use wealth with wisdom. The Lord concluded that instruction by saying, "No servant can serve two masters: for either he will hate the one, and love the other; or else he will hold to the one, and despise the other. Ye cannot serve God and mammon" (Luke 16:13).

He then spoke specifically to the Pharisees, whom, the account says, "were covetous." He said: "Ye are they which justify yourselves before men; but God knoweth your hearts: for that which is highly esteemed among men is abomination in the sight of God" (Luke 16:15). Rather than coveting their own possessions, the Pharisees should have been consecrating them unto God.

Joseph Smith made the context for this parable unmistakable. In the Joseph Smith Translation we can see that Jesus was having a forthright interchange with the Pharisees, saying, "You pervert the right way; and the kingdom of heaven suffereth violence of you; and you persecute the meek." Then he said, "Verily I say unto you, I will liken you unto the rich man," after which he presented the parable (see JST, Luke 16:21, 23).

Jesus' listeners may have been familiar with an old Egyptian folk tale that had been brought to the Holy Land by Alexandrian Jews and altered to fit the Jewish culture. In the story a rich publican and a poor rabbi (a Pharisee?) both died and were buried. In paradise, the rabbi wandered along the beautiful streams, drinking his fill, while the publican stood helpless next to the water, parched; the more he sought to obtain refreshing and life-giving drink, the more it receded from him.[1]

Commentary

Luke 16:19 *There was a certain rich man, which was clothed in purple and fine linen, and fared sumptuously every day:*

This parable begins with identical language to the parable found earlier in the same chapter: "There was a certain rich man" (see Luke 16:1).

The man's clothing indicates just how wealthy he was. Purple was an expensive dye; it was the color of royalty—and wealth. His underclothing was made of fine linen, much different from the coarse clothing worn by many. To fare sumptuously indicates rich and abundant meals, but not only that. One Bible version says that he "lived in luxury every day" (NIV). He had money and his goal was to spend it on his own pleasure and comfort.

It should be emphasized that there is no suggestion that the rich man was dishonest in any way, that he obtained his wealth illegally or inappropriately. The point is not that he was dishonest but rather than he was focused selfishly only on himself.

Luke 16:20 *And there was a certain beggar named Lazarus, which was laid at his gate, full of sores,*

This is the only parable where any of the characters is named (both Lazarus and Abraham). This Lazarus must not be confused with the Lazarus who was a friend of Jesus and was raised from the dead. Instead, the meaning of *Lazarus* gives a clue to why Jesus identified the man by name. Lazarus (from the Hebrew *Eleazar* or *Eliezer*) means "God is my help." The rich man would not help Lazarus during his mortal life, but ultimately God helped him.

Lazarus was a beggar, a common presence in the Middle East of that era. In ancient times the government offered no help to the poor, and charitable organizations were unknown. Those who were stricken with poverty and sometimes disease were forced to rely on the generosity of others for their daily sustenance. To help the poor was viewed as a religious requirement.

Apparently Lazarus had a disease that prevented him from walking and also gave him sores, perhaps from being unable to move about in bed. He was carried from his home to the gate of the rich man, where he was "laid" by his helpers. The fact that there was a gate suggests there was also a wall, and the fact that there was a wall suggests that the rich man lived in secure isolation, perhaps in a mansion.

Luke 16:21 *And desiring to be fed with the crumbs which fell from the rich man's table:*

Unable to walk, Lazarus lay by the rich man's gate dependent on the goodness of others for his daily sustenance. He would have been satisfied with just the crumbs from the rich man's table. It was the custom for the wealthy to use chunks of bread to wipe their hands and mouths on; the bread would then be thrown on the floor and swept out the door.

Lazarus desired only to receive some of that cast-off bread, but insensitive to the poor man's need, the rich man wouldn't even give him that. To make the condemnation of the rich man even worse, the rich man was aware of Lazarus's presence outside his gate; as we learn later in the parable, the rich man in fact knew both his face and his name.

Luke 16:21 *moreover the dogs came and licked his sores.*

Some commentators view this as the only kindness the beggar experienced in life, supposing that the licking of the dogs had a soothing effect. More likely it was an irritant, only making the sores worse. Further, these should not be viewed as friendly pets. It was common in the Middle East for semi-wild dogs to roam the streets of the towns, scavenging for whatever food they could find. For such dogs to lick Lazarus's sores as he lay there helpless would have been frightening and very uncomfortable and was an evidence of his pitiful state.

Luke 16:22 *And it came to pass, that the beggar died, and was carried by the angels into Abraham's bosom: the rich man also died, and was buried;*

There is a great contrast between the death and burial of the beggar and the rich man. The rich man was buried—he surely had all the respect and honors of the rich in death. He would have been carried by family and friends to the tomb of the wealthy. There probably was music and formal mourning.

The beggar's burial was not even mentioned. His body would have been carried without ceremony to the paupers' field. But his spirit was carried by angels into paradise, characterized here as into "Abraham's bosom," or the abode of Abraham as he awaited his resurrection.

The phrase *carried . . . into Abraham's bosom* conjures up an image of one man reclining companionably against another during a feast or banquet (see John 13:23). *Bosom* also suggests having close fellowship with another (see John 1:18). In paradise, Lazarus was able to have close association with Abraham, the revered father of all Israelites.

Luke 16:23 *And in hell he lift up his eyes, being in torments, and seeth Abraham afar off, and Lazarus in his bosom.*

Lazarus the beggar is with righteous Abraham, and the selfish rich man finds himself in hell.

The word for "hell" in this passage is *Hades,* the abode of the wicked in the spirit world. In latter-day terminology, we would call this place the spirit prison. Hell is a place of torment, which torments are symbolized by fire. It is a temporary place where the wicked await the judgment. It is also the place where those who did not in mortality receive the opportunity to receive the gospel can hear the message of salvation, accept it if they will, and have their eternity changed.

The rich man found himself in this hell and in torment. Off in the distance (in paradise) he saw Abraham and Lazarus, and he recognized them. We will indeed retain our identity in the spirit world; we will recognize one another and will be able to converse with each other.

Alma described the conditions in this hell when he said, "As soon as they are departed from this mortal body, . . . the spirits of the wicked, yea, who are evil . . . shall be cast out into outer darkness; there shall be weeping, and wailing, and gnashing of teeth, and this because of their own iniquity, being led captive by the will of the devil. Now this is the state of the souls of the wicked, yea, in darkness, and a state of awful, fearful looking for the fiery indignation of the wrath of God upon them; thus they remain in this state, as well as the righteous in paradise, until the time of their resurrection" (Alma 40:11, 13–14).

Luke 16:24 *And he cried and said, Father Abraham, have mercy on me, and send Lazarus, that he may dip the tip of his finger in water, and cool my tongue; for I am tormented in this flame.*

The rich man referred to Abraham as "father." The Jews took pride in their descent from Abraham (see Matthew 3:8; John 8:37). And, as we see in the next verse, Abraham also recognized that the rich man was one of his offspring, calling him "Son."

The combination of extreme heat and terrible thirst would have been familiar to people who lived in a desert climate. It would have been a source of torment indeed.

That the rich man wanted Lazarus to serve him indicates he still viewed Lazarus as inferior to him, someone who could be ordered around. Lazarus was willing to receive only crumbs when he was on earth, and the rich man now expresses his desire only for a drop of water. But as the rich man denied Lazarus's need on earth, so is the rich man denied his need in hell.

Luke 16:25 *But Abraham said, Son, remember that thou in thy lifetime receivedst thy good things, and likewise Lazarus evil things: but now he is comforted, and thou art tormented.*

It is the nature of parables that they cannot include all the possible details of a story. The truth is that God does not give his children rewards in the spirit world based only on the conditions and circumstances of their mortal lives. Instead, as the scriptures teach again and again, we receive rewards based on our choices, our works, and the intent of our hearts.

Accordingly, when Abraham draws on the law of retribution here, the explanation is abbreviated and needs to be expanded to be fully understood. A more complete statement would say, "In your lifetime you received good things, but you used them only for your own benefit, not helping the poor according to the commandment and your conscience. Lazarus's life was very difficult through no fault of his own, and yet he was good of heart and did his best under his circumstances. Because of this, you are being punished in the spirit world, while Lazarus is being rewarded."

> ***Luke 16:26*** *And beside all this, between us and you there is a great gulf fixed: so that they which would pass from hence to you cannot; neither can they pass to us, that would come from thence.*

According to divine law, there was a great separation or gulf between the righteous in paradise and the wicked in the spirit prison—those in one part of the spirit world could not associate with those in the other part. Hence, the rich man could not pass into paradise, nor could Lazarus go into the spirit prison. Once Christ conquered death, however, the gulf was bridged. Righteous emissaries of Christ could then visit, minister to, and teach those in the spirit prison, and those who repented with all their hearts and received the proffered ordinances (which are performed in mortal temples) could then leave the spirit prison and enter paradise (see 1 Peter 3:18–21; 4:6; D&C 138).

> ***Luke 16:27–28*** *Then he said, I pray thee therefore, father, that thou wouldest send him to my father's house: For I have five brethren; that he may testify unto them, lest they also come into this place of torment.*

Now that the rich man finds himself in the torments of hell, for the first time in the story he has concern and consideration for others: he wants Abraham to send Lazarus to warn his brothers to repent before it is too late. Apparently, like the rich man, the brothers are living a life of selfishness and self-absorption, oblivious to their religious duty and to the needs of those around them.

> ***Luke 16:29–31*** *Abraham saith unto him, They have Moses and the prophets; let them hear them. And he said, Nay, father Abraham: but if one went unto them from the dead, they will repent. And he said unto him, If they hear not Moses and the prophets, neither will they be persuaded, though one rose from the dead.*

Abraham is referring to the writings of the Old Testament, which teach over and over again that we should care for the poor. Deuteronomy 15:7–8, God's word received through Moses, is very plain: "If there be among you a poor man of one of thy brethren within any of thy gates in thy land which the Lord thy God giveth thee, thou shalt not harden thine heart, nor shut thine hand from thy poor brother: But thou shalt open thine hand wide unto him, and shalt surely lend him sufficient for his need, in that which he wanteth."

Likewise, Isaiah, one of the prophets, wrote: "Is not this the fast that I have chosen? to loose the bands of wickedness, to undo the heavy burdens, and to let the oppressed go free, and that ye break every yoke? Is it not to deal thy bread to the hungry, and that thou bring the poor that are cast out to thy house? when thou seest the naked, that thou cover him; and that thou hide not thyself from thine own flesh?" (Isaiah 58:6–7).

The rich man and his brothers had these teachings; they surely would have been taught them from their youth. But they had chosen to disregard them. If we ignore the writings of the prophets, we won't hearken to a visitor from the dead. Perhaps this seems extreme. But the fact is that when Jesus raised his friend Lazarus from the dead, the Jews tried to kill Lazarus (see John 12:10). When the Lord sent Moroni to the earth with a message for the latter days, most people who heard the message rejected it.

There is a sadly ironic additional meaning to these words, which Jesus himself was speaking through the mouth of his servant Abraham. A failure to care for the poor was not the only deficiency in the rich man's life. In some ways he represented the Pharisees as a group, as explained above. In their smug self-righteousness, the Pharisees also failed to care for the poor—but, more importantly, they refused to accept Jesus as the Christ.

With this reading in mind, when the rich man as a Pharisee dies and finds himself in hell because he did not accept Christ or his gospel, he pleads with Father Abraham that he will send a messenger to his brothers to tell them the truth. But Abraham says that they already have the testimony of Moses and the prophets, which testify of Christ.

When the resurrected Jesus walked the road to Emmaus with the two disciples, the disciples were telling him (not realizing it was Jesus) about the events of the previous days: how they thought they were following the Messiah, but that he had been killed—and now there were some reports that he was alive.

"Then he said unto them, O fools, and slow of heart to believe all that the prophets have spoken: Ought not Christ to have suffered these things, and to enter into his glory? And beginning at *Moses and all the prophets,* he expounded unto them in all the scriptures the things concerning himself" (Luke 24:25–27; emphasis added).

Later that same day, Jesus appeared to a group of disciples who were gathered in Jerusalem, showing them his resurrected body, and he said, "These are the words which I spake unto you, while I was yet with you, that all things must be fulfilled, which were *written in the law of Moses, and in the prophets,* and in the psalms, concerning me. Then opened he their understanding, that they might understand the scriptures" (Luke 24:44–45; emphasis added).

When we accept the teachings of Moses and the prophets, we also accept Jesus Christ. Even though the Old Testament prophets taught us much about our daily duty and a godly life, the burden of their message was that Jesus is the Christ. By rejecting the teachings of the Old Testament pertaining to the poor, the rich man was also rejecting the greater teachings regarding the Messiah. No wonder he found himself "in hell . . . , being in torments."

Personal Application

The rich man's sin was not found in what he did on earth, but in what he failed to do: he did not love God and man. One important manifestation of that love is caring for the poor. We in this dispensation are clearly commanded to assist the poor; in fact, it is a condition of our salvation. The Lord said through the Prophet Joseph Smith, in words that are reminiscent of those in the parable: "For the earth is full, and there is enough and to spare. . . . Therefore, if any man shall take of the abundance which I have made, and impart not his portion, according to the law of my gospel, unto the poor and the needy, he shall, with the wicked, lift up his eyes in hell, being in torment" (D&C 104:17–18).

On another occasion the Lord said (using words that recall his condemnation of the meridian-day Pharisees): "Wo unto you rich men, that will not give your substance to the poor, for your riches will canker your souls; and this shall be your lamentation in the day of visitation, and of judgment, and of indignation: The harvest is past, the summer is ended, and my soul is not saved!" (D&C 56:16).

The moral to this parable is clear: we must help those in need or we will stand condemned. We must not only hear the word of truth but also live it, embracing in our lives what James called "the royal law . . . , thou shalt love thy neighbor" (James 2:8).

But, as intimated earlier, this parable also has a broader meaning: we must find and follow Christ in our lives. As Jesus was teaching the Pharisees, immediately before giving this parable, they said they planned to follow "the law, and the prophets." Jesus responded, "The law and the prophets testify of me. . . . And why teach ye the law, and deny that which is written; and condemn him whom the Father hath sent to fulfill the law, that ye might all be redeemed?" (JST, Luke 16:16–17, 20). The rich man was unwilling to accept the testimony of the prophets when he was alive (and all the prophets have testified of Christ), and his five brothers also would not believe. The rich man wanted Abraham to send his brothers a dramatic sign so they would repent. But as Jesus said to the Pharisees, "You have said in your hearts, There is no God" (JST, Luke 16:21). Even though they professed to believe the law and the prophets, their performance was a sham.

Those who desire to be carried to paradise by angels, who hope to join Abraham in glory, must accept and follow Christ when they have the opportunity. Otherwise, just as the rich man, they may in the end lift up their eyes in hell.

CHAPTER 20

The Unprofitable Servant

Luke 17:7–10

But which of you, having a servant plowing or feeding cattle, will say unto him by and by, when he is come from the field, Go and sit down to meat?

And will not rather say unto him, Make ready wherewith I may sup, and gird thyself, and serve me, till I have eaten and drunken; and afterward thou shalt eat and drink?

Doth he thank that servant because he did the things that were commanded him? I trow not.

So likewise ye, when ye shall have done all those things which are commanded you, say, We are unprofitable servants: we have done that which was our duty to do.

This parable teaches us how we can increase our faith. After Jesus had taught his disciples various principles of the gospel, the apostles said to him, "Increase our faith" (Luke 17:5). Jesus responded by saying, "If ye had faith as a grain of mustard seed, ye might say unto this sycamine tree, Be thou plucked up by the root, and be thou planted in the sea; and it should obey you" (Luke 17:6). Then immediately after saying these words, Jesus spoke the parable of the unprofitable servant.

Commentary

Luke 17:7 *But which of you, having a servant plowing or feeding cattle, will say unto him by and by, when he is come from the field, Go and sit down to meat?*

In order to teach the apostles how to increase their faith, Jesus focuses on servants and their service to their master. Examples of service rendered include plowing the field, feeding the cattle, and preparing supper for the master. These examples are representative only. Servants at Jesus' time performed a great variety of services, both in the field and in the household. The parable's verb forms that refer to the servant's actions are *plowing, feeding, make ready, gird thyself, serve, did (the things that were commanded), shall have done, are commanded,* and *have done*.

For teaching purposes, Jesus opens the parable by employing a rhetorical question, a question that is set forth and then answered before the audience is able to respond. Jesus also uses the "what if" principle with his apostles, saying in effect: "What if you were the master and you had a servant, and your servant served all day plowing the field or feeding cattle, then at the end of the day you invited your servant to eat supper?" Both the rhetorical question and the "what if" principle draw the apostles into the story and encourage each to imagine himself as the master who has his own servant.

Luke 17:8 *And will not rather say unto him, Make ready wherewith I may sup, and gird thyself, and serve me, till I have eaten and drunken; and afterward thou shalt eat and drink?*

The servant works all day performing his duties, which are required of him because it is his role to serve. His duties vary according to the needs of his master and may include agricultural labor or domestic responsibilities. As one hired to do so, the servant is expected to submit to the master's wishes and commands. As Peter wrote, "Servants, be subject to your masters with all fear; not only to the good and gentle, but also to the froward [crooked or wicked]" (1 Peter 2:18).

Does the master in fact allow his servant to rest and to enjoy supper after spending the day in the field? No! As Jesus continues his parable by submitting a second rhetorical question, he explains that the master rightfully requires the servant to first provide him (the master) with supper, and only afterward may the servant partake of his. The master commands his servant, "Make ready wherewith I may sup, and gird thyself, and serve me, till I have eaten and drunken."

> ***Luke 17:9*** *Doth he thank that servant because he did the things that were commanded him? I trow not.*

In this parable the servant works all day in the field performing agricultural tasks and afterward attends to his master's domestic needs by preparing a meal. After the servant completes his day's labor, fulfilling all his master's commandments, does the master thank his servant? The answer is "I trow [think] not." The master does not thank his servant because the servant does what he has contracted to do. His payment is sufficient thanks, whether that payment comes in the form of coins, room and board, or protection. Furthermore, the master does not need to thank his servant for his service because, after all of his service, the servant is yet unprofitable (see verse 10).

> ***Luke 17:10*** *So likewise ye, when ye shall have done all those things which are commanded you, say, We are unprofitable servants: we have done that which was our duty to do.*

Jesus responded to the apostles' request, "Increase our faith," by presenting this parable. He gave the main idea in verses 7–9 and now in verse 10 offers the application and meaning of the entire parable, which are introduced with the words, "So likewise ye." Note the parable's role reversal. The "what if" principle first made the apostles imagine that they were the masters who had servants, but in verse 10, the role has been reversed and the apostles are told to concede, "We are unprofitable servants."

The parable's meaning is set forth in a straightforward manner. Although it was first directed to the Lord's apostles, it actually applies to all of his disciples in any age of the world, to all who would have him to be their Master. The parable clearly says regarding all of us that, even after we have "done all those things which are commanded" of us and after "we have done that which was our duty to do," we are yet "unprofitable servants." The parable emphasizes this by providing the example of a servant who labors for a period of time, first in the field and then in the home, and still he is unprofitable and undeserving of "thanks" from his master.

Even though we do all we have power to do, it still is not enough. We are still servants in need of our Master. Despite our best efforts, we can never save ourselves but will ever be in great debt to our Savior for his atonement.

A superficial reading of the parable may cause the reader to wonder how the parable taught the apostles how to increase their faith, since the parable focuses on an unprofitable servant. However, the servant's faithfulness and service to his master are instructive to all of us. Just as the servant served his master throughout the day and into the evening, we too must serve our Master day and night. And just as the servant received no thanks for his service from his master, we must not expect to receive the Lord's thanks for our service because, after all of our service, we are still unprofitable servants. In sum, our service to God and to others is the way to increase our faith.

Personal Application

In his famous speech at the temple, King Benjamin captured the full meaning of what it means to be "unprofitable servants":

"I say unto you that if ye should serve him who has created you from the beginning, and is preserving you from day to day, by lending you breath, that ye may live and move and do according to your own will, and even supporting you from one moment to another—I say, if ye should serve him with all your whole souls yet ye would be unprofitable servants.

"And behold, all that he requires of you is to keep his commandments; and . . . if ye do keep his commandments he doth bless you and prosper you.

"And now, in the first place, he hath created you, and granted unto you your lives, for which ye are indebted unto him.

"And secondly, he doth require that ye should do as he hath

commanded you; for which if ye do, he doth immediately bless you; and therefore he hath paid you. And ye are still indebted unto him, and are, and will be, forever and ever; therefore, of what have ye to boast?" (Mosiah 2:21–24).

Despite all our best efforts to serve and obey our Father in Heaven, we will yet remain unprofitable. He has created us and "granted unto [us our] lives." He "is preserving [us] from day to day"; he is "lending [us] breath"; and he is "supporting [us] from one moment to another." The phrase "lending [us] breath" is significant; it suggests that we must return or pay for that which is being loaned. We are unprofitable because we cannot return the air that we breathe, nor do we have sufficient funds to pay for it, especially since all that we possess belongs to God in any case.

President Joseph Fielding Smith said: "Do you think it will ever be possible for any one of us, no matter how hard we labor, . . . to pay our Father and Jesus Christ for the blessings we have received from them? The great love, with its accompanying blessings, extended to us through the crucifixion, suffering, and resurrection of Jesus Christ is beyond our mortal comprehension. We never could repay."[1]

Even though we are unprofitable servants, we still must work diligently to do the will of our Master. If we do it because we love him and want to please him, not concerning ourselves with that which we will receive in return, our faith truly will increase—and in time, unlike the servant in the parable, we will be invited to sit with the Master at his great supper.

CHAPTER 21

The Importunate Widow and Unjust Judge

Luke 18:1–5

And he spake a parable unto them to this end, that men ought always to pray, and not to faint;

Saying, There was in a city a judge, which feared not God, neither regarded man:

And there was a widow in that city; and she came unto him, saying, Avenge me of mine adversary.

And he would not for a while: but afterward he said within himself, Though I fear not God, nor regard man;

Yet because this widow troubleth me, I will avenge her, lest by her continual coming she weary me.

The parable of the importunate widow and unjust judge is set in the context of teachings about Jesus' second coming. Jesus responded to the Pharisees' request to know the time of the coming of the kingdom of God by providing a number of the signs of the times. He said in part, "For as the lightning, that lighteneth out of the one part under heaven, shineth unto the other part under heaven; so shall also the Son of man be in his day. . . . And as it was in the days of Noe, so shall it be also in the days of the Son of man. They did eat, they drank, they married wives, they were given in marriage, until the day that Noe entered into the ark, and the flood came, and destroyed them all. Likewise also as it was in the days of Lot; they did eat, they drank, they bought, they sold, they planted, they builded; but the same day that Lot went out of Sodom it rained fire and brimstone from heaven, and destroyed them all. Even thus shall it be in the day when the Son of man is revealed" (Luke 17:24, 26–30).

Immediately after presenting these and other signs of the times, Jesus delivered the parable of the importunate widow and unjust judge.

This parable describes a widow who lived in the same city as an unjust judge. She had been the victim of another's unfairness or wrongdoing and approached the judge for redress, but for a period of time he refused to help her. With his refusal, the judge was ignoring a Mosaic law that stated, "Thou shalt not pervert the judgment of the stranger, nor of the fatherless; nor take a widow's raiment to pledge" (Deuteronomy 24:17).

Commentary

> ***Luke 18:1*** *And he spake a parable unto them to this end, that men ought always to pray, and not to faint;*

The opening words of the parable instruct us to pray always. These opening words suggest that the parable is essentially about prayer, but the greater context must be considered. As noted, the passages that precede and follow Jesus' instruction that "men ought always to pray" are about Jesus' second coming. The preceding passage details a number of the signs of the times (see Luke 17:24–30) and the words immediately following the parable ask, "Nevertheless when the Son of man cometh, shall he find faith on the earth?" (Luke 18:8).

The parable of the importunate widow and unjust judge teaches us how to strengthen our faith so that we will know that the Lord really will return—and so that we will be prepared. We can and must pray in faith, "and not to faint," that we will be strong in the face of the trials of the last days, that the Lord will protect us from our enemies, that he will come and rescue a declining world—and that we will be worthy to stand with him when he appears.

Elder Bruce R. McConkie wrote, "Jesus now teaches, in a parable, how the preserving prayers of the saints will finally prevail in the day of his coming. He is not here speaking of the simplistic principle that earnest and repetitious importunings will eventually be heard and answered, though this may be true in some cases. . . . Rather, this parable . . . teaches that if the saints will continue to importune in faith for that which is right, and because their cause is just, though the answers to their prayers may be long delayed, yet, finally in the day of vengeance when he judges whose judgment is just, when he comes to rule and reign, the faithful will be rewarded."[1]

Three key words or phrases—*always, continual,* and *day and night*—parallel each other and help to define the parable. The words are mentioned in the opening phrase, "that men ought always to pray," the reference of the widow's "continual coming" to the city judge, and in the passage that follows the parable, which speaks of the elect who "cry day and night" to God (Luke 18:7). These parallel phrases suggest that God's elect, represented by the widow, must continually pray to the Father for all those things we deeply need. The elect must exercise faith while calling on God.

> ***Luke 18:2*** *Saying, There was in a city a judge, which feared not God, neither regarded man:*

At different times in the history of the Old Testament, kings (see 1 Kings 3:16–28; Proverbs 20:8), prophets (see Judges 4:4–5; 1 Samuel 7:15–17), and various charismatic leaders (in the book of Judges) served as judges. Moses, for example, served as Israel's judge during the wilderness period. As a judge he carried an extremely heavy workload, so he delegated some of his judicial responsibilities by appointing other judges. Moses retained the "hard cases" of judgment but relegated "every small matter" to others (Exodus 18:13–27). City judges also existed in the biblical world. These were officers who had authority to make judgments and to administer justice in legal cases. These judges, who were often appointed to their position (see Deuteronomy 16:18; Ezra 7:25), held a central role in ancient Israelite society (see 1 Chronicles 26:29). The judge identified in the parable of the importunate widow and unjust judge was such a city judge.

The book of Deuteronomy details Moses' instructions to Israel's judges: "And I charged your judges at that time, saying, Hear the causes between your brethren, and judge righteously between every man and his brother, and the stranger that is with him. Ye shall not respect persons in judgment; but ye shall hear the small as well as the great; ye shall not be afraid of the face of man; for the judgment is God's: and the cause that is too hard for you, bring it unto me, and I will hear it" (Deuteronomy 1:16–17). In addition to these instructions, Israelite judges were to "judge the people with just judgment" and they were commanded not to make partial judgments nor take bribes: "Thou shalt not wrest judgment; thou shalt not respect persons, neither take a gift: for a gift doth blind the eyes of the wise, and pervert the words of the righteous" (Deuteronomy 16:18–19).

Despite Moses' inspired instructions to the judges, some judges lacked righteous judgments, sought bribes (see Micah 7:3), and were prone to human weaknesses. A few judges were named "evening wolves" (Zephaniah 3:3), a reference to their ravenous and evil ways. On some occasions the judges sought to "turn aside the needy from judgment, and to take away the right from the poor of my people, that widows may be their prey, and that they may rob the fatherless!" (Isaiah 10:2). On other occasions, "they overpass[ed] the deeds of the wicked: they judge[d] not the cause, the cause of the fatherless, yet they prosper[ed]; and the right of the needy [did] they not judge" (Jeremiah 5:28).

The judge depicted in the parable under consideration was a judge who had a number of human weaknesses. He "feared not God," a phrase twice repeated in the parable, meaning that the judge lacked reverence and respect for or was indifferent to God. The parable says that the judge "neither regarded man," also a twice-repeated expression. A judge who lacks regard for humans is one who is deficient in judgelike qualities and effectiveness. The parable also describes him as "an unjust judge," indicating that he was either an unrighteous judge or that he lacked justice (or fairness or impartiality) in his judgments.

> ***Luke 18:3–4*** *And there was a widow in that city; and she came unto him, saying, Avenge me of mine adversary. And he would not for a while:*

God's interest in providing judgment to widows is set forth in the law of Moses: "For the Lord your God is God of gods, and Lord of lords, a great God, a mighty, and a terrible, which regardeth not persons, nor taketh reward. He doth execute the judgment of the fatherless and widow, and loveth the stranger, in giving him food and raiment" (Deuteronomy 10:17–18). In addition, the psalmist wrote, "The Lord preserveth the strangers; he relieveth the fatherless and widow: but the way of the wicked he turneth upside down" (Psalm 146:9).

The parable sets forth two figures from two ends of the social scheme, the judge at one end and the widow at the other. Judges were often socially powerful and widows were frequently powerless in the same system. The judge was respected, well stationed in society, belonged to the upper class, and likely had a large salary. Perhaps the widow lacked substance because her provider had passed away, and she was reliant upon others for maintenance. Conceivably, she lived in a lower-class neighborhood. Without familial, social, religious, or governmental assistance, she was somewhat helpless in the social system. For help against civil or social wrongdoings, she was forced to rely upon a judge for recourse. It was due to widows' extreme needs that James wrote, "Pure religion and undefiled before God and the Father is this, To visit the fatherless and widows in their affliction, and to keep himself unspotted from the world" (James 1:27; see Exodus 22:22–24; Isaiah 1:17; 1 Timothy 5:3).

In this parable the widow represents the Church of Jesus Christ as a body, as well as the individual members of the Church. A number of scriptures portray God's covenant people or the Church as a woman, wife, or widow, while the Lord himself is the Bridegroom. Isaiah, for example, connects God's covenant people to a widow and then explicitly states that the Lord of Hosts is her husband: "Fear not; for thou shalt not be ashamed: neither be thou confounded; for thou shalt not be put to shame: for thou shalt forget the shame of thy youth, and shalt not remember the reproach of thy widowhood any more. For thy Maker is thine husband; the Lord of hosts is his name; and thy Redeemer the Holy One of Israel; the God of the whole earth shall he be called" (Isaiah 54:4–5). As Elder McConkie explained, "We must not overlook the fact that the Church itself, in Christ's absence, is a widow."[2]

> **Luke 18:4–5** *but afterward he said within himself, Though I fear not God, nor regard man; Yet because this widow troubleth me, I will avenge her, lest by her continual coming she weary me.*

The unjust judge admits that he does not fear God nor does he give proper respect for humankind, when he states, "Though I fear not God, nor regard man." He provides two reasons why he determines to avenge the widow of her adversary. First, he admits that "this widow troubleth me." The widow's persistence in seeking was burdensome to him, and the matter may have also attracted undue attention to the judge and his position of trust, perhaps causing him political damage in the community or in the eyes of his peers. Second, the judge states that her "continual coming" had wearied him. Both of the judge's reasons for taking her cause had little to do with her and her needs. It was all about him. And for these selfish reasons, he finally agrees to avenge her.

In the parable of the importunate widow and unjust judge, Jesus introduced the parable's story in verses 1–5; then in verses 6–8 he gave its interpretation: "And the Lord said, Hear what the unjust judge saith. And shall not God avenge his own elect, which cry day and night unto him, though he bear long with them? I tell you that he will avenge them speedily. Nevertheless when the Son of man cometh, shall he find faith on the earth?"

This interpretation, with its sudden change of characters, may have surprised or even shocked Jesus' listeners. The parable told of an unrighteous city judge, but now the interpretation speaks of God. The parable conveyed information about a widow, but now the interpretation refers to God's elect. Perhaps Jesus' listeners were surprised as well when the Master introduced two new themes at the parable's conclusion, the Second Coming and faith: "Nevertheless when the Son of man cometh, shall he find faith on the earth?" In fact, the Joseph Smith Translation of verse 8 reinforces the theme of Jesus' coming, since it changed "I tell you that he will avenge them speedily" to read "I tell you that he will come, and when he does come, he will avenge his saints speedily."

How can the parable possibly compare the unrighteous city judge to God, who is the embodiment of perfection, light, and truth? The parable uses the "how much more so principle" to teach a significant concept. If the unjust judge, who does not have regard for humankind, finally hearkens to the persistent pleas of a widow, how much more so will a loving Father in Heaven, the righteous Judge (see Isaiah 33:22; 1 Peter 4:5), immediately provide impartial judgments on the widow's behalf? God's judgments, of course, are always right and true (see Genesis 18:25; John 8:16). Both the city judge and God render judgment in behalf of the widow, but the city judge did so after a long delay and God does so with haste. As Jesus explains in the parable, God "will avenge his saints speedily."

Personal Application

This parable has multiple applications, including the following three:

1. The parable's widow is likened to the latter-day Church during its infant days, when it was suffering from immense persecution. In Doctrine and Covenants 101, a revelation given to Joseph Smith on December 16, 1833, the Lord quoted part of the parable of the importunate widow and unjust judge and likened it to his Church, or the "children of Zion," at that time period. The heading of that revelation explains that "at this time the saints who had gathered in Missouri were suffering great persecution. Mobs had driven them from their homes. . . . Threats of death against individuals of the Church were many. The people had lost household furniture, clothing, livestock, and other personal property, and many of their crops had been destroyed."

Doctrine and Covenants 101:81–92 reads: "Now, unto what shall I liken the children of Zion? I will liken them unto the parable of the woman and the unjust judge, for men ought always to pray and not to faint, which saith—There was in a city a judge which feared not God, neither regarded man. And there was a widow in that city, and she came unto him, saying: Avenge me of mine adversary. And he would not for a while, but afterward he said within himself: Though I fear not God, nor regard man, yet because this widow troubleth me, I will avenge her, lest by her continual coming she weary me. Thus I will liken the children of Zion. Let them importune at the feet of the judge; And if he heed them not, let them importune at the feet of the governor; And if the governor heed them not, let them importune at the feet of the president; And if the president heed them not, then will the Lord arise and come forth out of his hiding place, and in his fury vex the nation; And in his hot displeasure, and in his fierce anger, in his time, will cut off those wicked, unfaithful, and unjust stewards, and appoint them their portion among hypocrites, and unbelievers; Even in outer darkness, where there is weeping, and wailing, and gnashing of teeth. Pray ye, therefore, that their ears may be opened unto your cries, that I may be merciful unto them, that these things may not come upon them."

As mentioned earlier, the Joseph Smith Translation of Luke 18:8 makes a strong connection between the parable of the importunate widow and unjust judge and Jesus' second coming. This verse reads, "I tell you that he [Jesus] *will come, and when he does come,* he will avenge his saints speedily" (emphasis added).

2. The parable also applies to each of us who has adversaries that are harmful to our spiritual life, whether the adversaries are other mortals, evil beings, or particular sins that continue to plague us. We, like the importunate widow, must pray always for help against these adversaries. As we do, our Heavenly Father will hear our prayers and bring us deliverance.

3. The parable speaks of every literal widow (and, by extension, every other individual) on the earth who has approached the Lord with the words, "Avenge me of mine adversary," or the like. She should follow the example of the importunate widow and continually approach God with her righteous desires and seek help from the Lord.

CHAPTER 22

The Pharisee and the Publican

Luke 18:9–14

And he spake this parable unto certain which trusted in themselves that they were righteous, and despised others:

Two men went up into the temple to pray; the one a Pharisee, and the other a publican.

The Pharisee stood and prayed thus with himself, God, I thank thee, that I am not as other men are, extortioners, unjust, adulterers, or even as this publican.

I fast twice in the week, I give tithes of all that I possess.

And the publican, standing afar off, would not lift up so much as his eyes unto heaven, but smote upon his breast, saying, God be merciful to me a sinner.

I tell you, this man went down to his house justified rather than the other: for every one that exalteth himself shall be abased; and he that humbleth himself shall be exalted.

Jesus directs this parable to a very specific group that is identified in the opening words: "And he spake this parable unto certain which trusted in themselves that they were righteous, and despised others." According to these opening words, members of this group are identified by three things: they "trusted in themselves," they thought themselves to be "righteous," and they "despised others." This parable may be likened to all of us who are prideful in trusting in ourselves rather than submitting to God and his plan of happiness, which is designed to bless us. In order to teach us not to trust ourselves and not to despise others, Jesus compares and contrasts the behavior of the publican and the Pharisee.

COMMENTARY

Luke 18:10 *Two men went up into the temple to pray;*

Jesus sets the stage for the parable by referring to the largest and most visible symbol of the Jewish faith, the temple, specifically the temple of Jerusalem. In the time of Jesus, as it is in our own day, the temple was a house of prayer, and Israelites for centuries made pilgrimages to the temple to worship and to pray. For Jesus to open the parable by telling of two men who went to pray at the temple would have piqued the curiosity of Jesus' audience; they would have wondered who the men were and why there was a story about them. This curiosity may have turned to surprise when Jesus identified one man as a Pharisee and the other as a publican.

Luke 18:10 *the one a Pharisee, and the other a publican.*

According to the historian Josephus, the Pharisees at the time of Herod numbered a little over 6,000.[1] Still, the Pharisees represented a particularly prominent Jewish religious party of the New Testament period. *Pharisee* means "separated one," and the word refers to the Pharisees' continual effort to separate themselves from the general population based on their understanding or practice of the law of Moses. The Pharisees believed that the Old Testament had significant authority in one's life and that studying the law of Moses constituted worship. They strongly emphasized rituals that pertained to purity and holiness. They also emphasized observance of the Sabbath and the payment of tithes. They were a monotheistic sect that believed in both the written and oral law, in angels and devils, and in missionary work. They were more concerned with the letter than the spirit of the law and with the exactness of the law than with worship involving the heart.

The Pharisees are frequently mentioned in the New Testament.

Paul was a Pharisee before he converted to Christianity (see Philemon 3:5). Nicodemus (see John 3:1–15) and Gamaliel (see Acts 5:34–39) were also identified as Pharisees. The Pharisees often challenged Jesus regarding his authority and his teachings, and on one occasion a group of priests and Levites affiliated with the Pharisees approached and interrogated John the Baptist (see John 1:19–28).

On several occasions Jesus spoke against the Pharisees (see Mark 7:5–13; 12:40; 23:7). Matthew 23 records one such occasion, where Jesus spoke directly to the Pharisees and the scribes and employed scathing words against them. He called them "blind guides," "serpents," and "vipers"; he four times declared, "Woe unto you, scribes and Pharisees, hypocrites!" He stated, "Ye are full of hypocrisy and iniquity." With regard to their hypocrisy, Jesus compared the Pharisees to beautiful "whited sepulchres" on the outside, with "uncleanness" and "dead men's bones" on the inside.

Publican is a word used by the King James translators, but recent English translations of the New Testament translate *publican* as "tax collector." Either the Roman government or other high-ranking officials employed the publicans (often Jews) to collect tribute money (see Matthew 17:24–27; Luke 20:22), meaning taxes or revenues. Because the publicans often worked for the hated Roman government, many Jews despised the publicans and saw them as collaborators and traitors. In addition, the act of collecting taxes was not carefully monitored, which allowed much opportunity for dishonesty, abuse, and fraud. Tax collectors were often desensitized and greedy and would appropriate the last item of value from the poor. Luke recorded that on one occasion publicans who came to John the Baptist to be baptized inquired of him, "Master, what shall we do? And he said unto them, Exact no more than that which is appointed you" (Luke 3:12–13; see also Luke 19:1–8).

The public's negative view of the publicans was so strong that publicans were often grouped with both sinners and harlots (see Matthew 9:10; 11:19; 21:31–32; Luke 7:34; 15:1).

Jesus occasionally ate meals with publicans, a practice that was roundly criticized by the Pharisees and others (see Matthew 9:10–11; Mark 2:15–16). Many publicans accepted Jesus' teachings and became his disciples: "And it came to pass, that, as Jesus sat at meat in his house, many publicans and sinners sat also together with Jesus and his disciples: for there were many, and they followed him" (Mark 2:15). Two notable publicans who followed Jesus were Matthew, who was called Levi (see Mark 2:14), and Zacchaeus, who was "chief among the publicans" (Luke 19:2), meaning that he served as an overseer of other tax collectors.

> ***Luke 18:11–12*** *The Pharisee stood and prayed thus with himself, God, I thank thee, that I am not as other men are, extortioners, unjust, adulterers, or even as this publican. I fast twice in the week, I give tithes of all that I possess.*

In the Pharisee's prayer, the Pharisee focuses on himself in a self-righteous and self-centered manner. Five times the Pharisee uses the personal pronoun "I," whereas he mentions God once only, in the prayer's opening address. He says, "I thank thee, that I am not [like the wicked]. . . . I fast . . . I give . . . of all that I possess." His words do not indicate a person who humbly approaches God in the attitude of worship, nor does he focus on love or compassion for his neighbors, friends, or humankind in general; rather, he speaks of others only in very negative terms, referencing extortioners, the unjust, adulterers, and a publican. The Pharisee contrasts others' wickedness with his own righteousness, which he expresses with the words, "I fast twice in the week, I give tithes of all that I possess."

Elder Howard W. Hunter compared this Pharisee to a prideful rabbi who is identified in the Jewish Talmud: "The boastful spirit and pride of this Pharisee is not unlike that of Rabbi Simeon ben Jochai, mentioned in the Talmud, who said: 'If there were only thirty righteous persons in the world, I and my son should make two of them; but if there were but twenty, I and my son would be of the number; and if there were but ten, I and my son would be of the number; and if there were but five, I and my son would be of the five; and if there were but two, I and my son would be those two; and if there were but one, myself should be that one' (Bereshith Rabba, s. 35, vol. 34)."[2]

Luke 18:13 *And the publican, standing afar off, would not lift up so much as his eyes unto heaven, but smote upon his breast, saying, God be merciful to me a sinner.*

Four things point to the publican's great humility as he offers his prayer. First, he stands a distance away from the temple, feeling unworthy to draw too close to the Lord's holy house. Second, recognizing his unworthiness before God, the publican does not raise his eyes to heaven. Third, by beating his breast he demonstrates his extreme anguish and deep emotion. And fourth, the publican's words indicate his humility: "God be merciful to me a sinner."

Luke 18:14 *I tell you, this man went down to his house justified rather than the other: for every one that exalteth himself shall be abased; and he that humbleth himself shall be exalted.*

Within the parable we see a series of parallels and contrasts between the Pharisee and the publican. The two are parallel in that they both are products of the social and religious scene of Palestine at the time of Christ, both are males, both pray at the temple, both stand during their prayer, and both begin their prayer by addressing God. The contrasts between the two are that the Pharisee drew closer to the temple and the publican stood "afar off." The Pharisee exhibited a prideful character by contrasting himself with the wicked, focusing on his own good works, while the humble publican beat his breast, lowered his eyes, and referred to himself as "a sinner." In the parable's final verse, Jesus presented yet another distinction between the Pharisee and the publican when he used the antonyms *exalteth* and *humbleth* and *abased* and *exalted.*

Jesus' usage of these four words is very skillful. The word *exalt* (e.g., exalteth, exalted) refers to both the Pharisee and the publican; and the synonyms *abased* and *humbleth* also refer to each of the parable's characters—*abased* pertains to the Pharisee and *humbleth* speaks of the publican. The referents of the four words, then, are as follows: "For every one that exalteth himself [the Pharisee] shall be abased [the Pharisee]; and he that humbleth himself [the publican] shall be exalted [the publican]."

At the end of the parable, the Pharisee was not justified but was abased, while the publican was both justified and exalted. Elder Howard W. Hunter explained what it meant to be justified: "Continuing the story, Jesus then said: 'I tell you, this man,' referring to the publican, the despised tax collector, 'went down to his house justified, rather than the other.' (Luke 18:14.) In other words, the Lord said he was absolved, forgiven, or vindicated."[3]

Personal Application

This parable demonstrates that not all things are really as they appear. People who observe the Pharisee's actions may assume that he is righteous because he fasts twice a week, pays tithing, and prays in the temple. They are not close enough to him to hear the words of his prayer, and they cannot look into his heart. Observers may also believe that the tax collector is not right before God because he does not station himself near the temple, he is not lifting his eyes to heaven, and he is beating his breast; besides all this, he belongs to a despicable occupational group. Only God knows who of the two characters is prideful and who is humble.

Although the parable speaks expressly of a Pharisee and a publican, the parable may be applied to each of us. The parable encourages us to ask ourselves, "Who do I resemble more, the Pharisee or the tax collector?" In fact, with reference to the Pharisee and the publican, Elder Howard W. Hunter taught that "it may be that one of them bears our name." This parable, wrote Elder Hunter, "was directed to more than just his disciples. Even though the subject matter was a Pharisee and a publican, it was not intended for Pharisees or publicans expressly, but for the benefit of the self-righteous who lack the virtues of humility and who use self-righteousness as a claim to exaltation. . . .

"Could there be greater contrast in the prayers of two men? The Pharisee stood apart because he believed he was better than other men, whom he considered as common. The publican stood apart also, but it was because he felt himself unworthy. The Pharisee thought of no one other than himself and regarded everyone else a sinner, whereas the publican thought of everyone else as righteous as compared with himself, a sinner. The Pharisee asked nothing of God, but relied upon his own self-righteousness. The publican appealed to God for mercy and forgiveness of his sins. . . .

"Humility is an attribute of godliness possessed by true Saints. It is easy to understand why a proud man fails. He is content to rely upon himself only. This is evident in those who seek social position or who push others aside to gain position in fields of business, government, education, sports, or other endeavors. Our genuine concern should be for the success of others. The proud man shuts himself off from God, and when he does he no longer lives in the light. . . .

"From the beginning of time there have been those with pride and others who have followed divine admonition to be humble. History bears record that those who have exalted themselves have been abased, but the humble have been exalted. On every busy street there are Pharisees and publicans. It may be that one of them bears our name."[4]

CHAPTER 23

The Laborers in the Vineyard

Matthew 20:1–16

For the kingdom of heaven is like unto a man that is an householder, which went out early in the morning to hire labourers into his vineyard.

And when he had agreed with the labourers for a penny a day, he sent them into his vineyard.

And he went out about the third hour, and saw others standing idle in the marketplace,

And said unto them; Go ye also into the vineyard, and whatsoever is right I will give you. And they went their way.

Again he went out about the sixth and ninth hour, and did likewise.

And about the eleventh hour he went out, and found others standing idle, and saith unto them, Why stand ye here all the day idle?

They say unto him, Because no man hath hired us. He saith unto them, Go ye also into the vineyard; and whatsoever is right, that shall ye receive.

So when even was come, the lord of the vineyard saith unto his steward, Call the labourers, and give them their hire, beginning from the last unto the first.

And when they came that were hired about the eleventh hour, they received every man a penny.

But when the first came, they supposed that they should

have received more; and they likewise received every man a penny.

And when they had received it, they murmured against the goodman of the house,

Saying, These last have wrought but one hour, and thou hast made them equal unto us, which have borne the burden and heat of the day.

But he answered one of them, and said, Friend, I do thee no wrong: didst not thou agree with me for a penny?

Take that thine is, and go thy way: I will give unto this last, even as unto thee.

Is it not lawful for me to do what I will with mine own? Is thine eye evil, because I am good?

So the last shall be first, and the first last: for many be called, but few chosen.

At one point in Jesus' ministry, a rich young ruler approached him and asked, "Good Master, what good thing shall I do, that I may have eternal life?"

Jesus responded that he should keep the commandments, but the young man was not satisfied.

Jesus then said, "If thou wilt be perfect, go and sell that thou hast, and give to the poor, and thou shalt have treasure in heaven: and come and follow me."

When the young man "went away sorrowful," Peter followed up with his own question: "Behold, we have forsaken all, and followed thee; what shall we have therefore?" In other words, Peter was saying, the rich young man was unable to meet the Lord's stringent requirements, but the apostles had done so. What reward would they receive?

Jesus responded, "Every one that hath forsaken houses, or brethren, or sisters, or father, or mother, or wife, or children, or lands, for my name's sake, shall receive an hundredfold, and shall inherit everlasting life." But then he added, "But there are many who make themselves first, that shall be last, and the last first. This he said, rebuking Peter" (Matthew 19:16, 21–22, 27, 29; JST, Mark 10:31).

That rebuke was followed by a unique story of a householder who needed laborers to work on his farm. He found them in the marketplace, as was the custom, and hired a group for the usual wage, one Roman penny (or denarius) for the day. Later, seeing he needed more help (or generously seeking to give additional laborers a chance to work), he hired more workers, which he did repeatedly at intervals throughout the day. When it was time to pay the workers, the householder did a very surprising thing: he paid everyone the same wage, regardless of how long they had worked.

Those who had worked the longest protested, but the householder was undeterred. "Is thine eye evil, because I am good?" he asked.

After telling the story, Jesus repeated the principle he had stated at the beginning: "So the last shall be first, and the first last," and then he added, "for many be called, but few chosen."

In some ways it is an enigmatic parable, one that is not readily understood. But it teaches an important truth about our Father's kingdom: our reward for service in the kingdom comes not only because of our efforts, though our work is essential, but also because of the goodness and graciousness of God, who will give each and all a full portion of blessings.

In the parable, the householder (also called the lord of the vineyard) represents our Father in Heaven. The laborers represent God's servants in the kingdom. The vineyard represents the earth; it may also represent the Church itself, since the Lord calls workers both to the world and to the Church (see D&C 39:13; 71:4; 72:2; see also D&C 33:3; 43:28).

Commentary

Matthew 20:1 *For the kingdom of heaven*

As in many of his parables, Jesus seeks to teach his listeners (in this case, his disciples) truths about the kingdom of heaven. The kingdom of heaven on earth is the Church of Jesus Christ, which helps to prepare the children of God to live in His kingdom in eternity, which is the celestial kingdom.

Matthew 20:1–2 *is like unto a man that is an householder, which went out early in the morning to hire labourers into his vineyard. And when he had agreed with the labourers for a penny a day, he sent them into his vineyard.*

It was customary for landowners to hire temporary, seasonal workers to help with the tasks on their farms. Potential laborers would gather in a central place hoping to be hired for the day. They would contract to work for one day at a time—or a part of a day. Their work lacked the security of an ongoing job, but they were anxious to obtain whatever work they could. The day's work typically lasted twelve hours, from 6:00 A.M. to 6:00 P.M., and the standard pay for such labor was one penny, or one denarius. In the story, the householder went into the marketplace at 6:00 A.M. and found a group of workers ready and willing to go to work for him. He hired them and sent them into his vineyard, probably to harvest the grapes.

It is significant that the householder went into the marketplace himself, rather than sending a trusted steward. When we are called to the Lord's work, even if by a mortal steward, the Lord speaks to us through his Spirit and confirms to us that we have indeed been called of God.

Matthew 20:3–5 *And he went out about the third hour, and saw others standing idle in the marketplace, And said unto them; Go ye also into the vineyard, and whatsoever is right I will give you. And they went their way. Again he went out about the sixth and ninth hour, and did likewise.*

The first hour of the working day was 6:00 A.M.; the third hour was 9:00 A.M.; the sixth hour was noon; and the ninth hour was 3:00 P.M. At each of those three-hour intervals the householder went into the marketplace and found others to work. Apparently as the day progressed, he was discovering that the harvesting wasn't progressing fast enough. Grapes were valued for their sugar content, and if they weren't harvested at exactly the right time the landowner would lose money.

Some may wonder why the householder didn't have more

foresight and appoint more workers in the beginning. In a literal vineyard that might be a legitimate question. But from a cosmic point of view, it is obvious that the needs of the day may change from one hour to the next, and that which is needed at one point in the harvest is quite different from that which is needed later.

The men the householder found were not "standing idle" by choice; they simply hadn't been hired by anyone that day. When they had the opportunity, they immediately took it. The householder did not promise them a specific amount of money for their work, but told them, "whatsoever is right I will give you." The denarius was not the smallest denomination of money in ancient Palestine, and the householder could have given fractions thereof to pay those who had labored only part of the day. Surely those who worked less than a full day would expect to be paid less than a full day's wage.

> ***Matthew 20:6–7*** *And about the eleventh hour he went out, and found others standing idle, and saith unto them, Why stand ye here all the day idle? They say unto him, Because no man hath hired us. He saith unto them, Go ye also into the vineyard; and whatsoever is right, that shall ye receive.*

The eleventh hour was 5:00 P.M., only an hour before it was time to stop working. The householder saw that he needed still more help to complete his harvest on time, and he went back into the marketplace at this late hour to find more workers. He saw some who had been idle all day—not because they were lazy, but "because no man hath hired us." Perhaps these workers did not show the same promise as those who had been hired by the householder and others during the day. Or perhaps they had not arrived as early as some of the others. Regardless, they had waited patiently for an opportunity to work, and the householder subsequently also hired them, making the same promise he'd made to the earlier groups: to pay them "whatsoever is right."

> ***Matthew 20:8*** *So when even was come, the lord of the vineyard saith unto his steward, Call the labourers, and give them their hire, beginning from the last unto the first.*

The evening represents the time of judgment, when all accounts will be settled. The steward who represents the lord of the vineyard is Christ. He is the one who administers the reward to each of those who work in his kingdom. It was required by the law of Moses that an employer pay a day-laborer at the end of the work day. "Thou shalt not oppress an hired servant that is poor and needy. . . . At his day thou shalt give him his hire, neither shall the sun go down upon it; for he is poor, and setteth his heart upon it: lest he cry against thee unto the Lord, and it be sin unto thee" (Deuteronomy 24:14–15; see also Leviticus 19:13).

It is unusual to pay first those who had worked the least. That sequence, however, reinforces the underlying truth of the parable: the last shall be first, and the first shall be last. In addition, paying the last first is necessary for the story. If the first had been paid first, they likely would have left immediately to go home, and they would not have known that the eleventh-hour workers were also paid a denarius.

> ***Matthew 20:9–10*** *And when they came that were hired about the eleventh hour, they received every man a penny. But when the first came, they supposed that they should have received more; and they likewise received every man a penny.*

Surely it was a surprise to everyone that those hired at the last hour were given a full day's wage. But it was even more of a surprise that those who had worked all day received exactly the same amount.

Those "hired about the eleventh hour" might include converts who find the Church late in life, a lifelong member who doesn't really catch fire until he or she is older, or someone who serves faithfully but for a much shorter time in a calling than others do. Some members are baptized at age eight, receive the priesthood at age twelve (if they are young men), graduate from seminary, serve a full-time mission, marry in the temple, and remain faithful and true all their days. Others, through initial disinterest or lack of understanding—or because they do not know about the restored gospel—may not do any of those things, perhaps receiving baptism and temple covenants only shortly before they die. If they do enter into those covenants with pure and repentant hearts, giving their all to Christ, their offering is fully accepted, and they will receive the full reward for their efforts.

From a broader point of view, those hired later might represent the Gentiles, who were called after the Jews, and after that the heathen. The word of the Lord will go forth to all nations, and as people find the Church and come to Christ they are called to join the work.

"We think here of those 'last,' the Gentiles from the east, west, north, and south (Luke 13:30); of the converted publicans and sinners; of those, a great part of whose lives has, alas! been spent somewhere else, and who have only come at a late hour into the market-place; nay, of them also whose opportunities, capacity, strength, or time have been very limited—and we thank God for the teaching of this Parable."[1]

The Lord promises his faithful ones that they will receive "all that my Father hath" (D&C 84:38). That promise is given to all; in that sense, everyone who works in the vineyard is paid the same. As the Lord said concerning those who gain exaltation: "And he makes them equal in power, and in might, and in dominion" (D&C 76:95; see D&C 88:107). When we receive everything, how can we expect more? And when we receive everything, how can we be envious if someone else receives the same? God is the judge, and he will mete out to each of us perfectly according to our works and his boundless grace.

> ***Matthew 20:11–12*** *And when they had received it, they murmured against the goodman of the house, Saying, These last have wrought but one hour, and thou hast made them equal unto us, which have borne the burden and heat of the day.*

Those who have worked all day are free in their criticism of "the goodman of the house." Their complaints are twofold: they have worked the entire day, and they worked when the conditions were hardest (they had "borne the burden and heat of the day"; in other words, they had lived and served when the trials were greatest). The landowner had given everyone equal pay, but because the work done varied so widely, what might appear to be equality was in fact gross inequality.

> ***Matthew 20:13–15*** *But he answered one of them, and said,*

Friend, I do thee no wrong: didst not thou agree with me for a penny? Take that thine is, and go thy way: I will give unto this last, even as unto thee. Is it not lawful for me to do what I will with mine own? Is thine eye evil, because I am good?

The landowner has a ready answer. He calls the spokesman of the group "Friend," which in the original Greek has a tone of reproach. That same word is used in the parable of the royal marriage feast (discussed in chapter 27), as well as in Matthew 26:50, when Jesus addressed Judas in the Garden of Gethsemane. The word is used when the person being addressed has actually been less than a friend.

The landowner does not directly respond to the charges of the disgruntled laborers. Instead, he points out that he truly fulfilled the agreement he had made first thing in the morning: to pay them a denarius for a day's work. He observes that the money is his to do with as he sees fit.

Then he asks a telling question: "Is thine eye evil, because I am good?" A clearer translation is found in the New International Version: "Are you envious because I am generous?"

This question gets to the heart of the issue. The landowner was generous to those who worked less than a day, and he was fair and ethical with those who worked all day. But those who were complaining were envious. They knew they had worked longer and harder than anyone else in the vineyard, and they wanted a better deal than they got. But their enviousness did not diminish the goodness of the landowner.

"My grace is sufficient," the Lord has said repeatedly (2 Corinthians 12:9; Ether 12:26–27; Moroni 10:32; D&C 18:31). The landowner knew that one denarius was sufficient payment to care for the daily needs of his workers and their families. He also knew that a fraction of a denarius would not be sufficient—they would go hungry if he paid them less than a full day's wage, regardless of how long they worked.

"For the kingdom of heaven is like . . ." Jesus said at the beginning of the parable. One key element of the kingdom of heaven is that in that kingdom all are equal and have all things in common. Another key element is that God, the landowner, is abundantly gracious and generous. He loves us, and demonstrates it by "*shewing mercy unto thousands of them that love me,* and keep my commandments" (Exodus 20:6; emphasis added).

Matthew 20:16 *So the last shall be first, and the first last:*

This phrase both opens (see Matthew 19:30) and closes the parable and thus becomes a vital key to its interpretation. Working the longest in the Lord's vineyard does not guarantee the greatest reward. There are many variables, and the King and Judge of all will judge perfectly. Some may work with a purer heart. Some may sacrifice more, even though they are laboring for a shorter amount of time on the clock (or calendar). Some, in the wisdom of the Lord, may have been reserved to serve at a later time.

Matthew 20:16 *for many be called, but few chosen.*

This phrase is used again in Matthew 22, in the parable of the royal marriage feast (see Matthew 22:14).

Latter-day revelation gives us a valuable insight into why some who are called may not be chosen. The Lord explained through Joseph Smith:

"Behold, verily I say unto you, that there are many who have been ordained among you, whom I have called but few of them are chosen. They who are not chosen have sinned a very grievous sin, in that they are walking in darkness at noon-day. . . . If you keep not my commandments, the love of the Father shall not continue with you, therefore you shall walk in darkness" (D&C 95:5–6, 12).

The Lord expanded that understanding in a revelation given six years later:

"Behold, there are many called, but few are chosen. And why are they not chosen?

"Because their hearts are set so much upon the things of this world, and aspire to the honors of men, that they do not learn this one lesson—That the rights of the priesthood are inseparably connected with the powers of heaven, and that the powers of heaven cannot be controlled nor handled only upon the principles of righteousness.

"That they may be conferred upon us, it is true; but when we undertake to cover our sins, or to gratify our pride, our vain ambition, or to exercise control or dominion or compulsion upon the souls of the children of men, in any degree of unrighteousness, behold, the heavens withdraw themselves. . . .

"Hence many are called, but few are chosen" (D&C 121:34–37, 40).

In other words, many are called to work in the vineyard, many are called to hold the priesthood, many are called to receive the endowment—but few are chosen to come unto the supreme blessing of exaltation. Why? Because, even though they may serve diligently, they do not develop a Christlike character, and they do not align themselves with the will and Spirit of God.

Some have noted a seeming discrepancy between this parable and the parable of the talents, which teaches that servants are rewarded based on their performance. This is the same concern that has been expressed about whether we are saved by grace or works. As these parables demonstrate, both are necessary. The parable of the laborers in the vineyard shows us that our efforts and our merits are overshadowed by the goodness of the Lord. Whatever we have to offer, it is inadequate when compared to the gifts we receive from the Lord. Even those who work all day, suffering the heat of the long midday hours, have to rely on the Lord's graciousness for their spiritual and temporal lives.

But we also are expected to be profitable servants, bringing our best efforts and all our hearts to the salvation process. We are not to view ourselves as independent of others, but are to reach out to love and strengthen and bless. And those who offer more to the Lord and his kingdom will, in the end, receive more. With his marvelous grace, the Lord rewards us according to our desires and our works.

Personal Application

In some ways, the parable of the laborers in the vineyard is quite similar to the parable of the prodigal son. In both cases, a master shows astonishing generosity to those who don't deserve it—and those who do feel they deserve it are offended because of envy and pride.

They feel that the master is being unjust to those who have worked long and hard because he is being so generous to those who have given less.

It is common to feel that we *earn* our place in God's kingdom. It is a true principle that we must work diligently to build the kingdom, to bless others, and to be personally obedient. If we fail to work, we will lose our reward.

But it is *not* true that our obedience and service qualify us for our place in the kingdom. In a strict sense, we are exalted not because of our own righteousness, but because of the righteousness of Christ (see 2 Nephi 2:3). We must rely on his grace, his merits, and his mercy, or we will be lost (see 2 Nephi 2:8; 31:19; Moroni 6:4).

We come into the kingdom and receive marvelous gifts through Christ. "My God shall supply all your need according to his riches in glory by Christ Jesus," wrote Paul (Philippians 4:19). We are His servants, and He is the Master, and He will give to each of us abundantly.

In the end, we should offer our service to God not because we expect reward (though much has been promised) but because we love him and want to bless his children. And we should realize that whatever reward is given, it truly is a gift. It is literally true that we could labor all our days for God and his kingdom and still be in his debt.

Our reward in the kingdom does not come because we have started first, or because we have "made ourselves first" (to paraphrase JST, Mark 10:31). It does not come through bargaining or some kind of equivalency between work done and pay given. "To impress upon [the apostles] still more fully and deeply that the kingdom of heaven is not a matter of mercenary calculation or exact equivalent—that there could be no bargaining with the Heavenly Householder—that before the eye of God's clearer and more penetrating judgment Gentiles might be admitted before Jews, and Publicans before Pharisees, and young converts before aged [members]—He told them the memorable Parable of the Laborers in the Vineyard. That parable, amid its other lessons, involved the truth that, while all who serve God should not be defrauded of their just and full and rich reward, there could be in heaven no murmuring, no envyings, no jealous comparison of respective merits, no base strugglings for precedency, no miserable disputings as to who had performed the maximum of service, or who had received the minimum of grace."[2]

Elder Dallin H. Oaks gave an inspired and very helpful interpretation of this parable:

"The Master's reward in the Final Judgment will not be based on how long we have labored in the vineyard. We do not obtain our heavenly reward by punching a time clock. What is essential is that our labors in the workplace of the Lord have caused us to *become* something. For some of us this requires a longer time than for others. What is important in the end is what we have become by our labors.

"Many who come in the eleventh hour have been refined and prepared by the Lord in ways other than formal employment in the vineyard. These workers are like the prepared dry mix to which it is only necessary to 'add water'—the perfecting ordinance of baptism and the gift of the Holy Ghost. With that addition—even in the eleventh hour—these workers are in the same state of development and qualified to receive the same reward as those who have labored long in the vineyard.

"This parable teaches us that we should never give up hope and loving associations with family members and friends whose fine qualities (see Moroni 7:5–14) evidence their progress toward what a loving Father would have them become. Similarly, the power of the Atonement and the principle of repentance show that we should never give up on loved ones who now seem to be making many wrong choices."[3]

One of our (the authors') grandfathers was an eleventh-hour laborer. He was baptized in the Church as a boy, but, following the example of his own less-active (and antagonistic) father, he fell away from the Church as a youth. He met and married a Latter-day Saint woman, but he continued to have no interest in the Church. They had two sons, both of whom were baptized by another man. Those sons advanced in the priesthood, eventually becoming elders. Grandpa was unable to ordain them and didn't seem to care.

Our father grew up and was sealed to his sweetheart in the temple. Grandpa wasn't present. Grandchildren were born, blessed, baptized. Grandpa didn't come. Our dad was made a bishop. Grandpa chose not to attend the meeting where Dad was sustained.

Grandpa Parry was a man of deep integrity. He was a hard and honest worker. Those who knew him had the highest regard for him. He was a caring father and grandfather. But he had no interest in the Church.

Then, late in his life, his heart was unexpectedly touched. He began to attend Church. When he was in his late sixties he was ordained an elder—by his son! He qualified for a temple recommend and took his lifelong sweetheart to the temple. Our father, then in his forties, had the privilege of kneeling at the altar with his parents and being sealed to them.

Grandpa Parry entered the vineyard at the eleventh hour, but he labored with all his might for the rest of his life. How grateful we are for the Lord's goodness, to give full wages to his eleventh-hour workers!

CHAPTER 24

The Pounds

Luke 19:12–27

He said therefore, A certain nobleman went into a far country to receive for himself a kingdom, and to return.

And he called his ten servants, and delivered them ten pounds, and said unto them, Occupy till I come.

But his citizens hated him, and sent a message after him, saying, We will not have this man to reign over us.

And it came to pass, that when he was returned, having received the kingdom, then he commanded these servants to be called unto him, to whom he had given the money, that he might know how much every man had gained by trading.

Then came the first, saying, Lord, thy pound hath gained ten pounds.

And he said unto him, Well, thou good servant: because thou hast been faithful in a very little, have thou authority over ten cities.

And the second came, saying, Lord, thy pound hath gained five pounds.

And he said likewise to him, Be thou also over five cities.

And another came, saying, Lord, behold, here is thy pound, which I have kept laid up in a napkin:

For I feared thee, because thou art an austere man: thou takest up that thou layedst not down, and reapest that thou didst not sow.

And he saith unto him, Out of thine own mouth will I judge thee, thou wicked servant. Thou knewest that I was an austere man, taking up that I laid not down, and reaping that I did not sow:

Wherefore then gavest not thou my money into the bank, that at my coming I might have required mine own with usury?

And he said unto them that stood by, Take from him the pound, and give it to him that hath ten pounds.

(And they said unto him, Lord, he hath ten pounds.)

For I say unto you, That unto every one which hath shall be given; and from him that hath not, even that he hath shall be taken away from him.

But those mine enemies, which would not that I should reign over them, bring hither, and slay them before me.

Jesus gave this parable in response to those who were anticipating that he would immediately establish the kingdom of God, serve as its king, and take over the present ruling power, the great Roman Empire. During this time period there was much turmoil in Palestine, and the Romans had already dealt with a number of uprisings and revolts.[1] Perhaps Jesus' hearers were anticipating Jesus to lead an insurrection, eventually become king, and bring forth a messianic rule. The verse that introduces the parable of the pounds also provides the setting: "And as they heard these things, he added and spake a parable, because he was nigh to Jerusalem, and because they thought that the kingdom of God should immediately appear" (Luke 19:11). Although Jesus would not at that time destroy the world's kingdoms, the parable does contain a kingdom of God theme. The three-time use of "kingdom" and two-time reference to "reign" alert the reader to this theme.

Jesus also delivered this parable to tell his disciples what they should be doing between his departure from mortality and his Second Coming. The parable certainly had direct application to Jesus' contemporaries, but it also applies to those of us in mortality who now await his coming. As Elder Bruce R. McConkie wrote, "Jesus was enroute to Jerusalem for the last time. In about ten days he would die upon the cross, and to the Jews generally it would appear that he had failed to set up the promise of the Messianic kingdom. To correct the false concept that 'the kingdom of God'—meaning the political kingdom, the kingdom which should rule all nations with King Messiah at its head, the millennial kingdom—'should immediately appear,' Jesus gave the Parable of the Pounds."[2]

Commentary

Luke 19:12 *He said therefore, A certain nobleman went into a far country to receive for himself a kingdom, and to return.*

In this parable, Jesus Christ referred to himself as "a certain nobleman" (or, as some modern English translations of the Bible read, "a man of noble birth") and "Lord." This nobleman traveled to a country that was far away in order to receive a kingdom. To receive a kingdom indicates that he would be made king through his coronation and enthronement. For Jesus the "far country" was none other than heaven, where Jesus went after his resurrection.

Many of Jesus' listeners may have misunderstood the parable, believing that the faraway country was Rome itself, because "in the world of the day, one went to Rome to gain the status of king before taking up one's rule. This is what Herod the Great had done (Josephus, *War* 1.282–85; *Ant.* 14.374–89) and it is what Archelaus had done as well (*War* 2.14–100; *Ant.* 17.224–340)."[3] What's more, Jesus' hearers may have believed that the parable spoke of Archelaus, Herod the Great's son, who traveled to see Augustus in Rome, or that the parable referred to any other noblemen who traveled to seek political support with the hopes of receiving a kingdom.

Nevertheless, Jesus would receive his kingdom in heaven and will remain there until his second coming. The parable provides four separate words that refer to his coming—*return, come, returned,* and *coming*. These four are dispersed throughout the parable: "to return" (Luke 19:12), "occupy till I come" (Luke 19:13), "when he was returned" (Luke 19:15), and "at my coming" (Luke 19:23). These references to Jesus' return would serve the purpose of giving confidence to his disciples that he would indeed come again to his people, after he had been enthroned in heaven. This confidence would be needful to those who would wonder if the Lord's plan had been changed or destroyed through the crucifixion of Christ.

> ***Luke 19:13*** *And he called his ten servants, and delivered them ten pounds, and said unto them, Occupy till I come.*

Several of Jesus' parables speak of money, treasure, wealthy people, business affairs, employers and employees, and masters and their stewards. See, for example, the parables of the hidden treasure (Matthew 13:44), the pearl of great price (Matthew 13:45–46), the foolish rich man (Luke 12:16–21), Lazarus and the rich man (Luke 16:19–31), the talents (Matthew 25:14–30), the unprofitable servants (Luke 17:7–10), the lost coin (Luke 15:8–10), and the unrighteous steward (Luke 16:1–18). His hearers, regardless of the occupational groups to which they belonged (shepherds, farmers, innkeepers, merchants, bakers, shop owners, and so forth) would have identified with these stories.

In Jesus' world were various banking institutions, commercialism, merchants and merchandising, trading and bartering systems, and coins and currency. There were investors, loans, and interest on loans. Although the parable speaks explicitly of "pounds," "money" (or Greek, *silver*), "trading," "bank," and "usury" (interest on money), these words symbolically refer to one's stewardship, spiritual gifts, callings, and talents.

In the parable, the nobleman entrusted a pound to each of his ten servants, giving a total of ten pounds. According to John Nolland, a pound "was worth two hundred denarii, and a denarius was a day laborer's wage."[4] To state it differently, a pound was worth a little more than six month's work for a common laborer at the time of Jesus Christ.

During his absence, Jesus entrusted his spiritual affairs in the mortal world to his servants and gave them stewardships over his possessions until his Second Coming. Jesus' servants are his apostles and his disciples, specifically those who have stewardships and callings in the Church.[5] Jesus delivers pounds, or silver, to his disciples. This silver signifies their responsibilities, stewardships, and callings in the earthly kingdom. During the King's absence, all of God's servants are to represent their master as agents in the business of his spiritual kingdom. They are to magnify, bless, testify, and build God's kingdom through love and hard work. They are to go beyond any minimal requirements and "should be anxiously engaged in a good cause, and do many things of their own free will, and bring to pass much righteousness; For the power is in them, wherein they are agents unto themselves. And inasmuch as men do good they shall in nowise lose their reward" (D&C 58:27–28).

Ten is emphasized several times in the parable. There are ten servants, ten pounds (mentioned three times), and ten cities. *Ten,* which represents wholeness or "completeness,"[6] is used to signify the entirety of the Lord's disciples (ten servants), their appointed stewardship (ten pounds), and their reward (ten cities). *Ten* is also used as a symbolic number in the parables of the lost coin (Luke 15:8–10) and the ten virgins (Matthew 25:1–13).

"Occupy" and "occupieth," as used in this parable, have the sense of "to employ; to busy one's self. Every man should be occupied, or should occupy himself, in some useful labor."[7] The ten servants are to remain busy occupying themselves in useful labor until he returns to receive their stewardship reports.

***Luke 19:14** But his citizens hated him, and sent a message after him, saying, We will not have this man to reign over us.*

The citizens who hated the nobleman in the parable represent all people, Jew or Gentile, who refuse and reject Jesus and his kingship. So emphatic is their rejection that they send a message stating, "We will not have this man to reign over us." The citizens are the Lord's enemies, so identified in Luke 19:27. Inasmuch as they refused to accept Jesus as their king, at the great Judgment they will be slain in the presence of the king. The citizens stand in contrast to the ten servants who accepted Jesus and with whom Jesus left the ten pounds.

***Luke 19:15** And it came to pass, that when he was returned, having received the kingdom,*

"And it came to pass" typically indicates the passage of time. In this verse the phrase indicates that much time had passed between the nobleman's journey to the far country to receive his kingdom and his return. Jesus' return refers to his Second Coming, when he will take an accounting of his servants' stewardships and when those who reject him and his kingship will be slain.

> ***Luke 19:15*** *then he commanded these servants to be called unto him, to whom he had given the money, that he might know how much every man had gained by trading.*

In addition to the nobleman, or the king who had received a kingdom, the parable classifies five groups of people:

1. The servant who multiplied one pound into ten.
2. The servant who multiplied one pound into five.
3. The servant who kept the pound in the napkin.
4. Those who "stood by."
5. The citizens who hated the Lord.

The first three groups are called before the king to give an accounting of their stewardships. Group four, who are standing by, are instructed to "take from him the pound." To this they responded, "Lord, he hath ten pounds." By implication, it seems that this group is the same that fulfill the Lord's command to bring the Lord's enemies to him and slay them. The fifth group is judged for not accepting the king's authority to rule. The king's judgment is plainly identified when he tells the third servant, "Out of thine own mouth will I *judge* thee" (Luke 19:22; emphasis added). This judgment, or accounting, will take place at the Second Coming.

> ***Luke 19:16–19*** *Then came the first, saying, Lord, thy pound hath gained ten pounds. And he said unto him, Well, thou good servant: because thou hast been faithful in a very little, have thou authority over ten cities. And the second came, saying, Lord, thy pound hath gained five pounds. And he said likewise to him, Be thou also over five cities.*

The Lord renders judgment on four of the five groups of people. First, to the servant who multiplied one pound into ten, the Lord gave "authority over ten cities," because he had been "faithful in a very little." "Well, thou good servant" is an abbreviated way of saying, "Well done, thou good and faithful servant," an expression found in the parable of the talents (see Matthew 25:21, 23). The ten cities belong to the Lord's new kingdom, with *ten* being a symbol of completeness. The servant will receive a full and complete reward in the kingdom. This reward of having authority over ten cities looks to the eternities rather than to the immediate future.

Second, the Lord renders judgment to the servant who multiplied one pound into five by promising him, "Be thou also over five cities." Although the Lord did not declare to this servant, "Well, thou good servant," the parable implies it. In the parable of the talents, a parable that closely parallels the parable of the pounds, Jesus commends both servants who multiply their talents by five and also by two by saying, "Well done, thou good and faithful servant" (Matthew 25:21, 23).

> ***Luke 19:20–26*** *And another came, saying, Lord, behold, here is thy pound, which I have kept laid up in a napkin: For I feared thee, because thou art an austere man: thou takest up that thou layedst not down, and reapest that thou didst not sow. And he saith unto him, Out of thine own mouth will I judge thee, thou wicked servant. Thou knewest that I was an austere man, taking up that I laid not down, and reaping that I did not sow: Wherefore then gavest not thou my money into the bank, that at my coming I might have required mine own with usury? And he said unto them that stood by, Take from him the pound, and give it to him that hath ten pounds. (And they said unto him, Lord, he hath ten pounds.) For I say unto you, That unto every one which hath shall be given; and from him that hath not, even that he hath shall be taken away from him.*

Next, the Lord judges the third servant. This servant had stored the Lord's pound in a piece of cloth or linen for the entire duration of the Lord's journey to and from the far country. The servant explains his reasoning: "For I feared thee, because thou art an austere man: thou takest up that thou layedst not down, and reapest that thou didst not sow." The NIV renders these last words as, "You take out what you did not put in and reap what you did not sow."

After listening to the third servant's excuses, the Lord responds with "Thou wicked servant" and asks two questions, one after the other: "You knew, did you, that I am a hard man, taking out what I did not put in, and reaping what I did not sow? Why then didn't you put my money on deposit, so that when I came back, I could have collected it with interest?" (NIV, Luke 19:22–23).

The Lord then commands the others to take the pound from this wicked servant and to give it to the servant who had ten pounds. Those who receive this command are surprised with this action and they exclaim, "Lord, he hath ten pounds." To this the Lord teaches a significant principle: "Unto every one who occupieth, shall be given; and from him who occupieth not, even that he hath received shall be taken away from him" (JST, Luke 19:25; see Matthew 13:12; 25:29; Mark 4:24–25; Luke 8:18). The verb "occupieth" in this verse (as translated by Joseph Smith) recalls the imperative "occupy" that is found in the beginning of the parable, which reads: "And he called his ten servants, and delivered them ten pounds, and said unto them, Occupy till I come" (Luke 19:13). Jesus teaches his disciples that they are to make good use of their time and their stewardships until he returns.

Luke 19:27 *But those mine enemies, which would not that I should reign over them, bring hither, and slay them before me.*

The king's final judgment is delivered to the citizens who hated him and sent him this message: "We will not have this man to reign over us" (Luke 19:14). The king commands those who do follow him to bring these citizens to him and kill them. "Slay them before me," he says.

This parable had immediate application to those who did not accept Jesus as their king. Many such were eventually slain or scattered during the rebellions and wars that followed Jesus' death and the temple's destruction.

But the parable has a greater application to when Jesus will return at his second coming and judge the world and slay the wicked, or those who do not accept him and his gospel. Paul wrote of such persons: "The Lord Jesus shall be revealed from heaven with his mighty angels, in flaming fire taking vengeance on them that know not God, and that obey not the gospel of our Lord Jesus Christ: who shall be punished with everlasting destruction from the presence of the Lord, and from the glory of his power" (2 Thessalonians 1:7–9).

Personal Application

The parable of the pounds applies to each of us who has received stewardships from the "certain nobleman" who is none other than Jesus Christ. He has given each of us, his servants, a pound, symbolizing the stewardships and gifts he grants to us. During his absence we are required to use this pound wisely in building up the nobleman's kingdom. We are not to hide it in a piece of cloth out of our fear that the nobleman is an austere man who will punish us if we fail in our stewardship.

The following story, related by Elder Thomas S. Monson, tells of a man who received a stewardship (a pound) and who faithfully employed it. We can visualize that the nobleman would say to this man, "Well [done], thou good servant: because thou hast been faithful in a very little, have thou authority over ten cities."

Said President Monson: "Years ago, President Spencer W. Kimball shared . . . an experience he had in the appointment of a patriarch for the Shreveport Louisiana Stake of the Church." President Kimball had diligently sought to know who he should call as a patriarch, but none of the proposed candidates seemed quite right.

That evening, as President Kimball sat in one of the sessions of conference, he suddenly asked the stake president "to identify a particular man seated perhaps two-thirds of the way back from the front of the chapel. The stake president replied that the individual was James Womack, whereupon President Kimball said, 'He is the man the Lord has selected to be your stake patriarch. Please have him meet with me in the high council room following the meeting.'"

The stake president was totally taken aback. James Womack didn't seem to be a reasonable candidate for the job of patriarch. While in combat during World War II, he had "lost both hands and one arm, as well as most of his eyesight and part of his hearing." Despite his disabilities, he had been able to earn a law degree, finishing third in his class. But how could a man without hands serve as patriarch?

"That evening as President Kimball met with brother Womack and informed him that the Lord had designated him to be the patriarch, there was a protracted silence in the room. Then Brother Womack said, 'Brother Kimball, it is my understanding that a patriarch is to place his hands on the head of the person he blesses. As you can see, I have no hands to place on the head of anyone.'

"Brother Kimball, in his kind and patient manner, invited Brother Womack to make his way to the back of the chair on which Brother Kimball was seated. He then said, 'Now, Brother Womack, lean forward and see if the stumps of your arms will reach the top of my head.' To Brother Womack's joy, they touched Brother Kimball, and the exclamation came forth, 'I can reach you! I can reach you!'

"'Of course you can reach me,' responded Brother Kimball. 'And if you can reach me, you can reach any whom you bless. I will be the shortest person you will ever have seated before you.'

"President Kimball reported to us that when the name of James Womack was presented to the stake conference, 'the hands of the members shot heavenward in an enthusiastic vote of approval.'"[8]

We may have fears or concerns about our ability to put our "pounds" to good use. But if we will trust in the Lord, he will enable us to serve him well, so that when he returns we can hear the words spoken to us personally: "Well [done], thou good servant: because thou hast been faithful in a very little, have thou authority over [much]."

CHAPTER 25

The Two Sons

Matthew 21:28–32

But what think ye? A certain man had two sons; and he came to the first, and said, Son, go work to day in my vineyard.

He answered and said, I will not: but afterward he repented, and went.

And he came to the second, and said likewise. And he answered and said, I go, sir: and went not.

Whether of them twain did the will of his father? They say unto him, The first. Jesus saith unto them, Verily I say unto you, That the publicans and the harlots go into the kingdom of God before you.

For John came unto you in the way of righteousness, and ye believed him not: but the publicans and the harlots believed him: and ye, when ye had seen it, repented not afterward, that ye might believe him.

When Jesus was teaching in the temple during the last week of his mortal ministry, the chief priests and the elders approached him and asked, "By what authority doest thou these things? and who gave thee this authority?"

Rather than answer them directly, Jesus responded with a question of his own: "I also will ask you one thing," he said, "which if ye tell me, I in like wise will tell you by what authority I do these things. The baptism of John, whence was it? from heaven, or of men?"

That was a most difficult question for these religious leaders, and Jesus knew it. Before they answered him, "They reasoned with themselves, saying, If we shall say, From heaven; he will say unto us, Why did ye not then believe him? But if we shall say, Of men; we fear the people; for all hold John as a prophet."

Finally, afraid to answer the question Jesus asked, they said, "We cannot tell."

Then Jesus said, "Neither tell I you by what authority I do these things" (Matthew 21:23–27).

But he did not let the teaching opportunity end there. Instead, he continued the discussion by telling them the parable of the two sons. A father asked each of his sons in turn to work in his vineyard. One refused but then repented and went. The other agreed to go but then went back on his word.

Which of the sons, Jesus asked, did their father's will? The answer was inescapable, and they said, "The first."

Jesus then made this stunning statement: "Verily I say unto you, That the publicans and the harlots go into the kingdom of God before you." How could that be? Because the publicans and harlots he was speaking of had accepted Christ and repented of their sins, however gross, while the chief priests and elders had not.

Jesus, continuing, said, "For John came unto you in the way of righteousness, and ye believed him not: but the publicans and the harlots believed him: and ye, when ye had seen it, repented not afterward, that ye might believe him" (Matthew 21:32).

The Joseph Smith Translation of this verse reads as follows: "For John came unto you in the way of righteousness, and bore record of me, and ye believed him not; but the publicans and the harlots believed him; and ye, afterward, when ye had seen me, repented not, that ye might believe him." Joseph Smith then added the following: "For he that believed not John concerning me, cannot believe me, except he first repent. And except ye repent, the preaching of John shall condemn you in the day of judgment."

Commentary

Matthew 21:28–29 *But what think ye? A certain man had two sons; and he came to the first, and said, Son, go work to day in my vineyard. He answered and said, I will not: but afterward he repented, and went.*

Our Heavenly Father has many kinds of children, including the following: (1) Those who say they will do his work and then follow through, enduring to the end; (2) those who say they have no interest in God or his work, and continue in that attitude throughout this mortal life; (3) those who say they will not serve God but then repent; and (4) those who say they will serve God faithfully but then refuse to do what he actually asks them to do. It is easy to say which of the first two did the will of the Father. The second two require a bit more thought.

This parable is about those last two categories of God's children.

The first son was like the publicans and sinners who repented when they heard the preaching of the word. The Pharisees were repeatedly scandalized that Jesus went into the homes of the publicans and sinners and ate with them (see, for example, Matthew 9:10–11). The reason Jesus did so, of course, was that he knew that some of them were like the son who initially chose a course contrary to God's will but then repented.

The vineyard in this parable, as in other places, represents God's kingdom—his Church and, ultimately, the field of the world.

Matthew 21:30 *And he came to the second, and said likewise. And he answered and said, I go, sir: and went not.*

The chief priests, elders, and Pharisees made a great show of righteousness. They prayed aloud on the street; they publicly paid much in offerings to the poor; they wore fine religious robes; they knew all the details of the law of Moses and observed them diligently. As Jesus said of them, "All their works they do for to be seen of men: they make broad their phylacteries, and enlarge the borders of their garments, And love the uppermost rooms at feasts, and the chief seats in the synagogues, And greetings in the markets, and to be called of men, Rabbi, Rabbi" (Matthew 23:5–7).

But they missed the true purpose of the law of Moses, which was to bring them to Christ. When John the Baptist preached of the coming Messiah, they rejected him. When Jesus himself came, they would not receive him. The scribes and Pharisees and their ilk honored God with their mouths, but their hearts were far from him (see Isaiah 29:13).

Matthew 21:31 *Whether of them twain did the will of his father? They say unto him, The first.*

The second son in this parable was more respectful than his brother. The first son did not address his father as "father" or "sir," but simply refused the request. He didn't even give any reasons or make excuses. The second son was polite, calling his father "sir," and readily agreeing to do what his father asked. But in the end he broke his promise, while the first son thought better of his disobedience, repented, and went into the vineyard as requested.

Personal Application

Later, in Jesus' discourse at the temple (apparently given the same day as when he taught the parable of the two sons), he castigated the scribes and Pharisees with particularly harsh language. He emphasized that they *seemed* to be like the son who said he was doing the Father's will, but in actuality they were nothing less than hypocrites and liars:

"Woe unto you, scribes and Pharisees, hypocrites! for ye shut up the kingdom of heaven against men: for ye neither go in yourselves, neither suffer ye them that are entering to go in.

"Woe unto you, scribes and Pharisees, hypocrites! for ye devour widows' houses, and for a pretence make long prayer: therefore ye shall receive the greater damnation. . . .

"Woe unto you, scribes and Pharisees, hypocrites! for ye pay tithe of mint and anise and cummin, and have omitted the weightier matters of the law, judgment, mercy, and faith: these ought ye to have done, and not to leave the other undone. . . .

"Woe unto you, scribes and Pharisees, hypocrites! for ye make clean the outside of the cup and of the platter, but within they are full of extortion and excess. . . .

"Woe unto you, scribes and Pharisees, hypocrites! for ye are like unto whited sepulchres, which indeed appear beautiful outward, but are within full of dead men's bones, and of all uncleanness.

"Even so ye also outwardly appear righteous unto men, but within ye are full of hypocrisy and iniquity. . . .

"Ye serpents, ye generation of vipers, how can ye escape the damnation of hell?" (Matthew 23:13–14, 23, 25–28, 33).

The repentant "publicans and harlots" will be admitted into God's kingdom before those who are outwardly religious but unrepentant. When John the Baptist preached repentance and the coming kingdom of God, "Then came also publicans to be baptized, and said unto him, Master, what shall we do?" (Luke 3:12). By contrast, "the Pharisees and lawyers rejected the counsel of God against themselves, being not baptized of him" (Luke 7:30).

The comparison is clear: those who were viewed by society as sinners repented and were baptized, and thereby did the will of the Father. Those who were viewed by society as righteous would not recognize their true sin and thereby remained estranged from God.

Certainly we have both kinds of people in the world today—those obviously in need of repentance who do indeed turn and come unto Christ, and those who seem to be righteous but hold darkness within.

James, the brother of Jesus, summed up our responsibility when he said, "Be ye doers of the word, and not hearers only, deceiving your own selves" (James 1:22). And Jesus himself said, "Ye are my friends, if ye do whatsoever I command you" (John 15:14). We are doers when we keep the promises we made at baptism, when we fulfill our responsibilities as home teachers or visiting teachers, when we accept and faithfully fulfill other callings, when we care for the poor, when we earnestly strive to obey all the Lord asks us to do.

Each of us can choose which kind of son or daughter we will be. If we have in one way or another chosen contrary to God's will in our lives (and who has not, in small or large things?), we can repent and begin to do what the Lord requires of us. If we do, we will be like the son who, in the end, made the better choice.

CHAPTER 26

The Wicked Husbandmen

Matthew 21:33–41

Hear another parable: There was a certain householder, which planted a vineyard, and hedged it round about, and digged a winepress in it, and built a tower, and let it out to husbandmen, and went into a far country:

And when the time of the fruit drew near, he sent his servants to the husbandmen, that they might receive the fruits of it.

And the husbandmen took his servants, and beat one, and killed another, and stoned another.

Again, he sent other servants more than the first: and they did unto them likewise.

But last of all he sent unto them his son, saying, They will reverence my son.

But when the husbandmen saw the son, they said among themselves, This is the heir; come, let us kill him, and let us seize on his inheritance.

And they caught him, and cast him out of the vineyard, and slew him.

When the lord therefore of the vineyard cometh, what will he do unto those husbandmen?

They say unto him, He will miserably destroy those wicked men, and will let out his vineyard unto other husbandmen, which shall render him the fruits in their seasons.

The setting for this parable was the temple of Jerusalem, where Jesus was teaching an organized gathering or group during the last week of his life. Matthew records that "when he was come into the temple, the chief priests and the elders of the people came unto him as he was teaching" (Matthew 21:23). The elders likely included Pharisees, who were also present in this setting (see Matthew 21:45). The temple had a number of chief priests, who supervised the administration of the temple's affairs. Jewish sources inform us that these included the anointed high priest (the presiding official), the deputy high priest (second in rank to the anointed high priest), the auditors (examiners of the temple's financial records), treasurers (administrators of the donations and monies), directors of the weekly courses (overseers of the temple's weekly sacrifices), and directors of the daily courses (overseers of the ordinary priests' temple work).[1] All of these officers and authorities were high priests in the Aaronic Priesthood. Any number of these religious authorities may have approached Jesus as he taught in the temple. Matthew groups them together by calling them "chief priests."

These chief priests and Pharisees went to Jesus and asked, "By what authority doest thou these things? and who gave thee this authority?" (Matthew 21:23). In response to these questions, Jesus gave the parables of the two sons (Matthew 21:28–32) and the wicked husbandmen (Matthew 21:33–41). The present parable, then, addresses Jesus' authority over his Father's vineyard. It also prophesies of Jesus' rejection by the Jewish people and of his subsequent death.

The principal characters and symbols of the parable are as follows: The householder (or landowner) represents God, and his vineyard is the house of Israel. The wicked husbandmen, or the vineyard's tenants, are the leaders of Israel in Jesus' day and probably at other time periods as well. The servants are God's messengers and prophets, and the beloved son is Jesus Christ. The landowner's punishment of the wicked husbandmen represents the destruction of many belonging to the house of Israel, through wars and through their being dispersed among the nations. The nation that replaces the Jewish nation as the vineyard's tenants refers to the Gentiles.

COMMENTARY

Matthew 21:33 *Hear another parable: There was a certain householder, which planted a vineyard, and hedged it round about, and digged a winepress in it, and built a tower,*

In this parable the householder refers to God, the owner of the vineyard, who performed many tasks in its behalf (see Isaiah 5:1–7).[2] First, he planted it, an effort that would have been preceded by removing large stones, leveling terraces, and otherwise preparing the ground. He then built a hedge consisting of stones or thorny bushes to deter thieves and animals. Next, he dug a winepress, perhaps out of solid rock. His creation of the winepress demonstrated that he anticipated a successful harvest of mature grapes that could be pressed into grape juice.

Inasmuch as the winepress was installed by the householder, rather than the tenants, it may be that the winepress is symbolic of the Atonement. The householder, or God, prepared the winepress knowing that his Beloved Son, during mortality, would trod the winepress as he performed the Atonement. The "blood of atonement is symbolized by the image of a man who treads red grapes in a winepress, staining his clothing with the juice. But, with Christ, not only his hem but his whole garment will be stained. His whole being was engaged in the work of atonement. He trod the winepress alone because he alone could and did perform the Atonement, kneeling alone in the Garden of Gethsemane, hanging alone on the cross. 'I . . . have trodden the winepress alone, even the winepress of the fierceness of the wrath of Almighty God' (D&C 76:107; 88:106)."[3]

The parable's winepress (Matthew 21:33) is directly associated with the death of the beloved son, a topic that is introduced later in the parable (see Matthew 21:37–39). The "winepress" hints at Jesus' atoning work in Gethsemane, while the death of the son in the parable refers to the cross.

Last of all, the householder built a tower that would have served multiple purposes. During the summer months and harvest season, according to custom, the householder may have slept in the tower, where he would have been protected from the elements, animals and insects, and the summer heat. The tower would also have served as a watchtower, from which he or his servants could protect the crops from predators or thieves.

Comparing the house of Israel to a vineyard would have been familiar to many of Jesus' listeners. Isaiah spoke of the same vineyard when he said, "For the vineyard of the Lord of hosts is the house of Israel, and the men of Judah his pleasant plant" (Isaiah 5:7; see also Isaiah 3:14; Jeremiah 12:10). In Jeremiah the Lord reminded his covenant people that "I had planted thee a noble vine" (Jeremiah 2:21). And the psalmist recalled the Lord bringing Israel out of Egypt when he declared to the Lord, "Thou hast brought a vine out of Egypt: thou hast cast out the heathen, and planted it" (Psalm 80:8).

> ***Matthew 21:33–34*** *and let it out to husbandmen, and went into a far country: And when the time of the fruit drew near, he sent his servants to the husbandmen, that they might receive the fruits of it.*

Husbandman is an archaic word for a tiller of the soil or a farmer, and *husbandry* is another word for farming. In this parable the landowner leased his vineyard out to farmers as he journeyed to a faraway land. It was a common practice in the ancient world, as it is in our own day, for absentee landowners to rent or lease out their properties to others. King Solomon, for example, owned a vineyard in Baal Hamon and leased it out to tenants, each of whom was to pay him a thousand shekels of silver from the harvested produce (see Song of Solomon 8:11).

Though the landowner was in a faraway country, he continued to oversee the affairs of his vineyard. Accordingly, he sent his servants at harvest time to obtain the payment for the lease. In this case, the payment was a portion or percentage of the harvested grapes. The fruit or the harvested grapes refer to Israel's works or the fulfillment of their responsibilities to God.

> ***Matthew 21:35–36*** *And the husbandmen took his servants, and beat one, and killed another, and stoned another. Again,*

he sent other servants more than the first: and they did unto them likewise.

To this point, the parable is a positive story about a householder who plants and cares for his vineyard and then leases it out to farmers. But at the time of harvest things take a bloody, violent, and unexpected turn. When the householder sends his servants to collect his portion of the fruits, which fruits represent his payment for the lease, the tenants beat, kill, and stone the servants. When he hears what happened, the householder sends even more servants, but these too are beaten or murdered.

The servants are God's prophets, whom God (i.e., the landowner) sent to his covenant people. That many of the prophets were killed is a historical reality and is recorded in scripture. Elijah related, "For the children of Israel have forsaken thy covenant, thrown down thine altars, and slain thy prophets with the sword; and I, even I only, am left; and they seek my life, to take it away" (1 Kings 19:10; see also 1 Kings 18:13). The author of Chronicles, too, wrote of the persecution of the prophets: "And the Lord God of their fathers sent to them by his messengers, rising up betimes, and sending; because he had compassion on his people, and on his dwelling place: But they mocked the messengers of God, and despised his words, and misused his prophets, until the wrath of the Lord arose against his people, till there was no remedy" (2 Chronicles 36:15–16).

Near the end of his ministry, Jesus lamented the killing of the prophets: "O Jerusalem, Jerusalem, thou that killest the prophets, and stonest them which are sent unto thee, how often would I have gathered thy children together, even as a hen gathereth her chickens under her wings, and ye would not!" (Matthew 23:37). When Paul wrote to the Hebrews, he also spoke of the persecution and destruction of God's prophets and messengers: "And others had trial of cruel mockings and scourgings, yea, moreover of bonds and imprisonment: They were stoned, they were sawn asunder, were tempted, were slain with the sword: they wandered about in sheepskins and goatskins; being destitute, afflicted, tormented" (Hebrews 11:36–37).

Matthew 21:37 *But last of all he sent unto them his son, saying, They will reverence my son.*

The householder commissioned two groups of servants to collect the harvest's fruits, but they were beaten, stoned, or killed by those who leased the vineyard. Finally the householder sent his own son to collect the money. "They will reverence my son," he said, meaning, "They will certainly pay respect to my own son." Mark's and Luke's accounts of the parable refer to the householder's son as "wellbeloved" and "beloved son." Mark writes, "Having yet therefore one son, his wellbeloved, he sent him also last unto them, saying, They will reverence my son" (Mark 12:6). And according to Luke, "Then said the lord of the vineyard, What shall I do? I will send my beloved son: it may be they will reverence him when they see him" (Luke 20:13).

The vineyard owner's son signifies Jesus Christ, who is God's "beloved son." God called Jesus his "beloved son" at Jesus' baptism: "And lo a voice from heaven, saying, This is my beloved Son, in whom I am well pleased" (Matthew 3:17). God also spoke from heaven at the Transfiguration and referred to Jesus as "my beloved Son": "And behold a voice out of the cloud, which said, This is my beloved Son, in whom I am well pleased; hear ye him" (Matthew 17:5).

The parable's hearers would have been shocked to hear of the husbandmen's abuse and murder of the servants. And they probably wondered why the landowner would send his own son to them, his beloved son, after hearing about the servants' mistreatment. Verse 37 provides the reason why God sent his beloved son to the vineyard—"They will reverence my son," he said.

Matthew 21:38–39 *But when the husbandmen saw the son, they said among themselves, This is the heir; come, let us kill him, and let us seize on his inheritance. And they caught him, and cast him out of the vineyard, and slew him.*

Upon seeing the landowner's son, the wicked tenants immediately concoct a plan among themselves that includes both the beloved son's death and a sizeable profit for themselves, the son's inheritance. The fact that the son was the landowner's heir may indicate one of the following: (a) the son was the landowner's only son, and for this reason he was the father's heir; or (b) the son was the firstborn son, and for this reason he was to receive a double portion of the inheritance. Either of these two possibilities fits the symbolism of the story, where Jesus Christ is the landowner's beloved son. Jesus Christ is the Only Begotten Son as well as the Firstborn Son.

After capturing the landowner's son, the wicked tenants "cast him out of the vineyard" and then kill him. The parable's description of the tenants' behavior fits the true-life scene of Jesus' crucifixion, which took place outside of the city of Jerusalem. As Paul wrote, "Wherefore Jesus also, that he might sanctify the people with his own blood, suffered without the gate" (Hebrews 13:12), meaning outside of the city's gate. John's testimony, too, speaks of Jesus' crucifixion outside of the city: "And Pilate wrote a title, and put it on the cross. And the writing was, JESUS OF NAZARETH THE KING OF THE JEWS. This title then read many of the Jews: for the place where Jesus was crucified was nigh to the city: and it was written in Hebrew, and Greek, and Latin" (John 19:19–20).

There is yet another point of comparison between the parable and Jesus' death. One biblical scholar has pointed out that the wording of the sentence "And they caught him, and cast him out of the vineyard, and slew him" suggests that the beloved son was not buried by those who killed him.[4] The same is true with Jesus, who was slain by one group and buried by another.

Who were the wicked husbandmen? In a broad sense, they include all who reject Jesus Christ and his message of salvation. In the narrow sense, they include all who participated in persecuting, brutalizing, and killing him. Matthew's record catalogs those involved with the mocking and slaying of Jesus—the governor, chief priests, elders, scribes, the multitude, soldiers, and those who looked on as Jesus was on the cross:

Pilate, the governor, had Jesus scourged and released to be crucified (Matthew 27:26);

The chief priests, elders, and multitude cried out, "Let him be crucified" (Matthew 27:23);

The soldiers stripped Jesus, placed a scarlet robe on him, mocked him, and hit him (Matthew 27:27–31);

The soldiers crucified him (Matthew 27:35);

While on the cross, many mocked and reviled Jesus; some wagged their heads and said, "If thou be the Son of God, come down from the cross" (Matthew 27:39–40);

The chief priests, scribes, and elders said, "He saved others; himself he cannot save" (Matthew 27:41–42);

The thieves, too, joined the others in mocking Jesus (Matthew 27:44);

Some onlookers said, "Let us see whether Elias will come to save him" (Matthew 27:49).

> ***Matthew 21:40–41*** *When the lord therefore of the vineyard cometh, what will he do unto those husbandmen? They say unto him, He will miserably destroy those wicked men, and will let out his vineyard unto other husbandmen, which shall render him the fruits in their seasons.*

To this point, Jesus has told the story of the landowner, his servants, his beloved son, and the wicked tenants. Now Jesus asks a question of his audience—the chief priests, elders, and Pharisees (see Matthew 21:23, 45): "When the lord therefore of the vineyard cometh, what will he do unto those husbandmen?" This question forces Jesus' audience into a position where they have to judge themselves. They, along with others, are the wicked husbandmen of the parable. They and their forefathers have persecuted and slain the prophets, the servants of the landowner. And very soon they will also slay God's Beloved Son.

The chief priests, elders, and Pharisees do judge themselves when they respond to Jesus' question by saying the Lord "will miserably destroy those wicked men," ironically having reference to themselves. That the chief priests, elders, and Pharisees knew that Jesus spoke of them is clear from verse 45: "And when the chief priests and Pharisees had heard his parables, they perceived that he spake of them." In fact, they were so incensed by the parable that they desired to arrest Jesus, but they held back because "they feared the multitude" (Matthew 21:46).

The fact that the chief priests and Pharisees try to "lay hands on him" reminds us of the part of the parable that states that the wicked husbandmen grabbed ("caught") the beloved son. Before the week is out, they will do exactly that and fulfill the next portion of the parable, where they kill the landowner's own beloved son.

The chief priests, elders, and Pharisees were correct when they stated that they would be destroyed. They also correctly stated that the landowner would "let out his vineyard unto other husbandmen, which shall render him the fruits in their seasons." These "other husbandmen" are none other than the Gentiles. The rights to lease the vineyard were be taken from the Jews and given to the Gentiles. In accordance with this, Jesus stated, "Therefore say I unto you, The kingdom of God shall be taken from you, and given to a nation bringing forth the fruits thereof" (Matthew 21:43).

Personal Application

After teaching this parable, "Jesus saith unto them, Did ye never read in the scriptures, The stone which the builders rejected, the same is become the head of the corner: this is the Lord's doing, and it is marvellous in our eyes? Therefore say I unto you, The kingdom of God shall be taken from you, and given to a nation bringing forth the fruits thereof. And whosoever shall fall on this stone shall be broken: but on whomsoever it shall fall, it will grind him to powder" (Matthew 21:42–44).

"Did ye never read in the scriptures" is an expression that Jesus used in other settings (see Matthew 12:3, 5; 19:4; 21:16; 22:31). The expression is rhetorical, meaning that Jesus did not expect a response from his audience. Of course, Jesus' hearers had read the scriptures, but Jesus meant, "Did you not *comprehend* the scriptures?"

After giving the parable, Jesus quoted Psalm 118:22–23: "The stone which the builders refused is become the head stone of the corner. This is the Lord's doing; it is marvellous in our eyes." At first glance, this quotation seems to be out of context. In his parable, Jesus spoke of a vineyard, winepress, husbandmen, and the vineyard's fruits, and then he unexpectedly quoted an Old Testament passage about stonemasons and a cornerstone. This passage, however, is not out of context, but instead ties in agreeably with the rest of the parable. The parable teaches of wicked husbandmen who rejected God's Beloved Son, Jesus Christ. The application then teaches of builders who rejected ("builders refused") the cornerstone, which also represents Jesus Christ. By citing Psalm 118:22–23, Jesus provides his audience, the chief priests and Pharisees, with a second witness that they are rejecting or refusing him. This second witness—the quotation of Psalm 118:22–23—is very subtle, and yet the chief priests and Pharisees were fully aware that Jesus was speaking of them (see Matthew 21:45–46).

Psalm 118:22–23, then, is a prophecy about Jesus Christ, who is likened unto a building's cornerstone. Isaiah used similar imagery when he prophesied that the Messiah would become a "precious corner stone" and a "tried stone," or a stone tested for its strength. Paul, too, wrote that "Jesus Christ himself [is] the chief corner stone" (Ephesians 2:20; see 1 Peter 2:4).

How is Jesus like a cornerstone? The cornerstone serves as part of a building's foundation, tying two of the walls together at the corner. In fact, the cornerstone is the principal stone of the foundation, upon which the integrity of the entire building rests. A weak, cracked, or fractured cornerstone results in a vulnerable structure, one that may crumble and fall. Jesus is likened unto a cornerstone in that he is the building's chief component of strength. With Jesus as the cornerstone of the building, his prophets and apostles can serve as the foundation (see Ephesians 2:19–20) and we, Jesus' disciples, serve as individual stones in the building's structure. As Peter wrote, "Ye also, as lively stones, are built up a spiritual house" (1 Peter 2:5; see also vv. 4–8). The cornerstone is stronger than all other parts of the building's structure. This cornerstone is strong enough to serve as a sure foundation so that the righteous can build upon it with confidence.

The stone imagery in this discourse continues, showing that Jesus is like a great stone that will destroy the wicked. "Whosoever shall fall on this stone shall be broken," he said, "but on whomsoever it shall fall, it will grind him to powder."

The first part of the parable makes it appear that the landowner (God) is weak because the wicked are able to slay his servants (the prophets) and his beloved son (Jesus Christ), but the latter part of the parable shows that He and his Son are stronger than all else: "He will miserably destroy those wicked men." The parable contrasts Jesus' invulnerability with all mortals. Like a great stone, he is permanent, indestructible, and everlasting, far beyond human capability. Mortals are helpless and vulnerable in comparison. By simply falling on the stone, mortals "shall be broken." If it falls on them, they will be ground into powder.

Peter used similar imagery when he wrote that Jesus is "a stone of stumbling, and a rock of offence, even to them which stumble at the word, being disobedient" (1 Peter 2:8). *Midrash Esther* sets forth words that are comparable: "If a stone falls on a pot, woe to the pot! If the pot falls on the stone, woe to the pot! Either way, woe to the pot!"[5]

The parable of the wicked husbandmen describes people who had a stewardship over a vineyard. These husbandmen not only failed as stewards, but, far worse, they abused their privileges and responsibilities by beating and killing the landowner's servants, symbols for the Lord's prophets. When the landowner sent his beloved son, or Jesus Christ, these husbandmen also slew him.

We are not among those who persecute or kill the prophets. Still, we can learn from this parable lessons about becoming better citizens in God's vineyard by accepting his servants, the prophets, and by demonstrating obedience to Jesus Christ.

On February 26, 1980, President Ezra Taft Benson gave an address at Brigham Young University titled "Fourteen Fundamentals in Following the Prophet." These fourteen fundamentals instruct us how to follow our prophets. If we faithfully follow the prophets, we will remove any similarity that exists between us and the parable's wicked husbandmen.

"To help you pass the crucial tests which lie ahead," President Benson said, "I am going to give you today several facets of a grand key which, if you will honor, will crown you with God's glory and bring you out victorious in spite of Satan's fury. . . . Here then is the grand key—follow the prophet—and here are fourteen fundamentals in following the prophet, the President of The Church of Jesus Christ of Latter-day Saints.

"First: *The prophet is the only man who speaks for the Lord in everything.*

"In . . . [D&C 21:4–6], the Lord states: 'Wherefore, meaning the church, thou shalt give heed unto all his words and commandments which he shall give unto you as he receiveth them, walking in all holiness before me; For his word ye shall receive, as if from mine own mouth, in all patience and faith. For by doing these things the gates of hell shall not prevail against you.'

"Second: *The living prophet is more vital to us than the Standard Works. . . .*

"Third: *The living prophet is more important to us than a dead prophet.*

"God's revelation to Adam did not instruct Noah how to build the Ark. Noah needed his own revelation. Therefore, the most important prophet, so far as you and I are concerned, is the one living in our day and age to whom the Lord is currently revealing His will for us. . . .

"Fourth: *The prophet will never lead the Church astray. . . .*

"Fifth: *The prophet is not required to have any particular earthly training or diplomas to speak on any subject or act on any matter at any time. . . .*

" . . . How much earthly schooling did Joseph Smith have? Yet he gave revelations on all kinds of subjects. . . . If there is ever a conflict between earthly knowledge and the words of the prophet, you stand with the prophet and you'll be blessed and time will vindicate you.

"Sixth: *The prophet does not have to say 'Thus saith the Lord' to give us scripture. . . .*

"Seventh: *The prophet tells us what we need to know, not always what we want to know. . . .*

"Eighth: *The Prophet is not limited by men's reasoning.*

"There will be times when you will have to choose between the revelation of God and reasoning of men—between the prophet and the professor. . . .

"Ninth: *The prophet can receive revelation on any matter—temporal or spiritual.*

"Said Brigham Young: ' . . . I defy any man on earth to point out the path a Prophet of God should walk in, or point out his duty, and just how far he must go, in dictating temporal or spiritual things.

Temporal and spiritual things are inseparably connected, and ever will be.' (*Journal of Discourses,* 10:363–64.)

"Tenth: *The prophet may be involved in civic matters. . . .*

"Eleventh: *The two groups who have the greatest difficulty in following the prophet are the proud who are learned and the proud who are rich. . . .*

"Twelfth: *The prophet will not necessarily be popular with the world or the worldly. . . .*

"Thirteenth: *The prophet and his counselors make up the First Presidency—the highest quorum in the Church. . . .*

"Fourteenth: *The prophet and the presidency—the living prophet and the first presidency—follow them and be blessed; reject them and suffer.*"[6]

CHAPTER 27

The Royal Marriage Feast

Matthew 22:1–14

And Jesus answered and spake unto them again by parables, and said,

The kingdom of heaven is like unto a certain king, which made a marriage for his son,

And sent forth his servants to call them that were bidden to the wedding: and they would not come.

Again, he sent forth other servants, saying, Tell them which are bidden, Behold, I have prepared my dinner: my oxen and my fatlings are killed, and all things are ready: come unto the marriage.

But they made light of it, and went their ways, one to his farm, another to his merchandise:

And the remnant took his servants, and entreated them spitefully, and slew them.

But when the king heard thereof, he was wroth: and he sent forth his armies, and destroyed those murderers, and burned up their city.

Then saith he to his servants, The wedding is ready, but they which were bidden were not worthy.

Go ye therefore into the highways, and as many as ye shall find, bid to the marriage.

So those servants went out into the highways, and gathered together all as many as they found, both bad and good: and the wedding was furnished with guests.

And when the king came in to see the guests, he saw there a man which had not on a wedding garment:

And he saith unto him, Friend, how camest thou in hither not having a wedding garment? And he was speechless.

Then said the king to the servants, Bind him hand and foot, and take him away, and cast him into outer darkness; there shall be weeping and gnashing of teeth.

For many are called, but few are chosen.

As Jesus taught at the temple during the last week of his life, the chief priests and Pharisees questioned his authority. Jesus responded by teaching three parables: first, the two sons; second, the wicked husbandmen; and third, the royal marriage feast. All three parables illustrate that those who thought they were righteous—the chief priests and Pharisees—were instead wicked, their works and hearts unacceptable to God.

This parable brings together in one story a testimony of the divine Sonship of Christ, a witness that the Jews would deny him, a prophecy of the destruction of Jerusalem, an indication that the gospel would be taken to the Gentiles, and a warning that those who hear and receive the call to come unto the Lord's kingdom must truly "put on Christ" or they will be cast out.

The Jews in Jesus' day knew of the prophecies of a great feast that would mark the beginning of the Messiah's reign in glory (see Zephaniah 1:7–8). But they believed only true descendants of father Abraham would be invited to that feast.

This parable has some similarities with the parable of the wedding guests found in Luke 14, and some have expressed the opinion that they are actually the same parable. The truth, however, is that Jesus taught the same parable in different settings to different people, and sometimes he taught similar but not identical parables to illustrate different principles.

Commentary

Matthew 22:1–2 *And Jesus answered and spake unto them again by parables, and said, The kingdom of heaven is like unto a certain king, which made a marriage for his son,*

As in other parables, the kingdom of heaven refers to God's kingdom on the earth, or The Church of Jesus Christ. The Church provides the marriage feast to God's children on the earth, giving them the bread of life, which enables them to never hunger again.

The king is God himself. And the son is Jesus Christ. In the scriptures, Jesus Christ is repeatedly referred to as the Bridegroom (see Matthew 25:1; D&C 33:17; 65:3; 88:92). The actual marriage symbolizes the opening of the great millennial reign of Christ.

Matthew 22:3 *And sent forth his servants to call them that were bidden to the wedding: and they would not come.*

The Joseph Smith Translation adds the following to the beginning of the verse: "And when the marriage was ready, he sent forth . . ."

It was traditional in weddings in the ancient Middle East to send out two invitations, each hand delivered by servants. The first was to announce the coming celebration, and the second was to inform the guests that the actual time had arrived for them to come.

When the potential guests refused the invitation, they were not merely being discourteous or ungrateful but were actually being treasonous. Such an invitation from the king—especially for the wedding of his own son, his heir—was more a command. For the guests to indicate they would not come was to say that they did not approve of the marriage or no longer gave allegiance to the king, or both.

Those who were first invited to the king's feast were the once chosen people of Israel. They were invited to come unto the true Messiah, but "they would not come," nor, in their apostate condition, would they accept the will of the Father.

This parable may have another application: when the Lord sends his servants to proclaim the word in any era of the world, some of those invited will reject the invitation—and will suffer the consequences.

> ***Matthew 22:4*** *Again, he sent forth other servants, saying, Tell them which are bidden, Behold, I have prepared my dinner: my oxen and my fatlings are killed, and all things are ready: come unto the marriage.*

The wedding feast is now ready; the food is prepared; it is time to come. The servants who take the invitation are a different group ("other servants") from those who took out the preliminary notice of the wedding. Such feasts in the ancient Middle East were not held for an hour or an afternoon or a day. Instead, the host would invite his guests to come and feast with him for seven or fourteen days. In the case of a rich and generous king, the length of the feast would almost certainly be the longer period.

The first invitation to the feast represents the call of the prophets of the Old Testament, issued to the people of the covenant. The second invitation, taken by different ("other") servants, was the same call, this time sent forth by the prophets, apostles, and missionaries of the New Testament. The third invitation, which went to all people (verses 9–10), is that of this dispensation.

> ***Matthew 22:5*** *But they made light of it, and went their ways, one to his farm, another to his merchandise:*

The Joseph Smith Translation changes the beginning of this verse to read, "But they made light of the servants . . ."

Even though the wedding feast is prepared, and even though the people are being invited by the king, they do not take the invitation seriously. They have what they perceive to be more important things on their minds. They have crops to attend to and shops to operate. Such people are all too easy to find in the world. They hear the gospel message, the invitation to come unto Christ, but they think they have better things to do. They are preoccupied with the things of the temporal world and ignore the infinitely more important things of the spiritual.

Matthew 22:6 *And the remnant took his servants, and entreated them spitefully, and slew them.*

Far worse than those who would not make the wedding a priority were those who actually abused the king's servants—they mistreated them and then killed them. These are the people who kill the prophets and persecute the Saints (see Matthew 23:35). They are not satisfied with simply turning their backs on the message of salvation; they feel driven to try to stop the messengers. Further, those who killed the king's servants were not participating only in murder, but they were rebelling against the king and all that his kingdom stood for.

Matthew 22:7 *But when the king heard thereof, he was wroth: and he sent forth his armies, and destroyed those murderers, and burned up their city.*

Fire is a traditional sign of judgment (see Isaiah 5:24–25). God himself was represented by such fire: "The Lord the God is a consuming fire, even a jealous God" (Deuteronomy 4:24).

The first group, those who were simply too busy or preoccupied to come, lost the privilege of associating with the king and his son and partaking of all the wonderful gifts they offered. But the second group, who actually persecuted and killed the king's messengers, were destroyed in the flesh.

This part of the parable served as a prophecy that received a literal fulfillment. After the Jews rejected and killed his Son, in his righteous wrath God allowed the Roman armies to descend on Jerusalem, which they sacked and burned in A.D. 70. They destroyed the holy temple and carried many of the surviving Jews away captive into distant lands. "Do I not hold the destinies of all the armies of the nations of the earth?" the Lord has asked (D&C 117:6).

The destruction and burning of the wicked also seems to have application to those events that will take place in the last days.

Matthew 22:8–10 *Then saith he to his servants, The wedding is ready, but they which were bidden were not worthy. Go ye therefore into the highways, and as many as ye shall find, bid* *to the marriage. So those servants went out into the highways, and gathered together all as many as they found, both bad and good: and the wedding was furnished with guests.*

Because those invited to the wedding will not come (and the more wicked part of them have been slain by the king's armies), the king sends out a third group of servants (the second group have been martyred). They are to go out into "the highways," the places where the people are, and invite them to come to the wedding feast, "as many as ye shall find." Those invited first were specially chosen, but now the king instructs his servants to talk to everybody. The servants obediently go forth and "gathered together all as many as they found, both bad and good." Through the efforts of these faithful servants, the royal wedding has plenty of guests to fill the hall.

After the Jews rejected the gospel, the word was to go to all nations, without distinction of where the people live or who they are. Even those who are considered "bad" are invited to come unto Christ and partake of the blessings of his atonement. As we read elsewhere, "the kingdom of heaven is like unto a net, that was cast into the sea, and gathered of every kind" (Matthew 13:47). But when the bad are pulled into the net, if they choose to let the power of the gospel work in their hearts, they can be counted among the "good" and will be heirs of salvation.

Matthew 22:11 *And when the king came in to see the guests, he saw there a man which had not on a wedding garment:*

It was traditional for the king to go into the hall after the guests had been served. In the parable the king enters the banquet hall to learn who has come to the wedding feast—and he sees one man who doesn't have on a wedding garment.

It is clear that the king is considering the guests one by one, rather than as simply a group. So it will be in the last judgment. The Lord will consider and judge us individually. We are not saved as congregations or groups but as individuals, who have come unto Christ, received his grace, and done the works required of us.

Some readers have wondered how anyone could be expected to

have the proper clothing under these circumstances. After all, weren't the wedding guests pulled in off the streets? The answer is that it was the custom for a wealthy host to provide the appropriate wedding garments for his guests. The man who "had not on a wedding garment" did not lack for one but willfully refused to put it on.

"The guest who did not have wedding clothes at the royal banquet unmistakably represents the self-righteous sinner. He wants to make it known that he does not need the sacrificial death and atoning blood of Jesus to enter heaven. He does not listen to Jesus' word, 'No one comes to the father except through me' (John 14:6), and thus he appears before God and is thrown out. It is an utter impossibility to appear before God without the protective clothing offered by Jesus Christ."[1]

A better translation of the Greek says of the last part of this verse: "He saw there a man not having been clothed [or endowed] by the garment of marriage." The word for *clothed* used here has the same root as the word for *endowed* (see Luke 24:49, "until ye be endued with power from on high"). Those who were dressed (or endowed) in the garment provided by the king were clothed in righteousness in the house of the king. But the righteousness came not only through their own efforts—it also required the power and blessings of Christ. When we partake of his righteousness, meaning we partake of his atonement, we "put on Christ" as a garment, to use an image from the writings of Paul (see Galatians 3:27).

Isaiah spoke of the blessing of the "garments of salvation" when he wrote, "I will greatly rejoice in the Lord, my soul shall be joyful in my God; for he hath clothed me with the garments of salvation, he hath covered me with the robe of righteousness, as a bridegroom decketh himself with ornaments, and as a bride adorneth herself with her jewels" (Isaiah 61:10).

Matthew 22:12 *And he saith unto him, Friend, how camest thou in hither not having a wedding garment? And he was speechless.*

When the king called the man "Friend," it was not a warm term, but one (in the original Greek) that indicated the man was being insolent and disrespectful.

Perhaps the man was speechless because he was surprised that he had been picked out of the large crowd, and he offered no acceptable answer when the king asked him why he was inappropriately clothed for such an important occasion. But the gospel does not save us in crowds or groups. We are saved as individuals, and we must as individuals put on the righteousness that the Lord invites us to receive.

The Old Testament prophet Zephaniah saw this same circumstance when he said, "Hold thy peace at the presence of the Lord God: for the day of the Lord is at hand: for the Lord hath prepared a sacrifice, he hath bid his guests. And it shall come to pass in the day of the Lord's sacrifice, that I will punish the princes, and the king's children, and all such as are clothed with strange apparel" (Zephaniah 1:7–8).

Matthew 22:13 *Then said the king to the servants, Bind him hand and foot, and take him away, and cast him into outer darkness; there shall be weeping and gnashing of teeth.*

All those who seek to come into God's kingdom deceitfully will be bound by their own sins. If they refuse to repent, when they enter into the spirit world they will be in a kind of outer darkness (which is different from the outer darkness that is the final state of those who are named sons of perdition). There they will have great anguish of soul, represented by weeping and gnashing of teeth.

Matthew 22:14 *For many are called, but few are chosen.*

The Joseph Smith Translation adds to the end of this verse, " . . . wherefore all do not have on the wedding garment."

This same teaching ("many are called, but few are chosen") is found in the parable of the laborers in the vineyard (see the discussion on pages 193–94). The Lord calls many to come to his feast, to participate in his gospel, to receive the blessings of salvation. And of those called, multitudes come through the gate of the kingdom by receiving the ordinance of baptism.

But even though they are called, and even though they may respond to the call, they are chosen only if thereafter they continue to be "alive in Christ" (2 Nephi 25:25), letting his Spirit and his power transform them from sinners to Saints (see Mosiah 3:19).

Elsewhere Jesus made a parallel statement: "Strait is the gate, and narrow is the way, which leadeth unto life, and few there be that find it" (Matthew 7:14).

Personal Application

This parable was spoken to the chief priests and Pharisees—but it actually has a very direct application to our day.

"For this cause I have sent you," the Lord said to the missionaries in this dispensation, "that a feast of fat things might be prepared for the poor; yea, a feast of fat things, of wine on the lees well refined, that the earth may know that the mouths of the prophets shall not fail; Yea, a supper of the house of the Lord, well prepared, unto which all nations shall be invited. First, the rich and the learned, the wise and the noble; And after that cometh the day of my power; then shall the poor, the lame, and the blind, and the deaf, come in unto the marriage of the Lamb, and partake of the supper of the Lord, prepared for the great day to come" (D&C 58:6, 8–11).

The cry therefore goes forth from the prophets and missionaries of our day, "Prepare ye the way of the Lord, prepare ye the supper of the Lamb, make ready for the Bridegroom" (D&C 65:3).

As we prepare to come to that feast, the Lord will help us to put on the wedding garment of righteousness. As part of his apocalyptic vision John heard "a great multitude" say, "Let us be glad and rejoice, and give honour to him: for the marriage of the Lamb is come, and his wife hath made herself ready. And to her was granted that she should be arrayed in fine linen, clean and white: for the fine linen is the righteousness of saints. And he saith unto me, Write, Blessed are they which are called unto the marriage supper of the Lamb" (Revelation 19:6–9).

But there are some who come to the feast unprepared. They hear the message of salvation taught by God's servants and join the Church, which brings them into the company of the Saints. But if they don't consistently apply the blessings of the Atonement to their lives, if they don't go forward with diligence and a pure heart, they will find themselves without the robes of righteousness when the king comes to judge them.

CHAPTER 28

The Fig Tree

Matthew 24:32–34

Now learn a parable of the fig tree; When his branch is yet tender, and putteth forth leaves, ye know that summer is nigh:

So likewise ye, when ye shall see all these things, know that it is near, even at the doors.

Verily I say unto you, This generation shall not pass, till all these things be fulfilled.

The Joseph Smith Translation changes these verses to read: "Now learn a parable of the fig tree: When its branches are yet tender, and it begins to put forth leaves, ye know that summer is nigh at hand. So likewise *mine elect,* when they shall see all these things, they shall know that *he* is near, even at the doors" (JST, Matthew 24:41–42; emphasis added; see also Joseph Smith—Matthew 1:38–39).

This is one of the few parables that is found in all three of the synoptic gospels (there are three other parables contained in all three: the sower and the soils, the mustard seed, and the wicked husbandmen). The Matthew and Mark versions are almost identical (see Mark 13:28–29). Luke's account, however, exhibits some significant differences. As Luke recorded the parable, Jesus said: "Behold the fig tree, *and all the trees;* When they now shoot forth, *ye see and know of your own selves* that summer is now nigh at hand. So likewise ye, when ye see these things come to pass, know ye that *the kingdom of God* is nigh at hand" (Luke 21:29–31; emphasis added).

The context of this parable is the Lord's instruction on the signs that will precede his second coming in glory. As he taught on the Mount of Olives shortly before his death, his disciples asked: "Tell us when shall these things be which thou hast said concerning the destruction of the temple, and the Jews; and what is the sign of thy coming, and of the end of the world, or the destruction of the wicked, which is the end of the world?" (Joseph Smith–Matthew 1:4). Jesus answered by giving them a number of signs to watch for:

- False Christs and false prophets will come forth and deceive many.
- Iniquity will abound, and "the love of many shall wax cold."
- Jerusalem will be destroyed.
- There will be wars and rumors of wars.
- There will be "famines, and pestilences, and earthquakes, in divers places."
- The gospel will be preached through the world, to all nations.
- "The abomination of desolation, spoken of by Daniel the prophet, [shall] be fulfilled."
- "The sun shall be darkened, and the moon shall not give her light, and the stars shall fall from heaven, and the powers of the heavens shall be shaken."
- The sign of the Son of Man will appear in heaven.

After these things, the Lord said, "they shall see the Son of Man coming in the clouds of heaven, with power and great glory" (Joseph Smith–Matthew 1:5–36).

Commentary

Matthew 24:32 *Now learn a parable of the fig tree; When his branch is yet tender, and putteth forth leaves, ye know that summer is nigh:*

The fig tree was common in ancient Palestine (see Deuteronomy 8:8). In fact, a town near Jerusalem was named Bethphage, which means "house of figs." The fig tree has broad green leaves that are a good source of shade in the summer. But it loses its leaves in the fall—unlike other trees of the area, such as the cedar, the palm, and the olive tree. In the spring, often during the first week of April—about when Jesus was speaking this parable—the new leaves begin to come forth.

Luke's account broadens the idea to "all the trees." When we see the leaves coming forth on the trees, we know without doubt that the long winter is over and summer is on its way.

> ***Matthew 24:33*** *So likewise ye, when ye shall see all these things, know that it is near, even at the doors.*

Jesus here teaches that the emerging leaves on the trees are like the signs of the times. When we see the signs he enumerated, we can know that the Second Coming is nigh.

When we read the version found in the Joseph Smith Translation, however, we see that watching the signs as an academic exercise will not bring us to a correct understanding. Even those who study the scriptures diligently and listen to gospel sermons may misunderstand if they fail to have the guidance of the Spirit in their lives. Hence, the Lord says, when *"mine elect"* see the signs—meaning, those who have drawn close him through ordinances, obedience, and pure hearts—they will know that the Lord's coming is nigh.

> ***Matthew 24:34*** *Verily I say unto you, This generation shall not pass, till all these things be fulfilled.*

The message is clear: when we see the signs come to pass, we can know that the Lord will come in that very generation. His coming will follow those signs as surely as the summer follows the appearance of leaves on the fig tree.

But generation has more than one meaning. As Elder Joseph Fielding Smith wrote: "There have been various interpretations of the meaning of a generation. It is held by some that a generation is one hundred years; by others that it is one hundred and twenty years; by others that a generation as expressed in this and other scriptures has reference to a period of time which is indefinite. The Savior said: 'An evil and adulterous generation seeketh after a sign.' This did not have reference to a period of years, but to a period of wickedness. A generation may mean the time of this present dispensation."[1]

Personal Application

In an 1830 revelation to Joseph Smith and Sidney Rigdon, the Lord referred to the parable of the fig tree: "The poor and the meek shall have the gospel preached unto them, and they shall be looking forth for the time of my coming, for it is nigh at hand—And they shall learn the parable of the fig-tree, for even now already summer is nigh" (D&C 35:15–16). In this passage, it is the poor in spirit and the meek that possess the gospel who will "learn the parable of the fig-tree" and who "shall be looking forth" for Jesus' second coming.

Later the Lord spoke again of those who would be "looking forth" for the signs of the times. Note the words that indicate these people are watching for his coming: "It shall come to pass that he that feareth me shall be *looking forth* for the great day of the Lord to come, even for the signs of the coming of the Son of Man. And they shall *see* signs and wonders, for they shall be *shown forth* in the heavens above, and in the earth beneath. And they shall *behold* blood, and fire, and vapors of smoke. And before the day of the Lord shall come, the sun shall be darkened, and the moon be turned into blood, and the stars fall from heaven. And the remnant shall be gathered unto this place [Zion]; and then they shall *look* for me, and, behold, I will come; and they shall *see* me in the clouds of heaven, clothed with power and great glory; with all the holy angels; and he that *watches* not for me shall be cut off" (D&C 45:39–44; emphasis added).

In a 1973 conference address, after reviewing the signs of the times, President Harold B. Lee said, "Brothers and sisters, this is the day the Lord is speaking of. You see the signs are here. Be ye therefore ready."[2]

And in 1976, Elder Bernard P. Brockbank quoted President Spencer W. Kimball as saying, "The leaves are commencing to show on the fig tree."[3]

Surely the signs are all around us. We can foolishly choose to ignore them, or we can recognize their reality and learn by the Spirit what the Lord would have us know. "If ye are prepared ye shall not fear," the Lord has said (D&C 38:30). If we watch the signs of the times, even as we might watch trees bearing their leaves in the spring, and if we do it as the Lord's elect, being pure in heart, we will be able to understand the seasons of the Lord's work—and we will be prepared for his coming.

President Marion G. Romney wrote: "It is my opinion that we Latter-day Saints, because of the knowledge we have received in the revelations, are better prepared to meet the perplexities of our times than are any other people. . . .

"'For they that are wise and have received the truth, and have taken the Holy Spirit for their guide . . . shall not be hewn down and cast into the fire, but shall abide the day.' [D&C 45:57] . . .

"Each one of us who is a member of the Church has had hands laid upon his head and has been given, as far as an ordinance can give it, the gift of the Holy Ghost. . . . If I receive the Holy Ghost and follow his guidance, I will be among those who are protected and carried through these troubled times. And so will you, and so will every other soul who lives under his direction."[4]

CHAPTER 29

THE TEN VIRGINS

Matthew 25:1–13

Then shall the kingdom of heaven be likened unto ten virgins, which took their lamps, and went forth to meet the bridegroom.

And five of them were wise, and five were *foolish.*

They that were *foolish took their lamps, and took no oil with them:*

But the wise took oil in their vessels with their lamps.

While the bridegroom tarried, they all slumbered and slept.

And at midnight there was a cry made, Behold, the bridegroom cometh; go ye out to meet him.

Then all those virgins arose, and trimmed their lamps.

And the foolish said unto the wise, Give us of your oil; for our lamps are gone out.

But the wise answered, saying, Not so; lest there be not enough for us and you: but go ye rather to them that sell, and buy for yourselves.

And while they went to buy, the bridegroom came; and they that were ready went in with him to the marriage: and the door was shut.

Afterward came also the other virgins, saying, Lord, Lord, open to us.

But he answered and said, Verily I say unto you, I know you not.

Watch therefore, for ye know neither the day nor the hour wherein the Son of man cometh.

Only days before his death, Jesus sat on the Mount of Olives (see Matthew 24:3) and related to his disciples a number of the signs that would be shown before his Second Coming (see Matthew 24:4–51). He prophesied of the coming of false Christs and false prophets, of the darkening of the sun and the moon, and the sign of the Son of man; he compared the "days of Noe" to the "coming of the Son of man" (Matthew 24:37). During this same discourse he gave the parables of the fig tree (Matthew 24:32–34), the ten virgins (Matthew 25:1–13), and the talents (Matthew 25:14–30). All three parables were designed to help the Lord's disciples prepare for the Savior's return. In fact, after revealing a number of the signs of the times, the Lord warned, "Watch therefore: for ye know not what hour your Lord doth come" (Matthew 24:42). Similar words come at the end of the parable of the ten virgins: "Watch therefore, for ye know neither the day nor the hour wherein the Son of man cometh" (Matthew 25:13).

Jesus frequently used parables to compare the kingdom of God to people or things that were part of life in the Holy Land. In the present parable, Jesus compares God's kingdom to ten virgins who had lamps and who were waiting for the bridegroom to come. The concluding verse informs us that the parable's primary theme is that all must watch and prepare for Jesus Christ's coming: "for ye know neither the day nor the hour wherein the Son of man cometh." The parable implies that each of us is responsible for his or her own spiritual life; and it tells us how to prepare for Jesus' second coming and what our course of life should be. As Wilford Woodruff summarized, "The parable of the ten virgins is intended to represent the second coming of the Son of man, the coming of the Bridegroom to meet the bride, the church, the Lamb's wife, in the last days."[1]

Commentary

Matthew 25:1 *Then shall the kingdom of heaven be likened unto ten virgins, which took their lamps, and went forth to meet the bridegroom.*

The first sentence of the parable introduces the parable's theme (the kingdom of heaven), the parable's principal characters (virgins and bridegroom), and the parable's chief additional elements (lamps). The bridegroom, virgins, and virgins' lamps work together to provide knowledge of the kingdom of heaven in the context of the Second Coming, at which time the marriage of the Bridegroom will take place. The parable's opening word, "then," connects the words from the previous passage to this one. It means "after that" or "subsequently." In this case "then" connects the parable of the ten virgins to signs of the times and the Second Coming, as presented in Matthew 24.

The bridegroom. In this parable Jesus explicitly refers to "marriage" (Matthew 25:10) and four times he speaks of the "bridegroom" (Matthew 25:1, 5, 6, 10). Because Jesus is "*the* bridegroom" instead of "a bridegroom," it seems he is referring to a specific rather than a generic bridegroom. That bridegroom is Jesus Christ[2] as the scriptures reveal (see Jeremiah 2:1–4; Matthew 9:15; Revelation 19:7; 21:9; D&C 33:17–18; 65:3; 133:10). He is the one who is betrothed to the covenant people (see Hosea 2:19–20); and he is called "husband": "For thy Maker is thine husband" (Isaiah 54:5); "I was an husband unto them, saith the Lord" (Jeremiah 31:32).

The bride. Although the parable does not explicitly mention a bride, her existence is certainly implied since there cannot be a bridegroom without a bride. The Lord's bride is variously the "holy city, new Jerusalem" (Revelation 21:2, 9), Zion (Isaiah 54:1–6), and the Church (D&C 109:73–74). His bride is represented by the faithful Saints, "they which are written in the Lamb's book of life" (Revelation 21:27), they who are the wise virgins (see Matthew 25:2, 4, 8–9), they who are "holy and without blemish" (Ephesians 5:27)—all these are the "Lamb's wife" (Revelation 21:9). At the Lord's coming, the Saints will cry out, "Let us be glad and rejoice, and give honour to him: for the marriage of the Lamb is come, and his wife hath made herself ready" (Revelation 19:7).

The virgins. Virgins were highly valued and held a distinct place in ancient Israelite society. A virgin's role was elevated socially, for example, becausc the law of Moses specified that a high priest could marry only a virgin. A high priest, an ecclesiastical authority in the ancient temple system, was not permitted to marry a widow, a divorcee, a harlot, or a profane woman (see Leviticus 21:13–14). His marriage to a virgin would have set her apart from other Israelite women. The high priest was a type and a shadow of Jesus Christ, who symbolically will marry his virgin bride, the faithful Saints, at his coming.

For another example, an Old Testament custom regarding a king's virgin daughters also made them special. According to 2 Samuel 13:18, these daughters were given robes "of divers colours." These robes, similar to the coat of many colors that Joseph of Egypt possessed,[3] would have made these virgins conspicuous in public life.

Scriptural passages also portray the Lord's covenant people as a "virgin" (2 Kings 19:21; Jeremiah 18:13; Lamentations 2:13; Amos 5:2): "the virgin, the daughter of Zion" (Isaiah 37:22; Lamentations 1:15), "the virgin daughter" (Jeremiah 14:17), and "the virgin of Israel" (Jeremiah 18:13; 31:4, 21). Paul, when writing to Church members, wished for them to become Jesus Christ's "chaste virgin." "For I am jealous over you with godly jealousy: for I have espoused you to one husband, that I may present you as a chaste virgin to Christ" (2 Corinthians 11:2).

The parable's ten virgins are members of the Church. According to Elder Marvin J. Ashton: "It can be properly and appropriately concluded that the ten virgins represent the people of the Church of Jesus Christ, and not alone the rank and file of the world. The wise and foolish virgins, all of them, had been invited to the wedding supper; they had knowledge of the importance of the occasion. They were not pagans, heathens, or gentiles, nor were they known as corrupt or lost, but rather they were informed people who had the saving, exalting gospel in their possession, but [the foolish virgins] had not made it the center of their lives. They knew the way, but were foolishly unprepared for the coming of the bridegroom. All, even the foolish ones, trimmed their lamps at his coming, but their oil was used up. In the most needed moment there was none available to refill their lamps. All had been warned their entire lives."[4]

President Spencer W. Kimball, too, explained that "these ten virgins were members of the Church. The bridegroom was the Lord Jesus Christ."[5]

The lamps. Most household lamps of the first century A.D. were small enough to be held in the hand. Made of potter's clay, the user filled them with olive oil and burned a floating wick to provide light. Although the five-time usage of the word "lamps" in the parable demonstrates its overall import in understanding Jesus' message, it is actually the lamp's oil that is the significant property, and that is because it symbolizes the Holy Ghost. Elder Bruce R. McConkie wrote that the oil-filled lamps are "symbolic of the Holy Spirit which lights the way before the saints."[6]

The scriptures symbolically connect olive oil with the Holy Ghost.[7] At King Saul's anointing with olive oil the "Spirit of the Lord" came upon him, which made him into "another man" (1 Samuel 10:1, 6, 9). Later the prophet Samuel anointed David with oil, and immediately "the Spirit of the Lord came upon David. . . . But the Spirit of the Lord departed from Saul" (1 Samuel 16:13–14; see 18:12). Isaiah's messianic prophecy also connects the Spirit with the anointing: "The Spirit of the Lord God is upon me; because the Lord hath anointed me to preach good tidings unto the meek" (Isaiah 61:1). This passage was fulfilled in Jesus, as he himself announced in Nazareth's synagogue (Luke 4:18, 21). Luke connected the anointing and the Holy Ghost when he wrote, "God anointed Jesus of Nazareth with the Holy Ghost and with power" (Acts 10:38; see also 2 Corinthians 1:21–22; JST, 1 John 2:20–27).

Additional references make implicit connections between olive oil and the Holy Ghost. Perhaps the fact that olive oil was employed in the temple's lamps for lighting purposes (see Exodus 27:20) points to the Holy Ghost, who provides light to God's faithful.[8] Similar symbolism is found in the two prophetic witnesses of the last days, who are called lamps (see Revelation 11); in King David, who is referred to as the "light of Israel" (2 Samuel 21:17); and in righteous individuals, who metaphorically are called the "light of the world" (Matthew

5:14–16).[9] These individuals receive their light from the Holy Ghost.[10] When the elders of the Church administer to the sick by anointing them with olive oil, the sick can experience both a physical and a spiritual healing (see James 5:14–15). Certainly the Holy Ghost plays a vital role in the spiritual recovery of sinful souls.

The number ten. The parable speaks of ten virgins and ten lamps. The number *ten* has a symbolic value and it is probably for this reason that Jesus selected this number, rather than six, eight, fifteen, thirty, or any other number. *Ten* is used to describe a number of spiritually significant things, such as tithing (one tenth), the ten plagues (see Exodus 9:14), and the ten commandments (see Exodus 20:1–17), as well as the ten pieces of silver in the parable of the lost coin (see Luke 15:8–10), the ten pounds (see Luke 19:12–27), and the ten virgins (see Matthew 25:1–13). In the parable of the ten virgins, the number *ten* represents completion or wholeness, signifying the entire Church.

> ***Matthew 25:2–4*** *And five of them were wise, and five were foolish. They that were foolish took their lamps, and took no oil with them: But the wise took oil in their vessels with their lamps.*

All ten of the virgins possessed lamps, and all ten carried their lamps as they went to meet the bridegroom. Five of the virgins are labeled "wise" because they took sufficient oil to last until the bridegroom came. The other five are "foolish" because they "took no oil with them."

"The arithmetic of this parable is chilling," wrote Elder Dallin H. Oaks. "The ten virgins obviously represent members of Christ's Church, for all were invited to the wedding feast and all knew what was required to be admitted when the bridegroom came. But only half were ready when he came. . . . We need to make both temporal and spiritual preparation for the events prophesied at the time of the Second Coming. And the preparation most likely to be neglected is the one less visible and more difficult—the spiritual. A 72-hour kit of temporal supplies may prove valuable for earthly challenges, but, as the foolish virgins learned to their sorrow, a 24-hour kit of spiritual preparation is of greater and more enduring value."[11]

The five foolish virgins' lack of oil proves to have a significant negative impact on them, since they are excluded from the marriage festivities after the arrival of the bridegroom. In fact, the door is shut on them, and they are not permitted to enter the Lord's home. The wise virgins' oil signifies that they have lived worthy of receiving the Holy Ghost in their lives. Modern scripture interprets the parable by saying: "And at that day, when I shall come in my glory, shall the parable be fulfilled which I spake concerning the ten virgins. For they that are wise and have received the truth, and have taken the Holy Spirit for their guide, and have not been deceived—verily I say unto you, they shall not be hewn down and cast into the fire, but shall abide the day" (D&C 45:56–57).

The light from each lamp is actually a representation of the spiritual preparedness of the virgin who owns the lamp. That is to say, the lamp's light symbolizes the light of the Holy Ghost that shines within each. "That which is of God is light; and he that receiveth light, and continueth in God, receiveth more light; and that light groweth brighter and brighter until the perfect day" (D&C 50:24). The foolish virgins possessed the light of the Holy Ghost for a season, but then their light went out because they failed to keep their lamps filled with oil.

Bildad, the Shuhite, provided this insight: "Yea, the light of the wicked shall be put out, and the spark of his fire shall not shine. The light shall be dark in his tabernacle, and his candle shall be put out with him" (Job 18:5–6). So, too, explains a proverb: "The light of the righteous rejoiceth: but the lamp of the wicked shall be put out" (Proverbs 13:9).

President Wilford Woodruff observed that the parable reflects the Church's situation, in terms of those Church members who are spiritually prepared for the Lord's coming: "I expect that the Saviour was about right when he said, in reference to the members of the church, that five of them were wise and five were foolish; for when the Lord of heaven comes in power and great glory to reward every man according to the deeds done in the body, if he finds one-half of those professing to be members of his church prepared for salvation, it will be as many as can be expected judging by the course that many are pursuing."[12]

Matthew 25:5 *While the bridegroom tarried, they all slumbered and slept.*

The parable does not explain why the bridegroom tarries. It may have been so that those of us in mortality would have sufficient time to repent and to obtain oil for our lamps. Or, inasmuch as no one knows the precise time of Jesus Christ's coming—a fact that is presented in the final verse of the parable (see vs. 13)—it is possible that the virgins were expecting him at a certain time and then he came later than expected.

Regardless of the reason why the bridegroom tarried, in 1875 Wilford Woodruff taught the Saints that the time had arrived for the "church and kingdom" to awake and arise and put oil in their lamps: "The word of the Lord to me is that it is time for Zion to rise and let her light shine; and the testimony of the Spirit of God to me is that this whole kingdom, this great kingdom of priests . . . who have borne the priesthood, have thoroughly fulfilled one part of the parable of the ten virgins. What is that? Why, that while the Bridegroom has tarried we have all slumbered and slept; as a church and kingdom we have slumbered and slept, and the word of the Lord to me is that we have slept long enough; and we have the privilege now of rising and trimming our lamps and putting oil in our vessels. This is the word of the Lord to me."[13]

Matthew 25:6 *And at midnight there was a cry made, Behold, the bridegroom cometh; go ye out to meet him.*

These words apply directly to us. A revelation given through Joseph Smith in 1831 refers to the parable of the ten virgins and makes the parable applicable to those who live during the last days: "Yea, let the cry go forth among all people: Awake and arise and go forth to meet the Bridegroom; behold and lo, the Bridegroom cometh; go ye out to meet him. Prepare yourselves for the great day of the Lord" (D&C 133:10).

This passage shares a number of parallels with the parable. Both feature a cry ("there was a cry made" and "let the cry go forth"), both speak of those who *rise* from their sleep ("all those virgins arose" and "awake and arise"); both mention the *meeting* of the bridegroom ("go ye out to meet him" and "meet the Bridegroom"); both feature the exclamation "Behold," followed by mention of the coming of the bridegroom ("Behold, the bridegroom cometh" and"behold and lo, the Bridegroom cometh"); and both speak of the Lord's second coming ("the Son of man cometh" and "the great day of the Lord").

It may seem curious that the bridegroom arrives for his wedding at such a late hour, but in first-century Palestine it was not unusual for various events to occur at midnight. For example, it was at midnight that Paul and Silas sang hymns and prayed while in prison (see Acts 16:25). On another occasion, Paul spoke to fellow Christians on the Sabbath day until midnight (see Acts 20:7). And in the parable of the friend at midnight, a late traveler stops by the home of his friend at a very late hour (Luke 11:5). But what about weddings at midnight? According to one biblical authority, weddings were held at night and "they usually began at the rising of the evening star."[14] If this was the case, it is possible that the wedding program (e.g., the ceremony, feast, and celebration) began soon after dark and continued until after the midnight hour. For the virgins to come "out in the night with their torches to meet the bridegroom probably reflects actual historical practice."[15]

An Old Testament scene of death also took place at midnight. Moses recorded that God sent the tenth plague, the smiting of the firstborn, upon the Egyptians at midnight (see Exodus 11:4; 12:29). Job, too, linked midnight to a time of death: "In a moment shall they die, and the people shall be troubled at midnight, and pass away: and the mighty shall be taken away without hand" (Job 34:20). The parable of the ten virgins also includes a midnight scene of woe. The five foolish virgins are shut out from participating in the marriage ceremony and are told by the Lord, "I know you not" (see Matthew 25:10–12). Being shut out from the Lord's presence constitutes spiritual death. The use of midnight seems to indicate that the Lord will allow people chances until the last possible moment.

> ***Matthew 25:7–9*** *Then all those virgins arose, and trimmed their lamps. And the foolish said unto the wise, Give us of your*

oil; for our lamps are gone out. But the wise answered, saying, Not so; lest there be not enough for us and you: but go ye rather to them that sell, and buy for yourselves.

The five foolish virgins ask the wise to give them some oil, but the wise virgins answer, "Not so; lest there be not enough for us and you." With this response the five wise virgins continue to demonstrate their good judgment. If they share their oil with others, none of the virgins will have sufficient oil to greet the bridegroom.

There is an additional reason why the wise cannot share their oil with the unwise. Inasmuch as the oil of the lamps represents the Holy Ghost, they lack the authority and the ability to provide the Holy Ghost to others. The five wise virgins, over a period of days, months, and years, had hearkened to the Holy Ghost, and for this reason they had oil in their lamps. President Spencer W. Kimball explained this principle:

"In [this] parable, oil can be purchased at the market. In our lives the oil of preparedness is accumulated drop by drop in righteous living. Attendance at sacrament meetings adds oil to our lamps, drop by drop over the years. Fasting, family prayer, home teaching, control of bodily appetites, preaching the gospel, studying the scriptures—each act of dedication and obedience is a drop added to our store. Deeds of kindness, payment of offerings and tithes, chaste thoughts and actions, marriage in the covenant for eternity—these, too, contribute importantly to the oil with which we can at midnight refuel our exhausted lamps."[16]

Matthew 25:10 *And while they went to buy, the bridegroom came; and they that were ready went in with him to the marriage:*

The parable's specific bridegroom ("*the* bridegroom") corresponds with one particular marriage ("*the* marriage"). Jesus is not speaking about an ordinary or generic wedding. He is referring to the marriage between Jesus Christ and his bride, which will take place at his Second Coming.

The marriage in this parable, of course, is symbolic. The marriage of the Lamb, who is Christ (see D&C 33:17–18), to his bride, who is the Church (see D&C 109:73–74) as well as the New Jerusalem (see D&C 21:2, 9–10), is a metaphor for the union between the Lord and his people, made possible through the atonement of Christ and sacred priesthood ordinances. In fact, the very name of Christ's sacrifice (*at-one-ment*) suggests the purpose of that sacrifice: to make us one with both the Father and the Son (see John 17:11, 19–23). To underscore the sweetness and blessing of that union, the Lord uses marriage as a symbol. There is no sweeter or more meaningful relationship on earth than that between a holy husband and a holy wife; that is the kind of relationship (in depth of feeling and completeness of union) that the Lord is inviting us to.

That marriage is between Christ and the Church—but the Church is not just an organization on the earth; it is also the individual souls who belong to that organization. Though we are to prepare for the marriage all our lives (see Matthew 25:1–13; D&C 45:56–57), it will be brought to its culmination (with the body of the Church) when Christ returns in glory. Of course, as individuals, we are bound to Christ as soon as we are ready. (For other references to the marriage of the Lamb, see Isaiah 54:4–5; 62:5; Jeremiah 31:32; JST, Matthew 22:1–14; Ephesians 5:23, 32; D&C 58:6–11; 65:3; 88:92; 133:10, 19.)

A passage in Revelation informs us that "his wife hath made herself ready. . . . To her was granted . . . she should be arrayed in fine linen, clean and white" (Revelation 19:7–8). This white clothing symbolizes the Saints' righteousness (see Revelation 19:8; 15:6) and it became white when it was "washed . . . in the blood of the Lamb" (Revelation 7:14), which means the Saints became sanctified through Christ's atonement. The wearing of special wedding garments accords with the customs of first-century A.D. weddings.[17]

One of the great blessings associated with this marriage between the Lamb and his bride is that those who are worthy to attend the marriage will partake of a marriage supper. This supper is called in scripture "the marriage supper of the Lamb" (Revelation 19:9). John the Revelator describes the gladness, rejoicing, and blessing that is associated with this marriage supper: "Let us be glad and rejoice, and give honour to him: for the marriage of the Lamb is come, and his wife hath made herself ready. . . . Blessed are they which are called unto the marriage supper of the Lamb" (Revelation 19:7, 9).

This marriage supper is also described in latter-day revelation, where the Lord describes it as being "a feast of fat things . . . for the poor; yea, a feast of fat things, of wine on the lees well refined, that the earth may know that the mouths of the prophets shall not fail; Yea, a supper of the house of the Lord, well prepared, unto which all nations shall be invited. First, the rich and the learned, the wise and the noble; And after that cometh the day of my power; then shall the poor, the lame, and the blind, and the deaf, come in unto the marriage of the Lamb, and partake of the supper of the Lord, prepared for the great day to come" (D&C 58:8–11; see D&C 65:3). As the passage just cited designates, the marriage supper will take place at the Bridegroom's home, "the house of the Lord" (D&C 58:9).

In a warning to the Saints, President Spencer W. Kimball spoke of this marriage supper: "The day of the marriage feast approaches. The coming of the Lord is nigh. And there are many among us who are not ready for the great and glorious event. . . . For those who heed the warning and make their preparations, for those found at midnight with the oil of righteousness in their lamps, for those with patience, long-suffering, and full dedication, the promise is that they shall sit down at the banquet with their Lord."[18]

Matthew 25:10–11 *and the door was shut. Afterward came also the other virgins, saying, Lord, Lord, open to us.*

Not everyone will be privileged to attend the marriage supper of the Lord, because the door will be shut on the foolish, meaning all those who are unworthy to attend. Joseph Smith described those who would be able to attend, using the Apostle Paul as an ideal example:

"Those who keep the commandments of the Lord and walk in His statutes to the end, are the only individuals permitted to sit at this glorious feast. . . . [Paul wrote:] 'I have fought a good fight, I have finished my course, I have kept the faith. . . . ' . . . His labors were unceasing to spread the glorious news: and like a faithful soldier, when called to give his life in the cause which he had espoused, he laid it down. . . . Follow the labors of this Apostle from the time of his conversion to the time of his death, and you will have a fair sample of industry and patience in promulgating the Gospel of Christ. Derided, whipped, and stoned, the moment he escaped the hands of his persecutors he as zealously as ever proclaimed the doctrine of the Savior. . . . Reflect for a moment, brethren, and enquire, whether you would consider yourselves worthy a seat at the marriage feast with Paul and others like him, if you had been unfaithful? Had you not fought the good fight, and kept the faith, could you expect to receive?"[19]

The foolish virgins' twofold repetition, "Lord, Lord" indicates their urgency to enter after the door was shut. The imagery of the door that is shut with the people on the outside calling, "Lord, Lord" is found elsewhere in Jesus' teachings. Once a disciple of Jesus asked him, "Lord, are there few that be saved?" Jesus responded, "Strive to enter in at the strait gate: for many, I say unto you, will seek to enter in, and shall not be able. When once the master of the house is risen up, and hath shut to the door, and ye begin to stand without, and to knock at the door, saying, Lord, Lord, open unto us; and he shall answer and say unto you, I know you not whence ye are" (Luke 13:23–25).

To John the Revelator, the Lord also revealed that he, the Lord, possessed "the key of David" and he alone held the power to open and shut. "These things saith he that is holy, he that is true, he that hath the key of David, he that openeth, and no man shutteth; and shutteth, and no man openeth; I know thy works: behold, I have set before thee an open door, and no man can shut it" (Revelation 3:7–8). The Lord through John continued to use the door imagery when he said, "Behold, I stand at the door, and knock: if any man hear my voice, and open the door, I will come in to him, and will sup with him, and he with me" (Revelation 3:20).

> ***Matthew 25:12*** *But he answered and said, Verily I say unto you, I know you not.*

The Joseph Smith Translation makes a significant change to the last phrase of this verse. Instead of reading "I know you not," the Joseph Smith Translation has "Ye know me not." The foolish virgins who are shut outside of the marriage and the supper are those who do not know the Lord. Knowing the Lord is a vital part of the covenant between God and his people. In his great intercessory prayer, offered just before he entered the Garden of Gethsemane, Jesus said, "This is life eternal, that they might know thee the only true God, and Jesus Christ, whom thou hast sent" (John 17:3).

The importance of knowing God is demonstrated in Hosea, chapters 1 and 2. In these chapters, the marriage of the prophet Hosea to Gomer symbolizes Jehovah's marriage to his covenant people, the house of Israel. God's people come to know him only after their betrothal to him and after they have proven to be faithful to him: "I will even betroth thee unto me in faithfulness: and thou shalt *know* the Lord" (Hosea 2:20, emphasis added).

Love, too, is a requirement to those who wish to know God: "Every one that loveth is born of God, and *knoweth* God. He that loveth not *knoweth not* God" (1 John 4:7–8, emphasis added).

> ***Matthew 25:13*** *Watch therefore, for ye know neither the day nor the hour wherein the Son of man cometh.*

Verses 1–12 communicate the parable's narrative, and verse 13 presents the Lord's command and admonition to us: "Watch," he said, because "ye know neither the day nor the hour wherein the Son of man cometh." "Watch" in this passage has the sense of "be prepared" or "be ready." How do we watch or prepare for his coming? A Doctrine and Covenants revelation that refers to the parable of the ten virgins explains that we prepare by becoming "faithful" and "praying always." "Wherefore, be faithful, praying always, having your lamps trimmed and burning, and oil with you, that you may be ready at the coming of the Bridegroom" (D&C 33:17).

The parable includes two phrases that place the fulfillment of the parable of the ten virgins at Jesus' second coming. The Joseph Smith Translation adds to verse 1, "and then, at that day, before the Son of man comes . . ." The final verse, too, sets forth the words "the Son of man cometh." Latter-day revelations also place the parable's fulfillment in the context of Jesus' coming. We read in Doctrine and Covenants 45: "And at that day, when I shall come in my glory, shall the parable be fulfilled which I spake concerning the ten virgins" (D&C 45:56). And the Lord revealed in Doctrine and Covenants 63:

"These things are the things that ye must look for; and speaking after the manner of the Lord, they are now nigh at hand, and in a time to come, even in the day of the coming of the Son of Man. And until that hour there will be foolish virgins among the wise; and at that hour cometh an entire separation of the righteous and the wicked; and in that day will I send mine angels to pluck out the wicked and cast them into unquenchable fire" (D&C 63:53–54; see also D&C 133:10).

Jesus' statement in verse 13 that "ye know neither the day nor the hour wherein the Son of man cometh" is expressed elsewhere in scripture. In Joseph Smith–Matthew 1:40, the Lord warned: "But of that day, and hour, no one knoweth; no, not the angels of God in heaven, but my Father only." In this verse Jesus Christ uses a triple negative ("no one knoweth; no not") to emphasize that even the angels do not know the precise time of his coming. In the Doctrine and Covenants the Lord reveals: "For the time is at hand; the day or the hour no man knoweth; but it surely shall come" (D&C 39:21); and again, "Which time is nigh at hand—I, the Lord God, have spoken it; but the hour and the day no man knoweth, neither the angels in heaven, nor shall they know until he comes" (D&C 49:6–7).

Personal Application

President Spencer W. Kimball, after citing part of the parable of the ten virgins, gave some instruction to help us know how to apply it in our lives:

"While the bridegroom tarried they all slumbered and slept. In the Church there are a great number of people who are slumbering and sleeping when they ought to be awake and doing their duties. They are resting on their oars. They plan to go 'tomorrow' to get oil for their lamps. Tomorrow they are going to be active!

"I was on a train one day going to the Northwest, and the conductor who took my ticket said, 'Oh, you're Brother Kimball.' I said, 'Yes. You must be a member of the Church.' He said, 'Well, I am.' And I said, 'What ward and stake do you live in?' He said, 'I hardly know.' And I asked him why, and his answer was: 'Well, when I came home from my mission I lived in Sanpete County. They loaded me so heavily with Church positions and obligations that when we moved to Salt

Lake I said to my wife, 'We're going to rest one year before we take any position of responsibility.' I said, 'How long ago was that?' 'Nine years,' was the answer. Nine years of inactivity, waiting to live."[20]

This conductor represents each of us, if we fail to keep oil in the lamps through Church activity, keeping God's commandments, and letting the Holy Spirit be our guide.

President Wilford Woodruff taught us how to keep oil in our lamps when he said: "Now the question is, how can we keep oil in our lamps? By keeping the commandments of God, remembering our prayers, do[ing] as we are told by the revelations of Jesus Christ, and otherwise assisting in building up Zion. When we are laboring for the kingdom of God, we will have oil in our lamps, our light will shine and we will feel the testimony of the Spirit of God. On the other hand, if we set our hearts upon the things of the world and seek for the honors of men, we shall walk in the dark and not in the light. If we do not value our priesthood, and the work of this priesthood, the building up of the kingdom of God, the rearing of temples, the redeeming of our dead, and the carrying out of the great work unto which we have been ordained by the God of Israel—if we do not feel that these things are more valuable to us than the things of the world, we will have no oil in our lamps, no light, and we shall fail to be present at the marriage supper of the Lamb."[21]

CHAPTER 30

The Talents

Matthew 25:14–30

For the kingdom of heaven is as a man travelling into a far country, who called his own servants, and delivered unto them his goods.

And unto one he gave five talents, to another two, and to another one; to every man according to his several ability; and straightway took his journey.

Then he that had received the five talents went and traded with the same, and made them other five talents.

And likewise he that had received two, he also gained other two.

But he that had received one went and digged in the earth, and hid his lord's money.

After a long time the lord of those servants cometh, and reckoneth with them.

And so he that had received five talents came and brought other five talents, saying, Lord, thou deliveredst unto me five talents: behold, I have gained beside them five talents more.

His lord said unto him, Well done, thou good and faithful servant: thou hast been faithful over a few things, I will make thee ruler over many things: enter thou into the joy of thy lord.

He also that had received two talents came and said, Lord, thou deliveredst unto me two talents: behold, I have gained two other talents beside them.

His lord said unto him, Well done, good and faithful servant; thou hast been faithful over a few things, I will make thee ruler over many things: enter thou into the joy of thy lord.

Then he which had received the one talent came and said, Lord, I knew thee that thou art an hard man, reaping where thou hast not sown, and gathering where thou hast not strawed:

And I was afraid, and went and hid thy talent in the earth: lo, there thou hast that is thine.

His lord answered and said unto him, Thou wicked and slothful servant, thou knewest that I reap where I sowed not, and gather where I have not strawed:

Thou oughtest therefore to have put my money to the exchangers, and then at my coming I should have received mine own with usury.

Take therefore the talent from him, and give it unto him which hath ten talents.

For unto every one that hath shall be given, and he shall have abundance: but from him that hath not shall be taken away even that which he hath.

And cast ye the unprofitable servant into outer darkness: there shall be weeping and gnashing of teeth.

While sitting on the Mount of Olives during the last days of his life (see Matthew 24:3), Jesus prophesied to his disciples of many signs that would signal the season of his Second Coming (see Matthew 24:4–51). It was in this setting that Jesus gave the parable of the fig tree (see Matthew 24:32–34) to provide his disciples with a greater understanding of how to interpret the signs of the times. That is to say, the disciples knew when summer approached because the fig tree's branch was tender and leaves began to appear. Similarly, when disciples see the signs of the times, they will know that the Second Coming "is near, even at the doors" (Matthew 24:33). On this same occasion, Jesus uttered the parable of the ten virgins (see Matthew 25:1–13) to encourage proper spiritual and temporal preparation for his coming. The parable of the ten virgins concludes with the warning,

"Watch therefore, for ye know neither the day nor the hour wherein the Son of man cometh" (Matthew 25:13).

The parable of the talents, which immediately follows that statement, belongs in the same context as the parables that precede it. All three parables are calculated to prepare the Lord's Saints for the end of the world and for the Lord's return in glory and power. The opening words of the parable of the talents set forth the theme of Jesus' departure from earth at the time of his death and resurrection and his eventual return. Jesus is "as a man travelling into a far country" (speaking of his postmortal journey to heaven) and, later, "after a long time the lord . . . cometh" (speaking of his Second Coming) (see Matthew 25:14, 19).

The parable of the talents resembles the parable of pounds. Elder James E. Talmage compared the two parables when he wrote that the parable of the pounds "was spoken to a mixed multitude in the course of our Lord's last journey from Jericho to Jerusalem; the [parable of the talents] was given in privacy to the most intimate of His disciples in the closing hours of the last day of His public preaching. The two should be studied together. In the story of the Pounds, an equal amount of capital is given to each of the servants, and men's diverse ability to use and apply, with commensurate results in reward or penalty, is demonstrated; in that of the Entrusted Talents, the servants received different amounts, 'every man according to his several ability'; and equal diligence, though shown in one instance by great gain and in other by small but proportionate increase, is equally rewarded. Unfaithfulness and negligence are condemned and punished in both."[1]

Commentary

> ***Matthew 25:14*** *For the kingdom of heaven is as a man travelling into a far country, who called his own servants, and delivered unto them his goods.*

This parable is one of the many "kingdom of heaven" parables, wherein the kingdom of heaven is likened unto something else, such as a farmer, a mustard seed, a treasure, a net, a king, a householder, and others. Most of the kingdom of heaven parables open with a similar formula, as shown with the following nine parables:

"The kingdom of heaven is likened unto a man which sowed good seed" (Matthew 13:24);

"The kingdom of heaven is like to a grain of mustard seed" (Matthew 13:31);

"The kingdom of heaven is like unto treasure hid in a field" (Matthew 13:44);

"The kingdom of heaven is like unto a merchant man, seeking goodly pearls" (Matthew 13:45);

"The kingdom of heaven is like unto a net" (Matthew 13:47);

"Therefore is the kingdom of heaven likened unto a certain king" (Matthew 18:23);

"The kingdom of heaven is like unto a man that is an householder" (Matthew 20:1);

"The kingdom of heaven is like unto a certain king, which made a marriage for his son" (Matthew 22:2);

"Then shall the kingdom of heaven be likened unto ten virgins" (Matthew 25:1).

In the parable of the talents, the opening words compare the kingdom of God to a man who journeys to a far country. This man is very wealthy, a fact that is evident because the journeying man (1) employs servants; (2) owns eight talents (see verse 15), which amounts to a great amount of wealth (see below); and (3) had the means to take a journey to a faraway country. This man represents Jesus Christ. His wealth is not of earthly riches, such as gold and silver, but spiritual riches and heavenly gifts. We, Jesus' disciples, are the parable's servants, and it is us that he provides with the talents, or spiritual gifts.

The parable states that the man journeyed to a far country, an image that portrays Jesus' going to heaven after his death and resurrection. Verse 19 records that "after a long time the lord of those servants cometh, and reckoneth with them." Jesus resides in heaven until, "after a long time," he will visit his servants at the time of the Second Coming.

Matthew 25:15 *And unto one he gave five talents, to another two, and to another one;*

Jesus uses the verb "gave" in this parable; the Lord *gave* the talents to his servants. They did not earn it through their own efforts, nor did they find, win, purchase, or inherit the talents, but the Lord gave the talents to them. He did it because of his supreme love, grace, and mercy.

In the scriptures, *talent* has three different representations of value—a standard of weight (see, for example, 2 Samuel 12:30; Revelation 16:21), a unit of money, and a natural or exceptional ability or gift. The weight of a talent in the Old Testament period was approximately 75.6 pounds,[2] but in the New Testament, a talent usually represented large units of money.[3] This evolution of the meaning of *talent* has been expressed in a commentary on the book of Matthew: "The talent was originally a measure of weight, and later a monetary unit of the highest denomination. . . . The word passed into English usage in the Middle Ages as a synonym for abilities and/or natural endowments."[4]

The eight talents mentioned in this parable refer to a form of currency because the parable specifically mentions "money" (Matthew 25:18, 27). Further, this money was a tangible item because one of the servants "digged in the earth, and hid his lord's money" (Matthew 25:18). Each talent had great value. One biblical commentator compares a talent to a million dollars: "It is difficult to know the value of the 'talent' (originally a measure of weight), but it was a very large amount of money, here probably silver coinage (see vv. 18, 27): one talent equaled 6,000 denarii (one denarius was the equivalent of a day's wages for a common laborer). The talent was thus analogous to the modern 'million.'"[5]

Though Jesus speaks explicitly of money, he refers metaphorically to abilities and gifts, spiritual and otherwise. The main point of the parable is that Christ's disciples of all ages must use their God-given talents, time, money, spiritual gifts, and all resources to build his kingdom and to serve and bless others while they await the coming of their Master. God requires that we use these talents and not make excuses. He knows our abilities and requires a return according to our ability, no more and no less. Those who have great abilities are required to give more, and those with lesser give less. As Paul taught, "For as we have many members in one body, and all members have not the same office: So we, being many, are one body in Christ, and every one members one of another. Having then gifts differing according to the grace that is given to us" (Romans 12:4–6).

A revelation to Joseph Smith instructs us that all of us are to improve our talent and to gain other talents, even to a "hundred fold." "And all this for the benefit of the church of the living God, that every man may improve upon his talent, that every man may gain other talents, yea, even an hundred fold, to be cast into the Lord's storehouse, to become the common property of the whole church" (D&C 82:18).

> ***Matthew 25:15*** *to every man according to his several ability; and straightway took his journey.*

After distributing the talents to his servants, the man immediately took his journey. The phrase "to every man according to his several ability" emphasizes individual skills, aptitude, and capacity. The man used judgment and wisdom in distributing the talents to the three servants because he knew the ability of each and distributed the talents accordingly.

> ***Matthew 25:16–19*** *Then he that had received the five talents went and traded with the same, and made them other five talents. And likewise he that had received two, he also gained other two. But he that had received one went and digged in the earth, and hid his lord's money. After a long time the lord of those servants cometh, and reckoneth with them.*

Through their industry, two of the servants double their talents, but fearing the consequence should he lose it, the third buries his single talent in the earth. When their lord returns from his journey, he rewards the two who doubled their talents and casts out the one who buried his talent. In the phrase "After a long time the lord of those servants cometh," the "long time" refers to the period before Jesus comes again at his second coming. After his return, the lord "reckoneth" with his servants, meaning, he will judge them to determine how they used their God-given talents while he was away.

> ***Matthew 25:20–21*** *And so he that had received five talents came and brought other five talents, saying, Lord, thou deliveredst unto me five talents: behold, I have gained beside them five talents more. His lord said unto him, Well done, thou good and faithful servant: thou hast been faithful over a few things, I will make thee ruler over many things: enter thou into the joy of thy lord.*

The servant who received five talents gives a stewardship report to his lord. He first declares what his stewardship was ("Lord, thou deliveredst unto me five talents") followed by the report of what he accomplished ("I have gained beside them five talents more"). The lord, after hearing the report, responds by saying, "Well done." The lord then calls his servant "good" and "faithful" and promises to make him a ruler. Inasmuch as the entire parable pertains to the kingdom of God, it is assumed that the Lord's promise to make the servant a ruler means that he will become a ruler in God's kingdom, where God himself rules as the King of all kings and rulers. Also, the promise to become a ruler suggests that the servant will have active authority in the kingdom; he will not simply be a puppet ruler or a young prince awaiting his opportunity to sit on the throne.

The idea of eventual rulership for Saints is in fact a common scriptural theme, describing the idea that the Saints will become kings or queens in God's eternal kingdom. John wrote in his Revelation that he and others were kings and priests unto God (see Revelation 1:6; 5:10; 20:6). According to Joseph Smith, "Those holding the fullness of the Melchizedek Priesthood are kings and priests of the Most High God, holding the keys of power and blessings."[6]

Elder James E. Talmage spoke of the eventual rulership of men and women: "When the frailties and imperfections of mortality are left behind, in the glorified state of the blessed hereafter, husband and wife will administer in their respective stations, seeing and understanding alike, and co-operating to the full in the government of their family kingdom. Then shall woman be recompensed in rich measure for all the injustice that womanhood has endured in mortality. Then shall [she] reign by Divine right, a queen in the resplendent realm of her glorified state, even as exalted man shall stand, priest and king unto the Most High God. Mortal eye cannot see nor mind comprehend the beauty, glory, and majesty of a righteous woman made perfect in the celestial kingdom of God."[7]

In the parable of the talents Jesus speaks the phrase, "Thou hast been faithful over a few things, I will make thee ruler over many things." The comparison between a few things and the five talents is significant. If "the talent was thus analogous to the modern 'million,'"[8] as one biblical commentator has written, then five talents would represent an enormous amount of money. And yet we notice that the Lord calls these five talents "a few things." However, in the eternal scheme of things, the five talents of silver, even if they equal five million, are but a "few things," especially when compared with the eternal glories, spiritual riches, and enormous endowments of honor God has in store for his faithful Saints. Those who are faithful over a few things will be blessed and made ruler over "many things"; "few" is an obvious contrast with "many" to show the magnitude of the blessings after the Judgment.

In addition to the blessings of rulership, the "good and faithful servant" is told to "enter into the joy of the Lord." This refers to perfect joy or fullness of joy that focuses on Jesus Christ (see D&C 101:36). It is reserved for the faithful and wise and is directly linked to the inheritance of eternal life: "And whoso is found a faithful, a just, and a wise steward shall enter into the joy of his Lord, and shall inherit eternal life" (D&C 51:19).

> ***Matthew 25:22–23*** *He also that had received two talents came and said, Lord, thou deliveredst unto me two talents: behold, I have gained two other talents beside them. His lord said unto him, Well done, good and faithful servant; thou hast been faithful over a few things, I will make thee ruler over many things: enter thou into the joy of thy lord.*

The servant who obtained and then doubled the two talents received the same blessing from his lord as the servant who doubled the five talents. The lord uttered the same words and promise to both servants: "Well done, good and faithful servant; thou hast been faithful over a few things, I will make thee ruler over many things: enter thou into the joy of thy lord." When the Lord blesses His servants, it does not matter how many talents each receives, but it does matter how each one uses those talents.

> ***Matthew 25:24–27*** *Then he which had received the one talent came and said, Lord, I knew thee that thou art an hard man, reaping where thou hast not sown, and gathering where thou hast not strawed: And I was afraid, and went and hid thy talent in the earth: lo, there thou hast that is thine. His lord answered and said unto him, Thou wicked and slothful servant, thou knewest that I reap where I sowed not, and gather where I have not strawed: Thou oughtest therefore to have put my money to the exchangers, and then at my coming I should have received mine own with usury.*

The servant who had received a single talent tried to excuse himself for not using his talent wisely by claiming that he was "afraid" and that his lord was a "hard man." To the servant's excuses, the lord replied with a charge followed by a question: "You wicked, lazy servant! So you knew that I harvest where I have not sown and gather where I have not scattered seed?" Then the lord said, "Well then, you should have put my money on deposit with the bankers, so that when I returned I would have received it back with interest" (NIV, Matthew 25:26–27).

Jesus' charge "Thou wicked and slothful servant" may have seemed harsh to those who heard the parable. This phrase, however, demonstrates that when we do not take care of our allotted stewardship, we are in that thing considered wicked. In the gospel, *wicked* refers to both sins of commission and omission; in the case of the parable of the talents, *wicked* pertains to those who fail to use their God-given talents.

This third servant hid his God-given talent in the earth. Once buried, the talent became hidden from the view of others. It could not be invested, used, multiplied, or magnified. It was of no use or blessing to anyone, even to the servant to whom it was entrusted. Others could not enjoy it or benefit from its usefulness or value. In the Church in these last days, some bury or hide their God-given talent, a thing that displeases the Lord. According to Doctrine and Covenants 60:2, the Lord said, "With some I am not well pleased, for they will not open their mouths, but *they hide the talent* which I have given unto them, because of the fear of man. Wo unto such, for mine anger is kindled against them" (emphasis added). In the same section of the Doctrine of Covenants, the Lord instructs, "Behold, [the elders of the Church] have been sent to preach my gospel among the congregations of the wicked; wherefore, I give unto them a commandment, thus: Thou shalt not idle away thy time, neither shalt thou *bury thy talent* that it may not be known" (D&C 60:13; emphasis added).

> ***Matthew 25:28–30*** *Take therefore the talent from him, and give it unto him which hath ten talents. For unto every one that hath shall be given, and he shall have abundance: but from him that hath not shall be taken away even that which he hath. And cast ye the unprofitable servant into outer darkness: there shall be weeping and gnashing of teeth.*

The owner of the talents commands his servants to take the single talent from the servant who buried it and to give it to the servant who had ten talents. The master then taught a significant principle: "For unto every one that hath shall be given, and he shall have abundance: but from him that hath not shall be taken away even that which he hath." Everyone who has received and used God-given talents and has magnified and exercised them will be given more talents. But everyone who does not utilize their God-given talents will lose what has been given them.

Moroni taught this principle in connection with the gift of charity: "Wherefore, I know by this thing which thou hast said, that if the Gentiles have not charity, because of our weakness, that thou wilt prove them, and take away their talent, yea, even that which they have received, and give unto them who shall have more abundantly" (Ether 12:35). If the Gentiles do not develop and magnify charity (which

Moroni calls a "talent"), then they will lose it and it will be given to others.

The master then describes the servant who buried his talent as an "unprofitable servant." His penalty for being unprofitable is severe but just. He is cast into a place of darkness—and not into darkness only, but to the outer edges of darkness, presumably farther away from any source of light. "Outer darkness" here likely refers to the portion of the spirit world often referred to as the spirit prison.

All those who seek to come into God's kingdom deceitfully will be bound by their own sins. If they refuse to repent, when they enter into the spirit world they will be in a kind of outer darkness (which is different from the outer darkness that is the final state of those who are named sons of perdition). There they will have great anguish of soul, represented by weeping and gnashing of teeth.

Personal Application

According to the parable of the talents, the Lord gives to each of us one or more talents: "And unto one he gave five talents, to another two, and to another one." He knows well our capacities and therefore gives "to every man according to his several ability." These talents may be of a physical, temporal, or tangible nature, such as playing a musical instrument, preparing and delivering talks, or having a gift for proper social interaction. Or these talents may refer to spiritual gifts and capacities, such as possessing great and unconditional love for all God's children, having great faith, or being fluent in the language of the Holy Ghost. One key is to always use your talents to bless others' lives, thus following President Gordon B. Hinckley's example: "My talents may not be great, but I can use them to bless the lives of others. I can be one who does [the Lord's] work with pride in that which comes from his hand and mind."[9]

Joseph Smith spoke to his contemporaries and likened the parable of the talents unto them and to us: "You know, brethren, that when the Master in the Savior's parable of the stewards called his servants before him he gave them several talents to improve on while he should tarry abroad for a little season, and when he returned he called for an accounting. So it is now. Our Master is absent only for a little season, and at the end of it He will call each to render an account; and where the five talents were bestowed, ten will be required; and he that has made no improvement will be cast out as an unprofitable servant, while the faithful will enjoy everlasting honors. Therefore we earnestly implore the grace of our Father to rest upon you, through Jesus Christ His Son, that you may not faint in the hour of temptation, nor be overcome in the time of persecution."[10]

Notes

Notes to Introduction

1. Hunter, "The Pharisee and the Publican," *Ensign,* May 1984, 64.
2. Hunter, "The Pharisee and the Publican," 64.
3. Brown, *The Eternal Quest,* 181.
4. LDS Bible Dictionary, 741. See also Marshall, "Parables," 877; and Jones wrote, "*Parable* means a putting alongside for purposes of comparison and new understanding." Jones, "Parables," 1071.
5. Hunter, "The Pharisee and the Publican," 64.
6. Clawson, in Conference Report, April 1922, 47.
7. LDS Bible Dictionary, 740–41.
8. Smith, *History of the Church,* 2:267.
9. Jones, "Parables," 1072.
10. Talmage, *Jesus the Christ,* 296–97. "Parabolic teaching is often an act of mercy," wrote Elder McConkie. "To offer truths to wicked and ungodly creatures, which they will most assuredly reject, is to do more than cast pearls before swine. It is to make possible a greater condemnation upon those who reject the greater light" (McConkie, *The Mortal Messiah,* 2:243).
11. McConkie, *The Mortal Messiah,* 2:239; see also, McConkie and Millet, *Doctrinal Commentary on the Book of Mormon,* 2:46.
12. The Old Testament also contains parables. God commanded Ezekiel, "Son of man, put forth a riddle, and speak a parable unto the house of Israel" (Ezekiel 17:2). Elder James E. Talmage identifies the following Old Testament parables (see *Jesus the Christ,* 304, note 11): Judges 9:7–15 (the trees and the bramble); 2 Samuel 12:1–4 (rich man with flocks of lamb and the poor man with a single ewe lamb); 2 Samuel 14:1–20; 1 Kings 20:35–43 (escaped captive); 2 Kings 14:9 (the thistle

and the cedar); Isaiah 5:1–7 (song of the vineyard); Ezekiel 17:3–21 (the eagles and the vine); Ezekiel 19:2–9 (the lions); Ezekiel 24:3–14 (the seething pot).

13. "Parable" in *Tyndale Bible Dictionary,* 988.
14. "The Gospels give credence to Mark's claim, for the bulk of Jesus' teaching in the Synoptic Gospels is presented in the form of parables," Evans, "Parables in Early Judaism," 51.
15. In terms of numbers, Joachim Jeremias lists thirty-seven parables in the index of his book *The Parables of Jesus*. In *Hear Then the Parable: A Commentary on the Parables of Jesus,* page 465, Bernard Brandon Scott lists twenty-five parables in his index of parable titles, but twenty-nine in the table of contents. T. W. Manson's *The Teaching of Jesus,* page 69, deals with a very high number of parables, at sixty-five; and Simon J. Kistemaker's *The Parables of Jesus* lists forty parables in the table of contents.
16. Wenham, *The Parables of Jesus,* 102–4, 199–201.
17. Wenham, *The Parables of Jesus,* 171–73.
18. Anderson, "How to Read a Parable," 58.
19. Latter-day Saint scholars, too, have differing opinions on how many parables exist in the New Testament. In the table of contents of his *Parables of the Kingdom,* Melvin R. Brooks presents forty-six parables. A table called "The Parables of Jesus," found in Elder J. Reuben Clark's *Our Lord of the Gospels,* pages 538–40, lists fifty-two parables.[25] Elder James E. Talmage's *Jesus the Christ,* page 560, indexes twenty-nine.[26] Elder Bruce R. McConkie presents thirty-one parables in the *Doctrinal New Testament Commentary* and *Mortal Messiah* series.[27] Elder McConkie identifies thirty parables in his "Doctrinal Harmony of Gospels," which prefaces volume 1 of his *Doctrinal New Testament Commentary,* 1:9–35. He does not there include the story of the friend at midnight as a parable, but he does refer to this story as a parable in his commentary. In his *The Mortal Messiah,* books 2 and 3, Elder McConkie lists thirty-one parables in the indices (see McConkie, *The Mortal Messiah,* 2:420 and 3:483). Elder McConkie's and Elder Talmage's lists are nearly identical, both in the number of parables and the name given to each. Talmage's indexed list, two short of those listed by Elder McConkie, does not include the parables of the wedding guests and fig tree. The LDS Bible Dictionary, page 741, references about twenty-five parables.

    Skinner and Marsh's *Scriptural Parables for the Latter Days* deals

chiefly with those parables that pertain to or have prophetic fulfillment in the last days (see pp. 1–5). Also, Millet's *Parables and Other Teaching Stories* comprises selected parables and is not designed to be inclusive.
20. Oaks, "Scripture Reading and Revelation," *Ensign,* January 1995, 8.
21. Millett, *Parables and Other Teaching Stories,* 6.
22. Smith, *History of the Church,* 5:261.
23. See, for example, Jones, "Parables," 1073; and Blomberg, "Parable," 656.
24. Anderson, "How to Read a Parable," 61.
25. Matthews, *Behold the Messiah,* 171.
26. Cited in Faulconer, *Scripture Study,* 1.

Notes to Chapter 1: The Sower and the Soils

1. The parable of the sower and the seeds is also recorded in Mark 4:3–8, 13–20; and Luke 8:5–8, 11–15.
2. Smith, *History of the Church,* 2:266.
3. McConkie, *Doctrinal New Testament Commentary,* 1:289.
4. Faust, "Of Seeds and Soils," *Ensign,* November 1999, 47–48.

Notes to Chapter 2: The Seed Growing by Itself

1. Parry, Parry, and Peterson, *Understanding Isaiah,* 256.
2. McConkie, *Mortal Messiah,* 2:254.
3. Haight, "Planting Gospel Seeds of Spirituality," *Ensign,* January 1973, 74, 79.

Notes to Chapter 3: The Wheat and the Tares

1. Smith, *Teachings of the Prophet Joseph Smith,* 97–98, 101.
2. McConkie, *Doctrinal New Testament Commentary,* 1:297.

Notes to Chapter 4: The Mustard Seed

1. On another occasion Jesus used a mustard seed, due to its smallness, as a point of comparison (see Matthew 17:20). He told his listeners that if they had faith the size of a mustard seed, or even a very small portion of faith, they would be able to accomplish great deeds.

2. Smith, *Teachings of the Prophet Joseph Smith,* 98–99.
3. Smith, *Teachings of the Prophet Joseph Smith,* 98.
4. Smith, *Teachings of the Prophet Joseph Smith,* 98.
5. Smith, *Teachings of the Prophet Joseph Smith,* 159.
6. Smith, *Teachings of the Prophet Joseph Smith,* 98.
7. Pratt, "Parables of Jesus," *Ensign,* January 2003, 62.

Notes to Chapter 5: The Leaven

1. Talmage, *Jesus the Christ,* 91–92.
2. Smith, *History of the Church,* 2:270.
3. Smith, *History of the Church,* 2:272.
4. Smith, *History of the Church,* 4:540.

Notes to Chapter 6: The Hidden Treasure

1. See Talmage, *Jesus the Christ,* 292–93 and McConkie, *Doctrinal New Testament Commentary,* 1:300.
2. Huffmann, "Atypical Features in the Parables of Jesus," 213.
3. Derrett, *Law in the New Testament,* 1–16.
4. Smith, *Teachings of the Prophet Joseph Smith,* 101.
5. Kimball, "Helping Others Obtain the Promises of the Lord," *Ensign,* June 1983, 3–4.

Notes to Chapter 7: The Pearl of Great Price

1. Smith, *Teachings of the Prophet Joseph Smith,* 101–2.
2. Hagner, *Matthew 1–13,* 397.
3. To protect the privacy of both the young man and his family, we have changed his name. The story is used by permission from the young man. The full story is contained in personal correspondence with the authors.

Note to Chapter 8: The Gospel Net

1. Smith, *Teachings of the Prophet Joseph Smith,* 102.

Notes to Chapter 9: The Lost Sheep

1. Johnson, *The People's New Testament,* commentary on Luke 15:1.
2. Edersheim, *Life and Times of Jesus the Messiah,* 2:256.
3. Talmage, *Jesus the Christ,* 390.
4. Hafen, *The Broken Heart,* 60.
5. Kimball, "Helping Others Obtain the Promises of the Lord," *Ensign,* June 1983, 3.
6. Faust, "Responsibilities of Shepherds," *Ensign,* May 1995, 45.

Notes to Chapter 10: The Lost Coin

1. Fitzmyer, *The Gospel According to Luke,* 1081.
2. Bullinger, *Number in Scripture,* 243.
3. Hales, "Some Have Compassion, Making a Difference," *Ensign,* May 1987, 77.
4. McKay, in Conference Report, April 1945, 121–22.
5. Clarke, "The Simplicity of Gospel Truths," *Ensign,* May 1984, 61.

Notes to Chapter 11: The Prodigal Son

1. Hinckley, in Conference Report, October 1980, 88.
2. Richard C. Trench, quoted in Jamieson, Fausset, and Brown, *Commentary Critical and Explanatory on the Whole Bible,* commentary on Luke 15:12.
3. Maxwell, in Conference Report, October 2000, 47.
4. Stuy, *Collected Discourses,* 5:52–53.
5. Talmage, *Jesus the Christ,* 460.
6. McConkie, *Doctrinal New Testament Commentary,* 1:512.
7. Hultgren, *The Parables of Jesus,* 86.

Notes to Chapter 12: The Unmerciful Servant

1. Jeremias, *The Parables of Jesus,* 210.
2. Ten Boom, *The Hiding Place,* 238.

Notes to Chapter 13: The Good Samaritan

1. Talmage, *Jesus the Christ,* 431.
2. Haight, "My Neighbor, My Brother!" *Ensign,* May 1987, 59.

3. Wenham, *The Parables of Jesus,* 157.
4. Hultgren, *The Parables of Jesus,* 99.
5. For an extended and fascinating discussion of these symbolisms, see Welch, "The Good Samaritan and Eternal Life," *BYU Magazine, BYU Studies,* 49–55; and Welch, "The Good Samaritan: A Type and Shadow of the Plan of Salvation," 51–115.
6. Hunter, "The Lord's Touchstone," *Ensign,* November 1986, 35.
7. Smith, *History of the Church,* 4:227.
8. Gregory Nazianzen of the fourth century, quoted in Jamieson, Fausset, and Brown, *Commentary Critical and Explanatory on the Whole Bible,* commentary on Luke 10:37.
9. Monson, "Your Jericho Road," *Ensign,* February 1989, 2, 4.

Notes to Chapter 14: The Friend at Midnight

1. See the discussion regarding *importunity* in Liefeld, "Parables on Prayer," 247–51.
2. Talmage, *Jesus the Christ,* 435.
3. Romney, in Area Conference Report—Taiwan, 7.

Notes to Chapter 15: The Foolish Rich Man

1. McConkie, *Doctrinal New Testament Commentary,* 1:474.
2. Kimball, in Conference Report, April 1968, 73–74.

Note to Chapter 16: The Barren Fig Tree

1. Lattimore, "Their Message Bore Fruit," *Ensign,* August 1983, 63.

Notes to Chapter 17: The Great Supper

1. McConkie, *The Mortal Messiah,* 3:235.
2. McCasland, "Travel and Communication in the New Testament," 693.
3. Hammond, "Parables of Jesus: The Great Supper," *Ensign,* April 2003, 52.

NOTES TO CHAPTER 18: THE UNRIGHTEOUS STEWARD

1. Fitzmyer, *The Gospel According to Luke,* 1101.
2. Nolland, *Luke 9:21–18:34,* 803.
3. Fitzmyer, *The Gospel According to Luke,* 1100.
4. Fitzmyer, *The Gospel According to Luke,* 1101.
5. Nolland, *Luke 9:21–18:34,* 799.
6. Nolland, *Luke 9:21–18:34,* 804; Fitzmyer, *The Gospel According to Luke,* 1110.
7. Nolland, *Luke 9:21–18:34,* 805.
8. Yang, "Parables of Jesus: The Unjust Steward," *Ensign,* July 2003, 29.
9. Fitzmyer, *The Gospel According to Luke,* 1106.
10. Kimball, "The False Gods We Worship," *Ensign,* June 1976, 5–6.
11. Talmage, *Jesus the Christ,* 463-64.

NOTE TO CHAPTER 19: LAZARUS AND THE RICH MAN

1. Kistemaker, *The Parables of Jesus,* 236.

NOTE TO CHAPTER 20: THE UNPROFITABLE SERVANT

1. Smith, in Conference Report, April 1966, 102.

NOTES TO CHAPTER 21: THE IMPORTUNATE WIDOW AND UNJUST JUDGE

1. McConkie, *The Mortal Messiah,* 3:287–88.
2. McConkie, *The Mortal Messiah,* 3:289.

NOTES TO CHAPTER 22: THE PHARISEE AND THE PUBLICAN

1. Josephus, *Antiquities,* 17.42.
2. Cited in Hunter, "The Pharisee and the Publican," *Ensign,* May 1984, 65.
3. Hunter, "The Pharisee and the Publican," 66.
4. Hunter, "The Pharisee and the Publican," 64–66

Notes to Chapter 23: The Laborers in the Vineyard

1. Edersheim, *Life and Times of Jesus the Messiah,* 2:418.
2. Farrar, *The Life of Christ,* 504.
3. Oaks, in Conference Report, October 2000, 44.

Notes to Chapter 24: The Pounds

1. Josephus, *Wars,* 2.1–112; *Antiquities,* 17.20–344.
2. McConkie, *Doctrinal New Testament Commentary,* 1:571.
3. Nolland, *Luke 18:35–24:53,* 913–14.
4. Nolland, *Luke 18:35–24:53,* 918.
5. McConkie, *Mortal Messiah,* 3:320–21.
6. Bullinger, *Number in Scripture,* 243–250.
7. This quotation is taken from the entry, "Occupy," in Webster, *American Dictionary of the English Language,* 25.
8. Monson, "Labels," *Ensign,* November 1983, 20–21.

Notes to Chapter 26: The Wicked Husbandmen

1. BT Horayot 13a; JT Horayot 3:5; T. Horayot 2:10; M. Kiddushin 4:1; T. Megillay 2:7; M. Horayot 3:8; BT Sanhedrin 51a.
2. Jesus alludes to Isaiah 5:1–7 in this parable. For parallels between Isaiah 5:1–7 and the parable the wicked husbandmen, see Evans, *Mark 8:27–16:20,* 224–28.
3. Parry, Parry, and Peterson, *Understanding Isaiah,* 555.
4. Evans, *Mark 8:27–16:20,* 236.
5. Cited in Nolland, *Luke 18:35–24:53,* 953. A midrash is a rabbinic or Jewish writing that comments on or explains one or more biblical passages.
6. Benson, "Fourteen Fundamentals in Following the Prophet," *Brigham Young University Speeches of the Year,* 1980, 26–29.

Note to Chapter 27: The Royal Marriage Feast

1. Kistemaker, *The Parables of Jesus,* 105.

Notes to Chapter 28: The Fig Tree

1. Smith, *Church History and Modern Revelation,* 2:102; see also Talmage, *Jesus the Christ,* 574–75.
2. Lee, "Closing Remarks," *Ensign,* January 1974, 129.
3. Brockbank, "The Leaves Are Commencing to Show on the Fig Tree," *Ensign,* November, 1976, 74.
4. Romney, "'If Ye Are Prepared Ye Shall Not Fear,'" *Ensign,* July 1981, 3, 5.

Notes to Chapter 29: The Ten Virgins

1. Woodruff, *Deseret News: Semi-Weekly,* February 29, 1876, 1.
2. See McConkie, *Doctrinal New Testament Commentary,* 1:684.
3. The Hebrew expression used to describe robes of the virgin daughters of the king is the same as that which describes Joseph's coat of many colors.
4. Ashton, "A Time of Urgency," *Ensign,* May 1974, 36.
5. Kimball, *Teachings of Spencer W. Kimball,* 183.
6. McConkie, *Doctrinal New Testament Commentary,* 1:684.
7. Several scholars have recognized a symbolic connection between olive oil and the Holy Ghost. Brock, "The Syrian Baptismal Ordines," 177–83, for instance, states "the oil is always very closely associated with the Holy Spirit" (181). Strand, "The Two Olive Trees," also maintains that oil represents the Holy Spirit.
8. Compare 2 Enoch 22:6, where Enoch describes the oil as being greater than the "greatest light."
9. It is well known that many peoples in the world of antiquity utilized oil lamps for lighting both domestic and public buildings. See, for example, Sussman, "Lighting the Way Through History," 42–56, which identifies a variety of oil lamp shapes and sizes and details the history of lamp making in Palestine.
10. Once individuals receive the anointing they have the ability to see spiritual things by the light of the Holy Ghost (see Revelation 3:18; Moses 6:35).
11. Oaks, "Preparation for the Second Coming," *Ensign,* May 2004, 8–9.
12. Woodruff, *Deseret News: Semi-Weekly,* February 29, 1876, 1.
13. Woodruff, *Deseret News: Semi-Weekly,* December 28, 1875, 1.
14. Clarke, *Adam Clarke's Commentary on the Bible,* 821.

15. Hagner, *Matthew 14–28,* 1995; see Jeremias, *Parables of Jesus,* 171–74.
16. Kimball, *Faith Precedes the Miracle,* 256.
17. Thompson, "Marriage," 788.
18. Kimball, *Faith Precedes the Miracle,* 257.
19. Smith, *History of the Church,* 2:19–20.
20. Kimball, *Teachings of Spencer W. Kimball,* 182.
21. Woodruff, *The Discourses of Wilford Woodruff,* 124–25.

Notes to Chapter 30: The Talents

1. Talmage, *Jesus the Christ,* 581.
2. LDS Bible Dictionary, 789.
3. LDS Bible Dictionary, 734.
4. Albright and Mann, *Matthew: A New Translation,* 304.
5. Hagner, *Matthew 14–28,* 734. For additional discussion on the value of a talent, see the commentary on the parable of the unmerciful servant.
6. Smith, *History of the Church,* 5:555.
7. Talmage; "The Eternity of Sex," *Young Woman's Journal,* October 1914, 602–3.
8. Hagner, *Matthew 14–28,* 734.
9. Hinckley, *Teachings of Gordon B. Hinckley,* 159.
10. Smith, *Teachings of the Prophet Joseph Smith,* 68.

Sources Consulted

Albright, W. F. and C. S. Mann. *Matthew: A New Translation*. New York: Doubleday, 1971.

Anderson, Richard Lloyd. "How to Read a Parable." *Ensign,* September 1974, 58–63.

———. "Parables of Mercy." *Ensign,* February 1987, 20–24.

Ashton, Marvin J. "A Time of Urgency." *Ensign,* May 1974, 35–37.

Benson, Ezra Taft. "Fourteen Fundamentals in Following the Prophet." In *Brigham Young University Speeches of the Year, 1980*. Provo, Utah: BYU Press, 1981, 26–30.

Blomberg, Craig L. *Interpreting the Parables*. Downers Grove, Ill.: Intervarsity Press, 1990.

———. "Parable." In *The International Standard Bible Encyclopedia,* vol. 3. Edited by Geoffrey W. Bromiley, et al. Grand Rapids, Mich.: Eerdmans, 1986, 655–59.

Brock, Sebastian. "The Syrian Baptismal Ordines." *Studia Liturgica* 12 (1977): 177–83.

Brockbank, Bernard P. "The Leaves Are Commencing to Show on the Fig Tree." *Ensign,* May 1976, 74–75.

Brooks, Melvin R. *Parables of the Kingdom*. Salt Lake City: Deseret Book, 1965.

Brown, Hugh B. *The Eternal Quest*. Salt Lake City: Bookcraft, 1956.

Bullinger, E. W. *Number in Scripture*. Grand Rapids, Mich.: Kregel Publications, 1967.

Carmack, John K. "Lord, Increase Our Faith." *Ensign,* March 2002, 53–57.

Carson, D. A. "Matthew." In *The Expositor's Bible Commentary: with the New International Version of the Holy Bible*. Edited by Frank E.

Gaebelein, et al. 12 vols. Grand Rapids, Mich.: Zondervan, 1984, 8:60–599.

Clark, J. Reuben. *Our Lord of the Gospels*. Salt Lake City: Deseret Book, 1974.

Clarke, Adam. *Adam Clarke's Commentary on the Bible*. Iowa Falls, Iowa: World Bible Publishers, 1967.

Clarke, J. Richard. "The Simplicity of Gospel Truths." *Ensign,* May 1984, 59–61.

Clawson, Rudger. In Conference Report, April 1922, 45–48.

Derrett, J. D. M. *Law in the New Testament*. London: DLT, 1970.

Draper, Richard D. "The Parables of Jesus (Matthew 13)." In *Studies in Scripture*. Vol. 5, *The Gospels*. Edited by Kent P. Jackson and Robert L. Millet. Salt Lake City: Deseret Book, 1986, 262–78.

Edersheim, Alfred. *The Life and Times of Jesus the Messiah*. 2 vols. McLean: Macdonald, 1983.

Evans, Craig A. *Mark 8:27–16:20. Word Biblical Commentary,* vol. 34B. Dallas, Tex.: Word Books, 2001.

———. "Parables in Early Judaism." *The Challenge of Jesus' Parables*. Edited by Richard N. Longenecker. Grand Rapids, Mich.: Eerdmans, 2000, 51–75.

Farrar, Frederic W. *The Life of Christ*. Portland: Fountain Publications, 1980.

Faulconer, James E. *Scripture Study: Tools and Suggestions*. Provo, Utah: FARMS, 1999.

Faust, James E. "Of Seeds and Soils." *Ensign,* November 1999, 46–48.

———. "Responsibilites of Shepherds." *Ensign,* May 1995, 45–48.

Fitzmyer, Joseph A. *The Gospel According to Luke X–XXIV*. New York: Doubleday, 1985.

Hafen, Bruce C. *The Broken Heart*. Salt Lake City: Deseret Book, 1989.

Hagner, Donald A. *Matthew 1–13. Word Biblical Commentary,* vol. 44A. Dallas, Tex.: Word Books, 1993.

———. *Matthew 14–28. Word Biblical Commentary,* vol. 33B. Dallas, Tex.: Word Books, 1995.

Haight, David B. "My Neighbor, My Brother!" *Ensign,* May 1987, 59–61.

———. "Planting Gospel Seeds of Spirituality." *Ensign,* January 1973, 74–79.

Hales, Robert D. "Some Have Compassion, Making a Difference." *Ensign,* May 1987, 75–77.

Hammond, F. Melvin. "Parables of Jesus: The Great Supper." *Ensign,* April 2003, 51–53.

Hinckley, Gordon B. In Conference Report, October 1980, 85–88.

———. *Teachings of Gordon B. Hinckley*. Salt Lake City: Deseret Book, 1997.

Holy Bible. Authorized King James Version. Salt Lake City: The Church of Jesus Christ of Latter-day Saints, 1979.

Holy Bible. New International Version. Grand Rapids: Zondervan Bible Publishers, 1989.

Huffmann, Norman A. "Atypical Features in the Parables of Jesus." *Journal of Biblical Literature* 97 (1978): 207–20.

Hultgren, Arland J. *The Parables of Jesus: A Commentary*. Grand Rapids, Mich.: W. B. Eerdmans, 2000.

Hunter, Howard W. "The Lord's Touchstone." *Ensign,* November 1986, 34–35.

———. "The Pharisee and the Publican." *Ensign,* May 1984, 64–66.

Jamieson, Robert, A. R. Fausset, and David Brown. *A Commentary Critical and Explanatory on the Whole Bible*. Grand Rapids, Mich.: Zondervan, 194(?).

Jeremias, Joachim. *The Parables of Jesus*. London: SCM Press, 1958.

Johnson, B. W. *The People's New Testament*. N.p., 1891.

Jones, Peter R. "Parables." In *Holman Bible Dictionary*. Edited by Trent C. Butler, et al. Nashville: Holman Bible Publishers, 1991, 1071–73.

Josephus, Flavius. *Josephus: Complete Works*. Translated by William Whiston. Grand Rapids, Mich.: Kregel Publications, 1981.

Judd, Frank F., Jr. "Parables of Jesus: The Priceless Parables." *Ensign,* January 2003, 56–59.

Kerr, W. Rolfe. "Parables of Jesus: The Unprofitable Servant." *Ensign,* October 2003, 44–47.

Kimball, Spencer W. In Conference Report, April 1968, 73–78.

———. *Faith Precedes the Miracle*. Salt Lake City: Deseret Book, 1972.

———. "The False Gods We Worship." *Ensign,* June 1976, 3–6.

———. "Helping Others Obtain the Promises of the Lord." *Ensign,* June 1983, 2–5.

———. *The Miracle of Forgiveness*. Salt Lake City: Bookcraft, 1971.

———. *Teachings of Spencer W. Kimball*. Edited by Edward L. Kimball. Salt Lake City: Bookcraft, 1982.

Kistemaker, Simon J. *The Parables of Jesus*. Grand Rapids, Mich.: Baker Book House, 1980.

Lattimore, J. Elaine. "Their Message Bore Fruit." *Ensign,* August 1983, 63.

LDS Bible Dictionary. In the Holy Bible LDS edition. Salt Lake City: The Church of Jesus Christ of Latter-day Saints, 1979.

Lee, Harold B. "Closing Remarks." *Ensign,* January 1974, 125–29.

Liefeld, Walter L. "Parables on Prayer (Luke 11:5–13; 18:1–14)." In *The Challenge of Jesus' Parables*. Edited by Richard N. Longenecker. Grand Rapids, Mich.: Eerdman's Publishing Company, 2000, 240–62.

Manson, T. W. *The Teaching of Jesus*. Cambridge: University Press, 1951.

Marshall, I. H. "Parables." In *New Bible Dictionary.* Edited by J. D. Douglas, et al., 932–34.

Matthews, Robert J. *Behold the Messiah*. Salt Lake City: Bookcraft, 1994.

Maxwell, Neal A. In Conference Report, October 2000, 45–49.

McCasland, S. V. "Travel and Communication in the New Testament." In *The Interpreter's Dictionary of the Bible*. 4 vols. Edited by George A. Buttrick, et al. Nashville: Abingdon Press, 1982, 4:690–93.

McConkie, Bruce R. *Doctrinal New Testament Commentary.* 3 vols. Salt Lake City: Bookcraft, 1965–73.

———. *The Mortal Messiah*. 4 vols. Salt Lake City: Deseret Book, 1979–81.

McConkie, Joseph Fielding and Robert L. Millet. *Doctrinal Commentary on the Book of Mormon*. 4 vols. Salt Lake City: Bookcraft, 1987–92.

McKay, David O. In Conference Report, April 1945, 119–24.

Millet, Robert L. *Lost and Found: Reflections on the Prodigal Son*. Salt Lake City: Deseret Book, 2001.

———. *Parables and Other Teaching Stories*. Salt Lake City: Shadow Mountain, 1999.

Monson, Thomas S. In Conference Report, October 1983, 19–21.

———. "Your Jericho Road." *Ensign,* February 1989, 2–5.

Nolland, John. *Luke 9:21–18:34. Word Biblical Commentary,* vol. 35B. Dallas, Tex.: Word Books, 1993.

———. *Luke 18:35–24:53. Word Biblical Commentary,* vol. 35C. Dallas, Tex.: Word Books, 1993.

Oaks, Dallin H. In Conference Report, October 2000, 40–45.

———. "Preparation for the Second Coming." *Ensign,* May 2004, 7–10.

———. "Scripture Reading and Revelation." *Ensign,* January 1995, 6–9.

Parry, Donald W., and Jay A. Parry. *Understanding the Signs of the Times*. Salt Lake City: Deseret Book Co., 1999.

Parry, Donald W., Jay A. Parry, and Tina M. Peterson. *Understanding Isaiah*. Salt Lake City: Deseret Book, 1998.

Parry, Jay A., and Donald W. Parry. *Understanding the Book of Revelation*. Salt Lake City: Deseret Book, 1998.

Pratt, Carl B. "Parables of Jesus: Prophecy for Our Day." *Ensign,* January 2003, 60–63.

Romney, Marion G. In Area Conference Report—Taiwan, August 1975, 6–8.
———. "'If Ye Are Prepared Ye Shall Not Fear.'" *Ensign,* July 1981, 2–5.
Scott, Bernard Brandon. *Hear Then the Parable: A Commentary on the Parables of Jesus*. Minneapolis: Fortress Press, 1989.
Skinner, Andrew C., and W. Jeffrey Marsh. *Scriptural Parables for the Latter Days*. Salt Lake City: Deseret Book, 2002.
Smith, Joseph. *History of the Church of Jesus Christ of Latter-day Saints*. Edited by B. H. Roberts. 2d ed. rev. 7 vols. Salt Lake City: The Church of Jesus Christ of Latter-day Saints, 1932–51.
———. *Teachings of the Prophet Joseph Smith*. Selected by Joseph Fielding Smith. Salt Lake City: Deseret Book, 1938.
Smith, Joseph Fielding. *Church History and Modern Revelation*. 4 vols. Salt Lake City: Council of the Twelve Apostles of the Church of Jesus Christ of Latter-day Saints, 1946–49.
———. In Conference Report, April 1966, 101–3.
Strand, Kenneth A. "The Two Olive Trees of Zechariah 4 and Revelation 11." *Andrews University Seminary Studies* 20 (1982): 257–61.
Stuy, Brian H., ed. *Collected Discourses*. Burbank: B. H. S. Pub., 1987–92.
Sussman, Varda. "Lighting the Way through History: The Evolution of Ancient Oil Lamps." *Biblical Archaeology Review* 11 (March/April 1985): 42–56.
Talmage, James E. "The Eternity of Sex." *Young Woman's Journal* 25 (October 1914): 600–604.
———. *Jesus the Christ*. 3d ed. Salt Lake City: The Church of Jesus Christ of Latter-day Saints, 1916.
Ten Boom, Corrie. *The Hiding Place*. New York: Bantam Books, 1974.
Thompson, J. A. "Marriage." In *New Bible Dictionary,* 2d ed. Edited by J. D. Douglas, et al. Tyndale House, Wheaton, Ill., 1988, 786–91.
Tyndale Bible Dictionary. "Parable." Edited by Walter A. Elwell and Philip W. Comfort. Wheaton, Ill.: Tyndale House, 2001, 988–90.
Webster, Noah. *American Dictionary of the English Language*. New York: S. Converse, 1828.
Welch, John W. "The Good Samaritan and Eternal Life." *BYU Magazine,* (Spring 2002): 49–55.
———. "The Good Samaritan: A Type and Shadow of the Plan of Salvation," *BYU Studies* 38, no. 2 (1999): 51–115.
Wenham, David. *The Parables of Jesus*. Downers Grove, Ill.: Intervarsity Press, 1989.
Woodruff, Wilford. In *Deseret News: Semi-Weekly,* February 29, 1876, 1.

———. In *Deseret News: Semi-Weekly,* December 28, 1875, 1.
———. *The Discourses of Wilford Woodruff*. Salt Lake City: Bookcraft, 1946.
Yang, Tsung-Ting. "Parables of Jesus: The Unjust Steward." *Ensign,* July 2003, 28–31.

INDEX